COINS AS CULTURAL TEXTS IN THE WORLD OF THE NEW TESTAMENT

COINS AS CULTURAL TEXTS IN THE WORLD OF THE NEW TESTAMENT

David H. Wenkel

Bloomsbury T&T Clark
An imprint of Bloomsbury Publishing Plc

B L O O M S B U R Y
LONDON • OXFORD • NEW YORK • NEW DELHI • SYDNEY

Bloomsbury T&T Clark
An imprint of Bloomsbury Publishing Plc

Imprint previously known as T&T Clark

50 Bedford Square
London
WC1B 3DP
UK

1385 Broadway
New York
NY 10018
USA

www.bloomsbury.com

BLOOMSBURY, T&T CLARK and the Diana logo are trademarks of Bloomsbury Publishing Plc

First published 2017

British Library Cataloguing-in-Publication Data
A catalogue record for this book is available from the British Library.

ISBN: HB: 978-0-5676-7073-1
ePDF: 978-0-5676-7074-8
ePUB: 978-0-5676-7075-5

Library of Congress Cataloging-in-Publication Data
A catalog record for this book is available from the Library of Congress.

Typeset by Forthcoming Publications (www.forthpub.com)
Printed and bound in Great Britain

Dedicated to Dr. James E. Davia

CONTENTS

Section II
THE WORLD OF THE COIN: PROPAGANDA

ABBREVIATIONS

AAW	Approaching the Ancient World
AB	Anchor Bible
ABS	Archaeology and Biblical Studies
ABYRL	Anchor Bible
AJA	*American Journal of Archaeology*
AJEC	Ancient Judaism and Early Christianity
AJN	*American Journal of Numismatics*
AJP	*American Journal of Philology*
BA	*Biblical Archaeologist*
BAR	British Archaeological Reports
BCAW	Blackwell Companions to the Ancient World
BCE	Before the Common Era (= BC)
BDAG	*A Greek–English Lexicon of the New Testament*, 3rd edn
BECNT	Baker Exegetical Commentary on the New Testament
BIS	Biblical Interpretation Series (Brill)
BJP	Brill Josephus Project
BMC	British Museum Catalogue
BPC	Biblical Performance Criticism
BSac	*Bibliotheca Sacra*
BSP	*Bible and Spade*
BTB	*Biblical Theology Bulletin*
CBR	*Currents in Biblical Research*
CCSS	Catholic Commentary on Sacred Scripture
CD	Cairo Damascus Document
CE	Common Era (= AD)
CIRC	Cambridge Introduction to Roman Civilization
CPS	Contributions to Phenomenology
CSCT	Columbia Studies in the Classical Tradition
DSS	Dead Sea Scrolls
EDEJ	*The Eerdmans Dictionary of Early Judaism*. Edited by J. J. Collins and D. C. Harlow. Grand Rapids, 2010
EDNT	*Exegetical Dictionary of the New Testament*. Edited by H. Balz, and G. Schneider. ET. Grand Rapids, 1990–93
EJL	Early Judaism and Its Literature
ESV	English Standard Version

FMPS	Financial and Monetary Policy Studies
FMRD	*Die Fundmünzen der römischen Zeit in Deutschland*
HMMS	History of Mechanism and Machine Science
INJ	*Israel Numismatic Journal*
INR	*Israel Numismatic Research*
IVPNTC	InterVarsity Press New Testament Commentary
JAJSup	Journal of Ancient Judaism: Supplement Series
JBL	*Journal of Biblical Literature*
JETS	*Journal of the Evangelical Theological Society*
JRA	*Journal of Roman Archaeology*
JSJSup	Journal for the Study of Judaism: Supplement Series
JSNTSup	Journal for the Study of the New Testament: Supplement Series
JSOTSup	Journal for the Study of the Old Testament: Supplement Series
KTAH	Key Themes in Ancient History
LCL	Loeb Classical Library
LNTS	Library of New Testament Studies
LSTS	Library of Second Temple Studies
LXX	Septuagint
MJT	*Midwestern Journal of Theology*
Neot	*Neotestamentica*
NET	New English Translation
NIDNTT	*New International Dictionary of New Testament Theology* Edited by Colin Brown. 4 vols. Grand Rapids, 1986
NIGTC	New International Greek Testament Commentary
NIV	New International Version
NovT	*Novum Testamentum*
NovTSup	Supplements to Novum Testamentum
NRSV	New Revised Standard Version
NSBT	New Studies in Biblical Theology
NT	New Testament
NTOA	Novum Testamentum et Orbis Antiquus
NTS	*New Testament Studies* (journal)
obv.	obverse
OCM	Oxford Classical Monographs
OGIS	*Orientis Graeci Inscriptiones Selectae*
OIS	Oriental Institute Seminars
OSCC	Oklahoma Series in Classical Culture
OT	Old Testament
PNTC	Pillar New Testament Commentary
ResQ	*Restoration Quarterly*
rev.	reverse
RevExp	*Review and Expositor*
RFCC	Religion in the First Christian Centuries
RIC	Roman Imperial Coinage

RPC	Roman Provincial Coinage
SCL	Sather Classical Lectures
SFMA	Studien zu Fundmünzen der Antike
SNTSMS	Society for New Testament Studies Monograph Series
STDJ	Studies on the Texts of the Desert of Judah
STI	Studies in Theological Interpretation
TAF	Tübinger Archäologische Forschungen
TENT	Texts and Editions for New Testament Study
TOTC	Tyndale Old Testament Commentary
TSAJ	Texts and Studies in Ancient Judaism
TynBul	*Tyndale Bulletin*
UBCS	Understanding the Bible Commentary
WBC	Word Biblical Commentary
WUNT	Wissenschaftliche Untersuchungen zum Neuen Testament

Josephus and Philo

Ant.	Josephus, *Jewish Antiquities*
Life	Josephus, *The Life of Flavius Josephus*
War	Josephus, *Jewish War*
Good Person	Philo, *That Every Good Person Is Free*

Classical Writers

Dom.	Suetonius, *Life of Domitian*
Galba	Suetonius, *Life of Galba*
Met.	Ovid, *The Metamorphoses*
Mor.	Plutarch, *Moralia*
NH	Pliny the Elder, *Naturalis Historia*

Introduction

Coins are best understood as cultural texts. This simple idea will help introduce coins to those interested in the New Testament and its first-century milieu. Our goal is to connect existing work on interpreting cultural artifacts (with the study of coins as an ancillary discipline) to the interpretation of the New Testament. This connection between coinage and the study of Christianity should be no surprise given the fact that "coinage was intimately bound up with religion" ever since coins first appeared in the seventh century BCE in Asia Minor.[1]

This study is written for the reader who is already familiar with the basics of New Testament theology, history, and hermeneutics but lacks familiarity with Greco-Roman and Jewish "numismatics" (the study of coins). This volume will provide an introduction to the relationships between numismatics and New Testament studies.

The first chapter will establish a basic framework for interpreting coins; we will outline how coins function as "cultural texts."[2] The second chapter is also introductory and seeks to describe briefly how coins functioned as currency in the first-century milieu. The rest of the book will be divided into four major sections: (1) the world *in front* of the coin (those who used the coinage for monetary purposes), (2) the world *of* the coin itself (a fixed combination of inscription and image), (3) the world *behind* the coin (the people who minted it and chose its features), and finally (4) the conclusion.

Only in the world of academia can people study the same general area and still be worlds apart. The worlds of biblical studies, archeology, and classical studies, like many other academic fields, are highly fragmented and often deeply isolated from one another. The growth of scholarly

1. Jonathan Williams, "Religion and Roman Coins," in *A Companion to Roman Religion*, ed. J. Rüpke, BCAW (Oxford: Blackwell, 2007), 163.

2. For a discussion of interpreting culture see Kevin J. Vanhoozer, "What Is Everyday Theology? How and Why Christians Should Read Culture," in *Everyday Theology: How to Read Cultural Texts and Interpret Trends* (Grand Rapids: Baker Academic, 2007), 15–60.

literature in any one area makes interdisciplinary work very difficult. In addition, there are only a handful of numismatics programs at the master's and doctoral levels.[3]

Those who have sought to connect New Testament studies with the study of coins have lamented for at least the past twenty-five years that they still remain relatively unconnected disciplines.[4] This is surprising given the fact that coins are primary sources that can aid the study of the New Testament. What is interesting is that those who specialize in numismatics also view it as an "isolated discipline."[5] The past twenty years of scholarship has seen an increase in the number of interdisciplinary studies between numismatics and history; plenty of studies about coins in the world of the first-century Mediterranean acknowledge that coins are tools of ideology and communication. Still, there have been few efforts to introduce the biblical studies specialist to the realm of numismatics. This may be one reason why iconography is still "underexploited for the study of ancient Judaism."[6] Of course, iconography on coins may be exploited for more than the study of the narrow field of Judaism, however defined. Throughout the book, we will generally focus on how coins may be used as a resource for interpretation of the New Testament canon.[7]

3. Some may use the term "metrology" which is the study of standards or measurements to include the study of coinage.

4. Marius Reiser, "Numismatik und Neues Testament," *Biblica* 81 (2000): 457. Richard E. Oster, "'Show me a denarius': Symbolism of Roman Coinage and Christian Beliefs," *ResQ* 28 (1986): 107. For a similar lament made several years earlier see Richard E. Oster, "Numismatic Windows into the Social World of Early Christianity: A Methodological Inquiry," *JBL* 101 (1982): 195–223. More recently, Larry J. Kreitzer also describes how rare it is to see numismatics connected with New Testament study in *Striking New Images: Roman Imperial Coinage and the New Testament World*, JSNTSup 134 (Sheffield: Sheffield Academic, 1996), 20–21.

5. Nathan T. Elkins, "The Trade in Fresh Supplies of Ancient Coins: Scale, Organization, and Politics," in *All the King's Horses: Essays on the Impact of Looting and the Illicit Antiquities Trade on Our Knowledge of the Past*, ed. P. K. Lazrus and A. W. Barker (Washington, DC: Society for American Archaeology Press, 2012), 94.

6. Michael E. Stone, *Ancient Judaism: New Visions and Views* (Grand Rapids: Eerdmans, 2011), 23.

7. For notes on the possible relationship between economics and interpretation see Peter Oakes, "Methodological Issues in Using Economic Evidence in Interpretation of Early Christian Texts," in *Engaging Economics: New Testament Scenarios and Earl Christian Reception*, ed. B. W. Longenecker and K. D. Liebengood (Grand Rapids: Eerdmans, 2009), 13.

In order to fill this void in contemporary scholarship, this volume will pursue one simple goal: to introduce coins as cultural texts that can aid those who specialize in studying the New Testament and its historical background. This volume also responds to the deep divides between mutually beneficial fields of study by integrating the fields of philosophy of language (particularly speech-act theory) and biblical studies. These various resources provide a deep well for interacting with the signs and symbols found on coins (the study of signs in general is called semiotics). I will also seek to interact with numismatic scholarship as well as New Testament scholarship.

Benefits of Numismatics for New Testament Studies

The student of the New Testament should be interested in the study of ancient coins (numismatics) for at least ten reasons:

1. Coins provide primary source materials—both images and inscriptions—that can supplement study of the biblical text. As primary sources, coins or photos of coins are readily accessible in museums, libraries, and on the internet.
2. Coins are an important part of secondary literature in New Testament studies. Journal articles in biblical studies and some commentaries are starting to interact with coins in footnotes and margins because of their ability to enlighten some difficult texts.
3. Coins provide inscriptions and data that is often critical to dating archaeological finds. Coins often make up "the majority of small finds" at Greco-Roman archaeological sites, Elkins says.[8] The dates on coins are also useful for adding precision to the timeline of events in antiquity.
4. Coins provide artistic and factual depictions of what people from antiquity actually looked like. This includes ancient hairstyles, jewelry, and even unique facial features.
5. Coins provide artistic and factual representations of ancient (and sometimes lost) artifacts such as the Ark of the Covenant.
6. Coins provide insight into complex political relationships in the Roman Empire. For example, says Kreitzer, the coins of Herod the Great (37–4 BCE) indicate that he was seeking to use his coins to present himself "as a legitimate ruler of the Jewish people."[9]

8. Elkins, "The Trade in Fresh Supplies of Ancient Coins," 93.
9. Kreitzer, *Striking New Images*, 22.

7. Coins are directly referenced several times in the New Testament, making them an even more relevant part of its historical background. Coins also relate to historical Jesus studies, as "much of Jesus' teaching reflects the village economy of the day."[10]
8. Coins may be relevant to contemporary historical controversies surrounding rituals and elements of Second Temple Judaism, such as placing coins on the eyes of the dead.[11]
9. Coins can provide strong evidence for those evaluating the historical accuracy of events, places, and culture referenced in biblical texts.[12] In fact, some have argued that the usefulness of coins for Christian apologetics is their most important value.[13]
10. Coins provide information for word studies, etymologies, and other philological studies. Important word-study tools for New Testament studies such as BDAG reference numismatic material, but these studies are mostly dated and further philological and linguistic research may benefit from interaction with fresh research into coins.

In addition to these ten points, one can add a somewhat negative observation: coins are historical sources that are not easily subject to "historical exaggeration or rewriting."[14] It is this historical information that informs and aids the exegete of the New Testament. For our purposes, apologetics are secondary to the interest of explaining and exegeting the New Testament.[15] In sum, knowledge of numismatics will help the biblical

10. Craig G. Bartholomew, *Where Mortals Dwell: A Christian View of Place for Today* (Grand Rapids: Baker, 2011), 94.

11. William Meacham, "On the Archaeological Evidence for a Coin-on-Eye Jewish Burial Custom in the First Century A.D.," *BA* (1986): 56–59. For a short comment on the relationship of coins to ancient rituals see Elkins, "The Trade in Fresh Supplies of Ancient Coins," 95.

12. Coins provide historical (apologetic) evidence for Pilate's responsibility for Jesus' death as the Roman procurator of the region (Darrell L. Bock, *Luke 9:51–24:53*, 2 vols., BECNT [Grand Rapids: Baker, 1996], 2:1809).

13. A. H. M. Jones, "Numismatics and History," in *Essays in Roman Coinage Presented to Harold Mattingly*, ed. R. A. G. Carson and C. H. V. Sutherland (Oxford: Oxford University Press, 1956), 14; John Paul Lotz, "The HOMONOIA Coins of Asia Minor and Ephesians 1:21," *TynBul* 50 (1999): 173–74.

14. Peter Brennan, Michael Turner, and Nicholas L. Wright, *Faces of Power: Imperial Portraiture on Roman Coins* (Sydney: University of Sydney/Nicholson Museum, 2007), 5.

15. For an argument that the discipline of New Testament studies must return to a focus on exegesis see Markus Bockmuehl, *Seeing the Word: Refocusing New Testament Study*, STI (Grand Rapids: Baker, 2006), 88.

scholar assess argumentations and assertions based on data that parallel the biblical text. In order to facilitate further research, each chapter will explore some implications for studying the New Testament.

Scope of This Study

There are four noteworthy limitations that define the scope of this study.

The first limitation is that we will focus on the world of the New Testament in the first century CE.[16] Many numismatic studies have a much wider date range. The phrase "world of the New Testament" is used quite regularly by those studying the cultural, social, and historical contexts of early Christianity.[17]

The second limitation is that we will focus exclusively on coinage. The study of numismatics technically covers coins, medals, stamps, tokens, and seals (also called *bullae*).[18] In this study we will focus solely on objects used for monetary exchange.[19]

The third limitation is that we will focus on coins and their communicative power as opposed to coins as components in economic systems. We cannot avoid the topic of the ancient economy, but we will not engage the very technical macro- and microeconomic discussions of taxes, credit, and circulation of money. When we use the term "money," we will be referring to coinage, unless otherwise noted. The word "money" is notoriously difficult to define.[20] Our emphasis on generalities stems from the interdisciplinary nature of this volume, focused as it is on making numismatics accessible to those who are not formally trained in the classics or numismatics.

16. For a recent study of coins, seals, and inscriptions related to the Old Testament see Meir Lubetski and Edith Lubetski, eds., *New Inscriptions and Seals Relating to the Biblical World*, ABS 19 (Atlanta: SBL Press, 2012).

17. For recent use of this phrase see J. B. Green and L. M. McDonald, eds., *The World of the New Testament: Cultural, Social, and Historical Contexts* (Grand Rapids: Baker, 2013).

18. For comments on the parallels between coins and seals see Michael H. Crawford, *Roman Republican Coinage*, 2 vols. (Cambridge: Cambridge University Press, 1974), 2:727–28.

19. For brief definitions of coins and medals see John Wilson Betlyon, "Numismatics and Archaeology," *BA* (1985): 162.

20. David B. Hollander, *Money in the Late Roman Republic*, CSCT (Leiden: Brill, 2007), 2.

The fourth limitation establishes some chronological boundaries. The first bookend of our timeline roughly corresponds with the period known as the Principate, as opposed to the Roman Republic which preceded it. The Principate begins with the rule of Augustus, the adopted son of Julius Caesar and the first ruler of the Roman Empire in 63 BCE.[21] The other bookend corresponds with the Roman Emperor Trajan who ruled from 98 to 117 CE, and the death of the Apostle John. This timeframe is similar to that known as the "Early Roman Period."[22]

Ancient Jewish coins were produced in Judaea in three non-contiguous periods that cover about three hundred years.[23] The first period of production aligns with the Maccabean revolt (139–137 BCE). The second period roughly parallels the reign of Herod the Great (37–4 BCE). The third period parallels the First Jewish Revolt against Rome (66–70 CE) and the fourth parallels the Second Revolt (132–135 CE). With respect to Jewish coins, we will be focused on the first century, which includes coins from Herod the Great and the First Jewish revolt.

A Word on Identification and Referencing

While the first goal of a numismatist (coin specialist) is to identify a coin correctly, the first goal of a biblical studies specialist is to understand how to correlate historical data, including an accurate understanding of the New Testament.[24] Despite these divergent interests, both will need to know how correctly to identify coins used in academic references.

One of the first challenges anyone will experience when delving into the area of numismatics is the unique nature of the citations used to reference coins. One of the tasks of those who specialize in numismatics is to examine as many similar coins as possible and then try to catalog them under some set of relationships or taxonomy. For example, coins

21. John Rogerson uses 63 BCE as the date from which Judah became a part of the Roman Empire in "Ancient Israel to the Fall of the Second Temple," in *A Handbook of Ancient Religions*, ed. John R. Hinnells (Cambridge: Cambridge University Press, 2007), 230.

22. Chancey, *Greco-Roman Culture and the Galilee of Jesus*, 17.

23. Paul Romanoff, *Jewish Symbols on Ancient Jewish Coins* (Philadelphia: Dropsie College, 1944), 7–8.

24. "The first goal of a numismatist is the correct identification of the coins" (Donald T. Ariel, "Identifying the Mints, Minters and Meanings of the First Jewish Revolt Coins," in *The Jewish Revolt Against Rome: Interdisciplinary Perspectives*, ed. Mladen Popović (Leiden: Brill, 2012], 373).

may be catalogued according to the ruler who minted them. But it is possible to see coins available in the marketplace that are designated as unidentified. This means that the specific coin has not been formally identified and labeled. There were literally thousands of different coins minted in the Roman Empire during the first century, so it is quite possible that new coins may be found or that unidentified coins may be recognized.

Citations and footnotes for coins may consist of three items. The first item is the reference book that provides the taxonomy. The second item is a unique number to identify specific coin issues. The third item is a label such as the emperor who was ruling over the minting of the coin (not the emperor who appears on the coin). For example, sources on ancient Jewish coins may make reference to a "Hendin" number which refers to David Hendin's *Guide to Biblical Coins*, now in its fifth edition.[25] Other approaches to identifying coins typically involve citing a well-known numismatic reference book.

The best way to identify a Greco-Roman coin for academic research is with a RPC (Roman Provincial Coinage) number or RIC (Roman Imperial Coinage) number. These numbers reflect a worldwide project that aims to provide a standard reference schema for coins from the Roman Empire. The project is based out of the Heberden Coin Room of the Ashmolean Museum, University of Oxford. The RPC project draws from collections in Vienna, Paris, New York, London, Copenhagen, and more.[26]

Those who specialize in biblical studies will also want to familiarize themselves with some of the monograph series engaged in first-century numismatics.[27] One series that focuses on coins, archaeology, and material culture is the *Studien zu Fundmünzen der Antike* (SFMA) by Philipp von Zabern in Mainz, Germany. A second important series worth noting is the on-going project of *Die Fundmünzen der römischen Zeit in Deutschland* (FMRD). This series has over 41 volumes and covers all ancient coins found in Germany, cataloguing over 300,000 coins. Another large series that may be valuable is the thirteen-volume *Jewish Symbols in the Greco-Roman Period* by Erwin R. Goodenough. An abridged version edited by Jacob Neusner is currently in print.[28] Researchers will also want to

25. David Hendin, *Guide to Biblical Coins*, 5th edn (New York: Amphora, 2010).

26. The RPC project will be composed of at least 10 volumes. As of 2013 only three volumes have been published.

27. Elkins, "The Trade in Fresh Supplies of Ancient Coins," 96.

28. Erwin R. Goodenough, *Jewish Symbols in the Greco-Roman Period: Abridged Edition*, trans. J. Neusner (Princeton: Princeton University Press, 1988).

investigate catalogues of museum collections.[29] One particular catalogue of interest may be the British Museum Collection, *Coins from the Roman Empire in the British Museum* (6 vols.; London, 1923–).

What to Expect

In this volume, the reader will encounter four sections. Within each chapter, most matters of scholarly debate are contained in the footnotes. This is because researchers from New Testament studies may not recognize some authors and issues that are particular to numismatics and Classical studies. This approach to citations will enable this work to become an accessible interdisciplinary text that nonetheless still provides avenues for further research. Another feature of this book is the inclusion of sections at the end of the chapters on implications for studying the New Testament. These sections on the New Testament are meant to be provocative and suggestive rather than exhaustive and conclusive. Their aim is to suggest further paths for research and to make clear the ways in which numismatics can support biblical studies.

Chapters 1 through 4 are set apart from the sections that follow because they focus on preliminary matters and establish the methodology used throughout this study. Chapter 1 argues that the coin is a cultural text that requires a robust and careful hermeneutic. This chapter engages with contemporary numismatic studies and finds that there is no general or generic hermeneutic that may be applied to the task of interpreting coins as cultural texts. The second chapter briefly considers speech-act theory as an approach to interpreting coins as cultural texts. This chapter seeks to make a contribution to the interdisciplinary study of the New Testament and its historical context by providing a general hermeneutic that may be applied to any coin. The third chapter introduces coins as currency, and the complexities of Roman and Jewish currency systems are described here. Chapter 4 focuses on coins as a literary and historical context for interpreting the New Testament and canvases all the references to coins in the New Testament.

The chapters in Section I focus on the world *in front* of the coin. This section locates the readers or audience of coins as the entire Roman Empire. This is one of the most challenging tasks to take up because we are seeking the most common socio-cultural denominators for most of the first-century Mediterranean. The vast swath of cultures and people

29. Jonathan Williams provides several suggestions for further reading, some of which I mention here, in "Religion and Roman Coins," 163.

groups make this almost an impossible task. Chapter 5 builds on this by arguing that a relational web of trust was required for coins to function as currency. Chapter 6 focuses on the universal emotion of fear and argues that this emotion played an important factor in how coins were used, carried, and stored—in light of the universal certainties called death and taxes. Chapter 7 demonstrates that the act of paying taxes could have serious theological and social implications.

The chapters in Section II argue that the world *of* the coin is that of a cultural text characterized by propaganda. Chapter 8 examines the relationship between propaganda and coinage. It argues that it is possible that an inscription on a coin is a symbol as well as a text to be read. Chapter 9 examines the relationship between propaganda and dates on coins. This chapter argues that coins served as cultural texts through which public conceptions of time could be manipulated. Chapter 10 examines how images on Roman coins encouraged or discouraged participation in a patron–client relationship. Chapter 11 considers Jewish coinage in the first century and presents a spectrum-oriented case for viewing the poles of Jewish independence and patronage to Rome as a fruitful way to capture the historical dynamics at work. Chapter 12 considers propaganda and metallurgy (or the metals used to make coins). It argues that the language of metals in the first century often communicated purity or a lack thereof.

The chapters in Section III argue that the world *behind* the coin or the author(s) of coins used them primarily to communicate something about their power. Chapter 13 argues that coins were an important tool used by those in power to shape their public identities. These public identities extended not only to themselves but to their families and previous emperors. Chapter 14 examines the relationship between coins, power, and presence. It demonstrates that the image of the emperor was designed to communicate omnipresence as defined by Roman religion. Chapter 15 examines the relationship between power and the production of coinage through mints, mining, and melting. This chapter argues that the ability of a province or city to mint its own money communicated an element of independence and power. The conclusion offers a final summary and concluding remarks for the New Testament specialist who wants to integrate numismatics into biblical research.

Chapter 1

Coins as Cultural Texts

The coin is a "text." That is the simple idea behind this volume. Coins are *cultural* texts that require a method of interpretation that is robust enough to capture the dynamics of author–text–reader interaction.

Introduction

This chapter will explain and outline a general methodology for reading coins as cultural texts. This methodology has two goals. First, it is designed to be *interdisciplinary*, drawing from the areas of hermeneutics and semiotics. Second, it is designed to be *introductory*.[1] The methodology presented here focuses on simple description and non-technical language so that those who are already involved in studying the New Testament will find an accessible pathway to enrich their knowledge of the first-century world. Understanding the cultural dynamics of the first century will especially help those pursing a historically accurate interpretation of the New Testament canon. On this, a quotation from the Roman art historian J. M. C. Toynbee is especially helpful: "To learn this [visual] language, to be able to translate it, and to apply the knowledge to the interpretation both of long-known and of newly revealed monuments is the business of all students of Roman civilization and history."[2]

Historically rigorous New Testament scholarship will seek to understand the culture in which the New Testament was written. The more we know about this era, the better we will be able to interpret the canon of scripture. This study seeks to utilize and apply this paradigm to bridge

1. For a more advanced overview of several approaches to iconography and hermeneutics for visual objects see Annette Weissenrieder and Friederike Wendt, "Images as Communication: The Methods of Iconography," in *Picturing the New Testament: Studies in Ancient Visual Images*, ed. A. Weissenrieder, F. Wendt, and P. von Gemünden, WUNT 2/193 (Tübingen: Mohr Siebeck, 2005), 3–49.

2. J. M. C. Toynbee as quoted by Oster, "'Show Me a Denarius,'" 108.

the study of the New Testament and the study of numismatics. And at the center of this interdisciplinary project is the concept that coins are cultural texts.

Culture

The task ahead of us requires us to define "culture"—not an easy task. Culture is, of course, "like the water fish swim in."[3] For our more technical purposes, however, culture will be defined as being "made up of 'works' and 'worlds' of meaning."[4] Culture consists of works because it consists of what people do because of their nature and their actions. Culture also consists of worlds of meaning because of the realms of interaction that naturally accompany communication. To speak of "worlds of meaning" is to speak of the competing worldviews within a given culture consists of competing worldviews. These competing worldviews all seek to "invite us in and encourage us to make our home there."[5] If culture is made up of works and worlds of meaning, then cultural hermeneutics (also called cultural exegesis) is the art and science of interpreting culture.

Another word requiring some definition is *propaganda*. While this term has negative connotations due to modern marketing and media spin, the term is used here in a more neutral sense. Here I follow the definition provided by a Classics scholar focusing on the use of media in the Roman republic, who defines propaganda as:

> The educational efforts or information used by an organized group that is made available to a selected audience, for the specific purpose of making the audience take a particular course of action or conform to a certain attitude desired by the organized group.[6]

This definition is a powerful reminder of just how broad and inclusive *propaganda* can be. Although our interest is limited to coins, the Romans used music, uniforms, games, and processions as tools of communication.[7] What is unique about coins is that they were the most common, easily

3. J. Todd Billings, *The Word of God for the People of God: An Entryway to the Theological Interpretation of Scripture* (Grand Rapids: Eerdmans, 2010), 137.

4. Vanhoozer, "What Is Everyday Theology?," 26.

5. Ibid., 27.

6. Jane DeRose Evans, *The Art of Persuasion: Political Propaganda from Aeneas to Brutus* (Ann Arbor: University of Michigan Press, 1992), 1, also 19.

7. Ibid., 4.

distributable, and pervasive means of communication to the audience of the Empire. Furthermore, the symbols and iconography on coins provided one way to communicate where written communication would fail.[8]

Cultural texts are the products of a culture that "communicates meaning and calls for interpretation."[9] Coins certainly communicate meaning, and they definitely require interpretation. Coins are cultural texts that can be read and used as worldview lenses. We need nothing less than a coin-oriented hermeneutic to accompany robust New Testament hermeneutics.

Coins as Texts

The notion that a coin is a "text" is not a radically unique idea. Scholars have been known to refer to coins as "historical documents."[10] Perhaps this has been done without realizing the significance of the parallel between a document and a coin, as both require interpretation. Of course coins are not texts in the same sense that books, scrolls, and parchment are. Yet coins are undoubtedly a medium of communication.

One scholar has suggested that "looking at a coin is like proofreading a letter."[11] Another states that "coins are iconographical texts."[12] But he does not tease out how coins as "texts" might be interpreted beyond some basic comments. The terminology of "text" is interchangeable with "document" and both terms can reflect the concept of coins functioning as primary source material. However, as this study makes clear, the rhetorical power of coinage was so powerful that it is difficult to treat coinage as a wholly different category than "the treatment of history by ancient writers" that

8. "There was another way to overcome the illiteracy rate: the use of visual propaganda." Ibid.

9. Vanhoozer, "What Is Everyday Theology?," 26.

10. "It is notoriously difficult to analyze any particular work of art as an historical document in and of itself" (Paul Zanker, *The Power of Images in the Age of Augustus*, trans. Paul Shapiro, Jerome Lectures 16 [Ann Arbor: University of Michigan Press, 1988], iv). "Coins are both historical documents and archeological objects" (Fleur Kemmers and Nanouschka Myberg, "Rethinking Numismatics: The Archaeology of Coins," *Archaeological Dialogues* 18 [2011]: 89).

11. Scott A. Travers has suggested that "Looking at a coin is like proofreading a letter." However, his suggestion that coins are like "books" is limited by his interest in their commercial value in: *The Coin Collector's Survival Manual*, 6th ed. [New York: Random House, 2008], 11).

12. Pieter J. J. Botha states that "coins are iconographical texts" but he does not develop how coins as "texts" might be interpreted beyond some basic comments in: *Orality and Literacy in Early Christianity*, BPC 5 (Eugene: Cascade, 2010), 52.

more clearly reflects subjective interpretation.[13] Coins are not rhetorically or ideologically neutral historical objects. Coins are indeed "universally treated as historical documents of the first degree" but they are not often subject to any consideration for a robust hermeneutic.[14] One school of thought has begun to approach the interpretation of coins through linguistics. This contemporary approach is associated with the *Lexicon Iconographicum Numismaticae* (LIN) and uses concepts such as grammar and syntax to categorize iconography in an objective manner.[15] In this approach, the main type is understood as a noun and the subtypes are understood as adjectives.[16] Those who utilize this approach view iconography or images as words that have the capacity to "say" something to their users.[17]

We have seen that many resources describe coins as texts. But these descriptions of coins as texts are often thin descriptions because they do not ask the vital question: What is a text?

This question about the definition of a "text" has received a great deal of attention in the discipline of philosophy of language. The definition of texts is often set in relation to speech. Thus, a text is defined as "any discourse fixed by writing."[18] It is the fixed nature of writing, its enduring quality, that sets it apart from speech. Indeed, coins provide a unique medium that allows writing to be fixed for centuries. What is unique

13. "In the case of Roman history, we typically mean by 'documents' the coins, inscriptions, and papyri that survive directly from the time, as distinct from the treatment of the history by ancient writers" (E. A. Judge, *The First Christians in the Roman World: Augustan and New Testament Essays*, WUNT 229 [Tübingen: Mohr Siebeck, 2008], 378).

14. Nikos Kokkinos, *Antonia Augusta: Portrait of a Great Roman Lady* (London: Routledge, 1992), 87.

15. For further information on the *Lexicon Iconographicum Numismaticae*, the Messina school and Maria Caltabiano see (in Italian): M. Caccamo Caltabiano, L. Campagna, and A. Pinzone, eds., *Nuove prospsettive della ricerca sulla Sicilia del III sec. a.C.: archeologia, numismatica, storia* (Messina: Dipartimento di Scienze dell'Antichità dell'Università degli Studi di Messina, 2004).

16. Marianna Spinelli, "The 'Soma' of the God: Subtypes as Qualification of the Corporal Gestures of the Main Subject on the *Kaulonia* Coins," in *Identity and Connectivity: Proceedings of the 16th Symposium on Mediterranean Archaeology*, BAR 2581 (Oxford: Aracheopress, 2013), 793.

17. "The image, therefore, must be understood as a word" (ibid., 794).

18. Paul Ricoeur, *Hermeneutics and the Human Sciences: Essays on Language, Action and Interpretation*, trans. John B. Thompson (Cambridge: Cambridge University Press, 1981), 145.

about understanding coins as texts is that they stretch this widely known definition of a text. While coins often have writing or inscriptions on them, they also typically have art or symbols on them. These two features work together.

The totality of what the coin says encompasses not only the literal text (inscriptions), but the imagery as well. In order to determine what a coin is communicating, two things must be accomplished: (1) the inscriptions must be translated, and (2) the images must be identified. The study and deciphering of ancient inscriptions is often called "epigraphy." By using the term "inscription" for any physical writing on the coin face, we will avoid any confusion about what the "text" is.[19] Once we have translated the inscription and identified the images on the coin, we may begin to see whole "text" of the coin as it was received in the first-century context.

The two aspects of inscription and image work in tandem to create one (two-sided) text.[20] The inscription is a text in its own right but it is uniquely related to the image on the coin. The art or image must be understood to be part of the entirety of what the text is and what the text is doing. What one scholar applies to coinage of the third century CE can also be applied to the first century: "cooperation between text and image facilitated not only illiterates' understanding of the messages present on coins, it also reduced the various possibilities" of how it could be interpreted.[21] What is unique about the textuality of coins is that they require the reader to engage in an act of interpretation that includes both image and inscription. The image and the inscription are dialectically related and cannot be completely severed from each other.

19. Bruce Corley, Steve Lemke, and Grant Lovejoy note that the term "inscription" usually excludes coins in: *Biblical Hermeneutics: A Comprehensive Introduction to Interpreting Scripture*, 2nd ed. (Nashville: B&H, 2002), 452. On the other hand, others use the term "inscription" as inclusive of numismatics in: Thomas M. Seebohm, *Hermeneutics: Method and Methodology*, CPS (Norwell: Kluwer Academic, 2004), 86.

20. "In most symbol schemes, inscriptions may be combined in certain ways to make other inscriptions. An inscription is *atomic* if it contains no other inscription; otherwise it is *compound*" (emphasis his; Nelson Goodman, *Languages of Art: An Approach to a Theory of Symbols* [Indianapolis: Hackett, 1976], 141).

21. Erika Manders, *Coining Images of Power: Patterns in the Representation of Roman Emperors on Imperial Coinage, AD 193–284* (Leiden: Brill, 2012), 30.

Coins, Authors, and Audience

When considering coins as texts, we may also speak of them having some type of author. One numismatic scholar states: "The emperor came to be regarded as the effective *author* of the Roman public coinage and the regulator of its system of production at the imperial mint in Rome."[22] In fact, when coins are catalogued for study or for collectors they are often classified by the emperor or leader who issued them. This is arguably the best "staging point" for creating easily understandable taxonomies for the myriad of coins issued during the Roman Empire.[23] Furthermore, some numismatic scholars refer to coins as products of a ruler's intentions and perceptions of the world: "They [coins] are a true reflection of their time—of a "face of power's" perception of what he had done, what he was going to do, what he was going to get others to do, or what others were going to get him or her to do."[24]

Not only do contemporary sources view legal authorizers as the authors of their coins, but it seems that some first-century citizens of Judaea did as well. Jesus' famous interaction with the scribes and chief priests about Caesar's denarius in Luke 20:19–26 indicates that Jesus understood Caesar's image to communicate ownership as well as authorship. Some argue that there are two ways to look at authorship of Roman coins. First, there was the common public perception that coins with the emperor's image and inscription meant that "this coin belongs to Caesar."[25] Second, there was the view that the Senate and the People were the ultimate author of coins because they granted the power to make coins to the emperor. This means that coins and mints were a public institution and not a royal institution. This view is part of a larger argument that Republican modes of government lasted well into the imperial era.[26] Whichever position one takes, the main point of our argument remains: there was an author who

22. Williams, "Religion and Roman Coins," 157. Emphasis mine.

23. "Roman coins are inextricably linked to those who issued them. Indeed, that is the very basis upon which they are classified in the most general terms and it is the staging point from which the other aspects of the coin can be explored. But it is important to remember that the emperor who issued the coin often is not the one who is portrayed" (David L. Vagi, *Coinage and History of the Roman Empire*, 2 vols. [London: Fitzroy Dearborn, 1999], 2:34).

24. Brennan, Turner, and Wright, *Faces of Power*, 5.

25. Williams, "The Republican Identity of Roman Imperial Coinage: 1st to mid-3rd Centuries AD," 71.

26. "It should not come as a surprise that the Roman imperial coinage maintained an essentially Republican identity. Because, after all, the Romans themselves could

actively sought to communicate something to someone with the inscriptions and images on his coinage.

Coins also had audiences who read the coins as texts. The act of reading a coin considers its inscriptions and images as an act of communication. This audience receives the communication of their authors. One author states:

> The pervasiveness of imperial iconography, and the extent to which it became insinuated even in private contexts makes it likely that some groups in society (above all in Rome itself) were well able to "read" the imagery on coins if they wanted to.[27]

Others have observed that the art and images of objects such as coins are powerful tools for communication. Coins were the equivalent of first-century "media."[28] One might say that coins represent how strong the connection is between "visual language" and "visual imagery."[29] We could call this audience the readers and interpreters of the language communicated by images and inscriptions on coins.

One last item remains for this brief coverage of the relationship between authors and audience: there were undoubtedly hermeneutical misunderstandings. The fact that a coin's author(s) had some sort of intended meaning does not mean that this intended meaning was always understood or received. People may simply have misunderstood what was being communicated. This means that scholarship that focuses exclusively on intended meaning will not be able to account for all of the ways in which coins functioned as cultural texts. Coins and their respective worlds of meanings may have been involved in debates or controversy in their historical settings. Krmnicek and Elkins have suggested that scholars respond to this possibility by focusing on the "living body of images that were manufactured, disseminated, and received by cognizant viewers."[30] Social and cultural context is vitally important for interpretation. However, there is a place to recognize *both* authors with their

never quite bring themselves to admit that they were living under a monarchy, or at least that the monarchy did not entail the abandonment of their Republican traditions of the rule of law and constitutionality" (ibid., 72).

27. Howgego, *Ancient History from Coins*, 77.

28. Warren Carter, *The Roman Empire and the New Testament: An Essential Guide* (Nashville: Abingdon, 2006), 4.

29. Zanker connects "visual language" and "visual imagery" in *The Power of Images*, 3.

30. Stefan Krmnicek and Nathan T. Elkins, "Dinosaurs, Cocks, and Coins: An Introduction to 'Art in the Round,'" in *Art in the Round: New Approaches to Ancient*

intentions and audiences with their various interpretations of cultural texts. The presence of hermeneutical misfirings in the process of communication does not undermine the importance of the authorial intention.

The fact that coins have a combination of inscriptions and images requires us to make a small but important distinction. A coin is particular kind of text: a cultural text. By defining coins as cultural texts we are acknowledging that they have the unique property of possessing both image and inscription—a quality that writing alone does not have. To speak of coins as cultural texts means we may refer to coins as texts that have authors and readers. This overly simplistic hermeneutical model does not account for a wide variety of scenarios but lays a foundation for further development. In a nutshell, we can state that coins are cultural texts that call out for interpretation.

Context

Those within the realm of biblical studies are familiar with the hermeneutical maxim: "context is king." The twin contexts of grammar and history are the basic building blocks of interpretation. Coins must simply be considered, like other texts, within their grammatical-historical context. When analyzing a sentence or paragraph one need only read the surrounding textual units (sometimes called "co-texts") in order to gain insight about what the author was trying to communicate. In addition, the text can be situated within a certain historical framework of people, places, and events. This approach is not always possible with coins, at least to the same extent—for several reasons.

Context in the area of numismatics is unique. The reason why coins may have an unidentifiable historical context is because they often survived for hundreds of years. One scholar notes that "coins in antiquity often remained in circulation for long periods—up to hundreds of years—after they were minted."[31] The Greek tetradrachm of Athens featuring an owl and the head of Athena was used from the fifth to the third century BCE because the wealth and power of Athens after the Persian wars made it the *de facto* international currency.[32] This is why studying coins can

Coin Iconography, ed. Nathan T. Elkins and Stefan Krmnicek, TAF 16 (Rahden: Marie Leidorf, 2014), 7.

31. Jodi Magness, *The Archaeology of Qumran and the Dead Sea Scrolls* (Grand Rapids: Eerdmans, 2002), 10.

32. Barclay V. Head, *Catalogue of Greek Coins in the British Museum: Attica, Megaris, Aegina* (London: British Museum, 1888), xxii.

be somewhat different from studying texts that have identifiable original audiences. With respect to studying ancient coins from the Mediterranean one must be aware that the context is often unclear and as a result, there is no definitive context to be crowned as king. One of the ways to mitigate this difficulty is to locate coins within larger religious or social contexts and movements such as Hellenism or Judaism.

Context is difficult to define and is often complex. Using large religious and social movements as contexts for interpretation has obvious difficulties. With respect to the New Testament, the discussion continues in many circles about how best to capture the essence of Hellenism—particularly in the area of Judaea. Which elements of life were more Greek, and which were more Jewish? And one must be careful not to refer to only one type of Judaism! On the one hand, we must not suppose that Judaism in Judaea was cut from a wholly different cloth than Judaism in the diaspora (such as North Africa).[33] On the other hand, the land of Judaea was still understood by Jews to be sacred and the orbit of the temple in Jerusalem was surely a powerful presence. Ed Sanders explains this succinctly: "The historian begins with the basic commitment either to read X in light of X's own day or to determine how X was understood during some subsequent period. But...people live simultaneously in multiple contexts."[34] The matter of continuity and discontinuity between Greco-Roman culture and Jewish culture is not an easy issue and it certainly cannot be resolved here. Keeping the trees (the parts) and the forest (the whole) appropriately balanced is a delicate matter.

Context is often based on limited historical data. The attempt to "read" coins alongside the New Testament may lead to despair. The historical context of coinage is often unclear because the horizons of coinage are often very broad. Coins lasted a long time and were often distributed over a large geographical era. One scholar even suggests that we consider each coin as having its own biography.[35] This presents a methodological challenge to any study of coinage, especially as cultural texts, as coins may have been received by a wide range of cultures and contexts. It may seem as though there are so many simultaneous contexts that interpretation is impossible.

33. Mark A. Chancey, *Greco-Roman Culture and the Galilee of Jesus*, SNTSMS 134 (Cambridge: Cambridge University Press, 2005), 1–5.

34. Ed Sanders, "Paul Between Judaism and Hellenism," in *Saint Paul Among the Philosophers*, ed. Jack Caputo (Bloomington: Indiana University Press, 2009), 74.

35. Stefan Krmnicek, "Das Konzept der Objektbiographie in der antiken Numismatik," in *Coins in Context I: New Perspectives for the Interpretation of Coin Finds*, ed. H. V. Kaenel and F. Kemmers, SFMA 23 (Mainz: Philipp Von Zabern, 2009), 51.

One solution to this problem is to focus on the archaeological context in which a coin was discovered.[36] The reality is that hundreds of thousands of coins have been found and removed from their "grave" without any note. An extreme view on this matter will relegate too many coins to historical insignificance. But not all is lost in the matrix of historical contexts for the simple reason that we do not need to have exhaustive knowledge to have partial and even vital historical knowledge.

Context is important when defining economic value. The cultural conditions are, of course, sometimes difficult to ascertain. For example, Exod 30:13 states that there are 20 *gerahs* to the *shekel*. However, the *shekel* standard, like any other currency, would have changed in value depending on economic factors. There are several *shekels* mentioned in the Old Testament and one must be careful not to assume that every *shekel* was worth 20 *gerahs* in all the various time periods in which the *shekel* gets mentioned.[37] Economic value is not static or inherent in any object across time.

Economic systems and coins are contextual and dynamic. One numismatist states: "To produce a more complete picture of the past, coins must be studied in multiple contexts and in conjunction with other disciplines."[38] That means that the value of a given coin is relative to a culture—a certain time period and geographic location. Coins cannot be interpreted as cultural texts that communicated something to someone about something unless they are located in some cultural milieu.

Intertextuality

When scholars approach the biblical text it is now customary to use the term "intertextuality" to refer to one text's use of another. Just *how* a text is used by another text is a difficult idea to describe with precision. However, the concept of intertextuality and the term itself can arguably be appropriated by those seeking to understand how coins function as cultural texts.

Most books on ancient coins make reference to the origins of currency. But it is not always clear how the origins of coin-based currency impacts the era of history being considered. By approaching coins as cultural texts and appropriating the concept of intertextuality, we can explain how

36. Ibid., 47.

37. David Hendin, "Current Viewpoints on Ancient Jewish Coinage: A Bibliographic Essay," *CBR* 11 (2013): 259.

38. Elkins, "The Trade in Fresh Supplies of Ancient Coins," 95.

ancient coins relate to their antecedents. For example, early Roman coins borrowed heavily from the designs of the Greeks.[39] In this case we would state that the Greek coins were the antecedents of the Roman.

Our working definition of intertextuality as it applies to numismatics is as follows: coins are utilized intertextuality when contemporary coins imitate coins from a historically antecedent or contemporary era. Imitations of great rulers such as Alexander the Great were common, for example, and coins with his image were struck long after his death.

There are several reasons why the authors (minters) of coins sought to draw close connections between contemporary currency and antecedent currency. The first and most prominent reason is that an economic system that uses coins must rely to some degree on public trust and authority. Second, when a new mint or political power comes into existence, it must seek to instill confidence in its power.[40]

The authors of coins in the first century often imitated coins they considered historically trustworthy and well known. Intertextuality is likely a helpful concept to approach the way in which coins functioned as templates for other coinage. One scholar notes that "designs on Greek coins typically remained unchanged for decades or even centuries, varying only in style or detail over time."[41] Coins are cultural texts that drew heavily from tradition. Those traditions were sometimes strong enough to last millennia.

We will treat coins as cultural texts that have communicative power. A coin is not like a papyri or scroll, but it is a text nonetheless and a text that must be interpreted. As a text, it consists of the semantic features of the inscriptions and images upon it. Each coin is a text with pragmatic features: it had an author who sought to communicate meaning to someone about something. New Testament texts receive rigorous hermeneutical and methodological considerations as we interpret them. As we seek to locate the New Testament in the cultural milieu of the first century we will want to understand and compare other cultural artifacts and extant aspects of visual culture. This hermeneutical spiral requires that coins be approached with an equally rigorous methodology.

39. "The character of images on early Roman coinage was heavily influenced by the coinage of its Greek neighbors" (Elkins, "Coins, Context, and an Iconographic Approach," 25). Similarly, Williams, "Religion and Roman Coins," 144.

40. "It was the usual practice in the ancient world to imitate existing types that were current locally, in order to secure greater confidence in and prestige for a new coin minted by a recently established authority" (Meshorer, *Jewish Coins of the Second Temple Period* [Tel-Aviv: Am Hassefer, 1967], 58).

41. Williams, "Religion and Roman Coins," 143.

Summary

This chapter establishes a major pillar of the methodology behind this interdisciplinary study of coins in the world of the New Testament: *coins are cultural texts*. By providing a simple framework for robust and holistic scholarly analysis of ancient coins, those who specialize in biblical studies may find it easier to integrate these important artifacts into their work. Developing the idea that coins are cultural texts meant defining notoriously difficult concepts such as "culture" and "propaganda." Next we asserted that coins may be understood as a kind of text that calls out for interpretation, and this chapter introduced some of the challenges involved in interpreting coins in their historical context. The last section sought to create an analogy between the concept of intertextuality and the importance of tradition and imitation in ancient coinage.

Chapter 2

Coins as Speech-Acts

Interpreting coins requires a robust interpretive methodology. Speech-act theory offers an explicit account of their communicative power and their social context.

Introduction

Thus far we have established two salient points. First, coins are products of culture that reflect meaning and call out for interpretation. Second, coins may be considered texts in some sense because they present a discourse that integrates image and inscription. This has brought us to the conclusion that coins may be considered cultural texts. But how does one begin this process of interpreting coins as cultural texts? We observed above that many works of scholarship on coins conceive of coins as a type of text but fail to articulate a method for interpreting those texts. What is surprising about this lacuna in the scholarship is the widespread acknowledgment that coins are a type of text. This introductory study seeks to utilize elements of speech-act theory in order to establish a basic hermeneutical framework for interpreting coins.[1]

Speech-act theory states that language has three components: (1) locution, (2) illocution, and (3) perlocution. First, the *locution* is typically defined in linguistics as the utterance itself. When applied to numismatics we will nuance this definition to include images and inscriptions, the content on the coin. Second, the *illocution* is defined in linguistics as the force of the communication. In order to understand illocution one needs to ask: what is the person *doing* with what they are saying? When applied to coinage, one asks: what was the author or those in power *doing* with what they are communicating on this coin? Thus, speech-act theory asks

1. The credit for originating speech-act theory belongs to the linguistic philosopher J. L. Austin, *How to Do Things With Words*, 2nd ed. (Oxford: Oxford University Press, 1962).

us to situate coins within the social context lived by the users of the coinage.[2] A helpful equation states that "illocution is to locution as speech acts are to speech."[3] Third, the *perlocution* is typically defined as the response or reception of the communication, which may also be referred to as a perlocutionary effect. This consequential effect might include persuading, motivating, challenging, or moving someone to action. With these definitions in place, we can see that there are three important reasons why speech-act theory provides a source of foundational concepts for interpreting coins.

First, speech-act theory is an explicit approach to understanding communication—both spoken and written. It has been stated before that the major strength of speech-act theory is that it "offers a relatively explicit theory of communicative actions."[4] When applied to numismatics, this approach provides an underutilized but possibly significant source of integration for those understanding numismatic data and ancillary disciplines of the humanities. Integration is an important goal because coins are works and worlds of meaning that call out for interpretation. In other words, a methodology is required to explain the communicative power of coins. Coins are cultural texts with authors and audiences. One numismatist describes coins as occupying "a privileged place in the discourse between king and subjects."[5]

Second, speech-act theory is also quite appropriate for analyzing coins. It recognizes that the dialectical discourse between image and inscription and provides a lens through which the world can be viewed. For example, those coins that had an image of Caesar's bust on one side and on the other a depiction of symbols associated with military victory projected a world in which Caesar was the most honorable, powerful man in the known world. The reader or audience of the coin could accept or reject this discourse and then react to the world around them based on their response.

2. "Speech-act theory brings illocution to the fore by situating language within the relationships lived by its users" (Sandy Petrey, *Speech Acts and Literary Theory* [New York: Routledge, 1990], 13).

3. Ibid.

4. Michael L. Geis, *Speech Acts and Conversational Interaction* (Cambridge: Cambridge University Press, 1995), xii.

5. Andrew Meadows, "The Spread of Coins in the Hellenistic World," in *Explaining Money and Financial Innovation*, ed. P Bernholz and R. Vaubel, FMPS 39 (London: Springer, 2014), 173. Emphasis mine.

Third, speech-act theory emphasizes communicative action. The combination of inscriptions and images on coins provide communicative action. The meaning of a sentence is more than the sum of its words; likewise the communicative power of a coin is more than the sum of its parts. The authors of a given coin may be plural (minters, administrators, Caesar) and may be described on more than one level, yet they are authors nonetheless. (The fact that more than one person was involved in the production of coinage during the first century is likely a moot point because of the strong autocratic nature of the Empire—the Emperor had to approve everything.[6])

In sum, speech-act theory provides the tools for answering the question: what was the author or those in power *doing* with this coin as a cultural text? We will now expand and apply what each component of speech-act theory means for studying coins.

The World in Front of the Coin

We are moving through the three aspects of text, reader, and author. The world *of* the coin is a world of meaning conveyed by symbols and inscriptions, among other things. We now turn to the world *in front* of the coin to understand the role of the reader. We use the term "reader" to highlight the fact that the designs on coins had to be received and interpreted. In speech-act theory this act of reception is called the perlocutionary aspect of communication. The first section of this book focuses on this perlocutionary aspect of speech-act theory.

When we refer to the "world in front of the coin" we are seeking to understand the role of the reader of coins in the first century. This is the most difficult section because it is the most broad and general by its very nature. The world *behind* coins is rather limited to public officials and the world *of* the coin is limited to its physical qualities. But the world *in front* of the coin is as broad and diverse as the entire Roman Empire.

Given the broad range of those in front of the coin, we can only hope to draw attention to certain cultural and historical dynamics. Drawing attention to select data will enable those who are involved in biblical studies to make connections with numismatic (coin-based) historical data.

6. "In periods of autocracy, at any rate, whether coin types were dictated from above to present an official image, or chosen by lower officials to flatter, the result will have been the same. The coins showed what was desirable to the regime. That is what matters" (Howgego, *Ancient History from Coins*, 70).

In order to keep this chapter manageable, we will focus on the numismatic concept that would have resonated most with those who lived in the first century: payment. The world in front of the coin did not have to receive the communication the coin offered in order to find practical value in the coin.

The world in front of the coin was nothing less than the entire Roman Empire. A brief perusal of maps will indicate how far Paul's missionary journeys took him. After all, Paul is charged in Thessalonica with turning the whole known "world" upside down (Acts 17:6). If our date range spans 37 BCE to 100 CE, then the scope of the world in front of the coin will be quite large.

There was no uniform approach to wealth and money in the Roman Empire. Various social networks, especially religious sects, had unique perspectives on wealth and how it should be handled. It is unlikely that any one model will be "universally valid" and able to encompass the interactions of Greek, Roman, and local cultures.[7] In an area and time as complex as the Roman Empire in the first century, this requires a perspective that provides as much breadth as possible.

There is clear evidence to suggest that people were aware of the images and inscriptions on coins, as attested by the following quotation from the stoic philosopher Epictetus (ca. 100 CE):

> The stamps with which a man comes imprinted on his disposition [are] like the stamps we look for on coins too: if we find them we accept their value, if we don't, we chuck them out. "Whose stamp does this sesterce bear? Trajan's? Take it. Nero's? Chuck it out, it will not pass, it is rotten." (Arrian, *Discourses of Epictetus* 4.5.15–17)[8]

One scholar concludes, "Coin types were no doubt often 'misunderstood,'" but there is no doubt they had an impact.[9] This can be seen in the changing hairstyles of women in the first century, influenced by the images on coins of prominent Roman women such as Livia (the wife of Augustus).[10]

7. Chancey, *Greco-Roman Culture and the Galilee of Jesus*, 11.

8. Quoted by Olivier Hekster, "Coins and Messages: Audience Targeting on Coins of Different Denominations?," in *Representation and Perception of Roman Imperial Power*, ed. L. de Blois et al. (Leiden: Brill, 2003), 20.

9. Howgego, *Ancient History from Coins*, 74.

10. Ibid.

Another piece of evidence of the impact of coinage on the ancient audience is specific to Judaism. Images of deities, animals, humans, and especially Caesar were considered forbidden by the Law of Moses. With respect to the population of Jews in the Empire, we have clear literary evidence that images on coins had a significant impact (e.g. Mark 12:17). While there is little information about the effect of coins upon the audience in antiquity, the first-century context affords *some* historical data. (Thus, it would be an exaggeration to conclude as Evans does that "as far as the effect of coins on the audience, we are at an almost complete loss."[11])

The Civil War of 68–69 CE is a further example of how coins were used to communicate messages to specific audiences. The civil war followed the suicide of the emperor Nero in 68 CE. This was also called the Year of the Four Emperors, as Galba, Otho, Vitellius, and Vespasian vied for the throne. Galba's silver and gold coinage focused on garnering provincial support while bronze coins focused on rallying the urban citizens and featured urban themes.[12] Otho did not strike bronze coinage but Vitellius struck all denominations with themes of peace and harmony amongst the citizens and soldiers. Vespasian's gold *aureus* and silver *denarius* feature a victorious general.[13] The coins of this era portray the fact that "different types of legends on the different types of coins" reflected "a difference of primary audience."[14] The Civil War of 68–69 CE demonstrates that coins were used to communicate specific messages to specific people groups and that political crises created a context in which the messages on coins were politically forceful. Why would would-be emperors bother to mint coinage bearing their likenesses if they did not view coins as an important expression of their claim to rule?

Last, there is a case to be made that the ideal or implied readers of most imperial Roman coins from the first century were legionary soldiers. One scholar explains that the complexity and symbols on coins "seem to have been designed for the appreciative intelligence of a reasonably well-educated mind accustomed to weighing the nuances of imperial policy."[15] This may further be supported by the fact that high-ranking soldiers were one of the direct recipients of government payments. This thesis about the implied readers of coins being the educated soldiers cannot be proven but remains a viable starting point when tackling interpretative difficulties.

11. Evans, *The Art of Persuasion*, 19.

12. Hekster, "Coins and Messages," 26.

13. Ibid.

14. Ibid.

15. C. H. V. Sutherland and R. A. G. Carson, *The Roman Imperial Coinage: From 31 BC to AD 69* (London: Spink & Son, 1984), 13.

When considering the world in front on the coin, one should consider the maxim: "liveliness on coins reflects political instability."[16] In order to examine the wide-ranging purposes for coins in the first-century marketplace across the entire Roman Empire, we will keep our focus on those things which everyone had in common: trust, fear, and taxes. We will examine how the monetary system relied upon a web of trust and how the storage of coins expressed fear of robbers, war, and even death. We will also consider how coins related to the stresses and dynamics of paying taxes, especially in the context of Judaea.

The World of the Coin

One of the overarching concerns of this volume is to highlight the three "worlds" that must be considered in order to interpret coins properly. Each "world" can be considered independently, but none can be divorced completely from the other worlds. These three worlds correspond, of course, to the triple dynamic of text–reader–author. In this chapter we will consider the world *of* the coin. *Section II will develop the idea that the world of the coin is a world of propaganda.*

It is widely agreed upon that coins were ideological tools for those in power. If "ideology" may be defined as "worldview with an attitude" we might say that coins in the world of the New Testament had attitude.[17] But it has not always been the case that coins have been viewed as propaganda. As recently as half a century ago, prominent numismatists argued against this view.[18] But this minimalist approach to interpreting coins has been widely overturned in recent scholarship. The debate that remains today turns on the difference between the idea of "propaganda" and the more basic idea of "communicating a message."[19]

The following paragraphs directly address directly addresses the ideology of coins by referring to the world of the coin. Cultural texts invite the reader or viewer into a "meaningful environment in which humans dwell… imaginatively."[20] The "government-sponsored art" on coins quickly became

16. A. Wallace-Hadrill, "Image and Authority in the Coinage of Augustus," *JRS* 67 (1986): 66–87; also quoted by Hekster, "Coins and Messages," 26.

17. For the definition of "ideology" as "worldview with attitude" see David Wells, *Above All Earthly Pow'rs: Christ in a Postmodern World* (Grand Rapids: Eerdmans, 2005), 25.

18. Jones, "Numismatics and History," 13–33.

19. Hekster, "Coins and Messages," 22.

20. Vanhoozer, "What Is Everyday Theology?," 26.

a tool that used symbols to communicate propaganda.[21] For example, a coin that portrays the head of Caesar might be projecting an imaginative world upon the viewer in which Caesar is at the center of the world, the savior of humankind, the most honorable man, and the greatest benefactor.

Because coins were so widespread in the Roman Empire, they could easily communicate messages to vast amounts of semi-literate and illiterate people. This was particularly important for those in power because the images on coins could create relationships with authorities of greater power or with predecessors. The relationships created with the coins served the purpose of establishing honor in the benefactor hierarchy.

When we speak of "propaganda" in the first century, we must do so with an important qualifier. The messages that those in power intended to communicate through coins was not as "systematically developed" as contemporary propaganda machines.[22] This is largely a reflection of the technology available. Whereas modern propaganda often overwhelms the senses with sounds and images, ancient propaganda was generally limited to static images. Although ancient propaganda was less systematic than it is today, this should not be assumed as a reflection of intention but a reflection of technological limitation.

Roman coins are widely viewed as a form of propaganda.[23] Our goal is to cast a wide net and include Jewish coins as well as Roman coins. In this section we will examine the physical properties of coinage, the world of the coin itself. We will see that the world of the coin, its form, inscriptions, images, and metallic content could be offered to the world as a lens through which to view the Empire; together these properties could be used to communicate something to someone about something.

The very form of the coin was used to communicate propaganda. There are two sides to every coin, with each side playing a special role in communication. One side, generally speaking, was used to communicate something about a person and the other about their attributes or

21. "Coins are government-sponsored art, and coin iconography therefore usually reflects the official ideology by means of recognizable symbols. The wide circulation of these coins thus affords an opportunity for political propaganda" (Catherine M. Murphy, *Wealth in the Dead Sea Scrolls and in the Qumran Community*, STDJ 40 [Leiden: Brill, 2001], 316).

22. "Self-representation in this way was never as systematically developed as the products of modern propaganda machines, but, as with the study of portraiture, it can be very revealing about the aspirations and claims of any regime, matters which are as interesting to the historian as the reality of what actually happened" (Andrew Burnett, *Coins*, Interpreting the Past [Berkeley: University of California Press, 1991], 37).

23. Kreitzer, *Striking New Images*, 22.

achievements. Some coins were issued in sets so that the imagery and symbolism corresponded to each other. For example, around 30 BCE, six denarii were issued together that idealized Octavian (Augustus) and the peace he achieved through military victory.[24]

When it comes to the scientific and historical study of coins the terms get a little more complicated. Each side of the coin has its own term and most literature that interacts with coin-based data will refer to the *obverse* (the front of the coin, abbreviated as "obv.") and the *reverse* (the back of the coin, abbreviated as "rev."). In modern language, the *obverse* is equivalent to "heads" and the *reverse* is equivalent to "tails." In photographs, it is now standard to display the *obverse* on the left and the *reverse* on the right. Knowing which side is which is important because most coins use the significance of *obverse* and *reverse* to communicate something to someone.

The World Behind the Coin

The world *behind* the coin refers to those people, powers, and institutions that created, designed, stamped, and minted the coin. If a coin is a "text," then the world behind the coin refers to the communicative action of the "author(s)" behind the coin. This is in contrast to the world *of* the coin which generally refers to those elements of inscriptions and images on the coin and the world *in front* of the coin that focuses on how the coin was received. *This section will argue that the author(s) of coins used them primarily to communicate something about their power*.

Arguably the best word to capture the dynamics of the world behind the coin in the first century is *power*. The power to mint coins was only possible through significant political control. Those who had military or civilian political control often wanted to use coins to communicate something to those underneath them. One scholar explains, "coins provide a clear example of government-sponsored inscriptions, their designs chosen by and expressing the values of social elites."[25]

Coinage in the context of the first century has been likened to present-day billboards.[26] One scholar explains it this way: "Coinage was a

24. Ibid., 31.

25. Mark A. Chancey, "The Epigraphic Habit of Hellenistic and Roman Galilee," in *Religion, Ethnicity, and Identity in Ancient Galilee: A Region in Transition*, ed. J. Zangenberg, H. W. Attridge and D. B. Martin, WUNT 210 (Tübingen: Mohr Siebeck, 2007), 86.

26. Oster, "'Show Me a Denarius,'" 108.

pervasive symbol of the authority responsible for its issue."[27] Perhaps a case could be made that the images on coins were used like webpage pop-up advertisements; most of the general public was exposed to the visual message.

The world behind the coin focuses on what the powers behind the coin *meant to say* with each particular combination of images and inscriptions. It is precisely because we can use the images and inscriptions, along with other historical evidence, to attempt to ascertain what the "author" of the coin was trying say that numismatics intersects with hermeneutics—the art and science of interpretation.

The reference to the "world behind the coin" is designed to be either broad in scope or narrow in scope. Broadly speaking, this world is the world of production. This includes artisans, engravers, miners, smelters, blacksmiths, carvers, and so on.

The more narrow application of the "world behind the coin" refers to those in power who made the decision(s) about what the coin looked like and what was going to be communicated. When we view coins as cultural texts we can identify this person (or people) as *authors*. The authors of coins in the first century were communicative agents who selected images and inscriptions that would communicate something to someone about something.[28]

By "author," we are not referring to the person who provided the manual or skilled labor needed to produce coinage. Rather, we are using the term "author" to refer to those in power who directed and controlled the images and inscriptions. The term "author" is meant to be flexible so that it can refer to the collective of those in power. In some contexts it could refer to a single individual in power, often cultural or political elites. Section III of this book argues that the authors of coins in the era surrounding the writing of the New Testament were largely interested in using coins to communicate something about their power.

This approach to referring to the "author" of coinage is intentionally vague and flexible because of the limitations of historical data. We do not know who was responsible for the entire process of making coins. One scholar lists the types of questions that remain unanswered. He

27. Burnett, *Coins*, 29.

28. "For, with the notion of meaning as a form of action, the author returns, not in his or her Cartesian guise as an all determining self-conscious subject, but as a communicative agent" (Kevin J. Vanhoozer, *Is There a Meaning in This Text? The Bible, the Reader, and the Morality of Literary Knowledge* [Grand Rapids: Zondervan, 1998], 203).

asks, was it a group of officials? A single bureaucrat? The coin makers?[29] Furthermore, he notes that "the process for design selection may have varied from city to city."[30] The only thing we do know in broad terms is that a single person or group of people had the authority to create, approve, and implement the minting of coinage. Where more specific information is available, it should be used to identify who was engaged in the act of communication through the coinage.

To clarify, the term "author" is used by necessity, as a collective. This is particularly true for identifying coinage from Palestine/Judaea.[31] While there was a certain ethnic and religious unity amongst Jews in power during the First Jewish Revolt, there were also sects and factions that are difficult to identify with precision. To illustrate, we might refer to Jews as the collective authors of the coins minted in or near Jerusalem during the First Jewish Revolt. By doing so, we would be highlighting their unity as a people-group and the idea of authorship is more collective in nature.

Summary

This chapter took the idea that coins are cultural texts one step further by utilizing speech-act theory to articulate the relationship between authors, coins, and their audiences. We concluded that this is appropriate because coins are cultural texts that were embedded in the "discourse" between Caesar and the subjects of the Empire.[32] As such, coins require a robust and holistic hermeneutic that can consider their communicative powers. This chapter suggests a modified form of speech-act theory to understand the relationship between rulers, coins, and the Empire. Speech-act theory consists of three aspects: the locutionary, the illocutionary, and the perlocutionary. These three aspects correspond to the following three sections of this book: (1) the world *in front* of the coin (those who used the coinage for monetary purposes), (2) the world *of* the coin itself (a fixed combination of inscription and image), and (3) the world *behind* the coin (the people who stamped it and chose its features).

29. Chancey, "City Coins and Roman Power in Palestine," 104.

30. Ibid.

31. I use "Judaea" as a geographical term that is interchangeable with the more politically charged term "Palestine."

32. Meadows, "The Spread of Coins in the Hellenistic World," 173.

Chapter 3

COINS AS CURRENCY

The currency systems of the first-century Roman Empire were complex. They were a mixture of conventions old and new, east and west, provincial and Empire-wide.

Introduction

The first place to start understanding the "world of the coin" is with standard denominations of value and the framework of the currency system. The problem is that few ancient writers said anything about currency or the motifs featured on them.[1] The ancient historian Pliny in his *Natural History* is an exception.[2] This fact forces historians to rely upon archaeological finds and make extrapolations based on known data. Because our study focuses upon the communicative power of coinage in the Jewish and Roman world's we will not delve into the various economic theories and issues (e.g. price movements, monetization, etc.) which might otherwise be relevant. Although the Jewish currency system was technically subservient to Rome's control, I treat it here under a separate heading for the sake of simplicity and because most New Testament scholars will want to see a specific focus on this region.

The Roman Currency System

The Roman currency system of the first century defies simple explanation because it was as complex as the Empire itself. As a system of currency it was composed of six base denominations with various fractions and multiples: (1) gold aureus, (2) silver denarius, (3) sestertius,

1. Richard Duncan-Jones, *Money and Government in the Roman Empire* (Cambridge: Cambridge University Press, 1994), 97.

2. Ibid.

(4) dupondius, (5) as, and (6) quadrans.[3] In order to make this system of currency accessible for our interdisciplinary study we will use a series of simplistic but helpful generalizations.

First, the Roman currency system was characterized by differences in coinage in the two major halves of the Empire. The Roman Empire can be broken down into two large geographical areas: east and west. The one exception to this was Egypt, which used its own currency.[4] In the eastern cities, the coins were smaller in size and denomination and composed of bronze and copper.[5] In the east, local gods were common on provincial coins whereas they were not normally integrated into the Roman pantheon in the west.[6] In the east, monuments do not commonly appear on coins till the end of the first century. In the west, client kings often echoed the architecture and buildings of Rome throughout the first century.[7] When buildings do appear on coins in the east, they are generic in nature whereas buildings in the west are more specifically related to the temples and cultic activities of Roman public religion.[8] The mixing of eastern Greek coins and western Roman coins is also evident in Mark's need to inform the reader that two Greek lepta are equivalent to a Roman quadrans (Mark 12:42). The flow of Greek drachma and other coins through the Roman economy was not dictated by imperial policy but rather by normal patterns of trade around the Mediterranean.[9]

Second, the Roman currency system was practically based on the denarius (δηνάριον) as the standard coinage. This was the case for nearly five hundred years (264 BCE to 238 CE).[10] The silver denarius was effectively the standard coin of the Empire even though it was not technically

3. Sutherland and Carson, eds., *The Roman Imperial Coinage*, 3.

4. Reiser, "Numismatik und Neues Testament," 458. In Egypt, the term "denarius" referred to the Egyptian tetradrachm and the "as" referred to the obol (Bradley H. McLean, *An Introduction to Greek Epigraphy of the Hellenistic and Roman Periods from Alexander the Great Down to the Reign of Constantine [323 BCE–CE 337]* [Ann Arbor: University of Michigan Press, 2002], 372).

5. Marcus Sigismund, "Small Change?: Coins and Weights as a Mirror of Ethnic, Religious and Political Identity in First and Second Century C.E. Tiberias," in Zangenberg, Attridge and Martin, eds., *Religion, Ethnicity, and Identity*, 317.

6. Christopher Howgego, "Coinage and Identity in the Roman Provinces," in *Coinage and Identity in the Roman Provinces*, ed. C. Howgego, V. Heuchert, and A. Burnett (Oxford: Oxford University Press, 2005), 3.

7. Ibid., 4.

8. Ibid.; Williams, "Religion and Roman Coins," 148.

9. Kenneth W. Harl, *Coinage in the Roman Economy, 300 B.C. to A.D. 700*, Ancient Society and History (Baltimore: The Johns Hopkins University Press, 1996), 106.

10. Ibid., 6.

a universal currency, the exceptions being Asia and Egypt.[11] The silver denarius was equal to a typical day's wage. It was often distributed directly to soldiers for services rendered. It is estimated that a farm worker might have earned 0.5 denarius per day whereas a Roman solider would have earned 0.66–0.8 denarius per day.[12] Over the centuries, the denarius varied in its silver content.[13] The fineness of the silver remained relatively constant through the reigns of Augustus, Tiberius, Caligula, and Claudius.[14] Current scientific evidence points to the conclusion that "emperors were anxious to restore the fineness" of coinage or increase the metallic purity whenever they could.[15] The imperial mint likely moved from Lyon (in what is now France) to Rome during the reign of Caligula.[16] It was not until the reign of Nero that the fineness of silver in denarii was reduced to about 93%.[17] Obols (a Greek silver coin worth one sixth of a drachma) were not minted after the reign of Augustus.[18] Where locally minted coins were minted and preferred, such as the drachmas minted in Egypt, Asia Minor and Syria, they would probably have been converted into denarii before being used in wider geographical contexts.[19]

Third, the Roman currency system used gold for accounting and large-scale currency transfers. The standard gold coin of the Roman Empire was the Aureus (plural: Aureii). The Aureus was worth about 25 denarii.[20] Gold coins might have been a rare sight in the marketplace but that does not mean they did not play an important role in government transactions. Under the Principate of Rome, the Empire had enough access to gold to use it for shipping currency. This would have been important for

11. Richard Duncan-Jones, *Structure and Scale in the Roman Economy* (Cambridge: Cambridge University Press, 1990), 39.

12. Some numismatic scholars use the weight of coins and their respective silver content to chart issues such as metal scarcity. This work may provide historical evidence of social issues such as war and poverty.

13. McLean, *Introduction to Greek Epigraphy*, 375.

14. For a chart on the fineness of denarii from Lyon see Kevin Butcher and M. Ponting, "The Denarius in the First Century," in *Proceedings of the XIV International Numismatic Congress: Glasgow 2009*, ed. N. Holmes (Glasgow, 2011), 558.

15. Ibid., 567.

16. Ibid., 558.

17. Ibid., 559.

18. Daniel Sperber, "Palestinian Currency Systems During the Second Commonwealth," *Jewish Quarterly Review* 56 (1966): 282; Karl Christ, *Antike Numismatik: Einführung und Bibliographie* (Darmstadt: Wissenschaftliche Buchgesellschaft, 1972), 18.

19. McLean, *Introduction to Greek Epigraphy*, 372–73.

20. Reiser, "Numismatik und Neues Testament," 458.

long-distance shipments because gold is lighter that silver.[21] One numismatist argues that we should not read too much into the lack of gold coins found in hoards when ascertaining the importance of gold coins in the first century.[22]

Fourth, the Roman currency system was a mix of old and new coinage. The silver coinage from the Republic did not simply disappear with the rise of the Empire. Even though some old currency was melted or re-stamped, the first half of the first century saw little intentional government action to recall old coinage. The value of silver coins was based in part on their weight. This meant that they could retain value for decades if not centuries. Such moves to remove old currency were not enacted till the reigns of Nero and Trajan.[23] The motives for such government intervention were based on the ability to melt down older coinage with a higher concentration of silver and produce more coinage with smaller concentrations.[24]

Fifth, the Roman currency system of the first century was a relatively new phenomenon. Following the principle of numismatic intertextuality described earlier, the images on coins in Greece remained fundamentally unchanged for decades and even centuries. This consistency transferred into the Roman era of the republic. The late second century BCE "did not differ fundamentally from its Greek civic counterparts with regard to form or design."[25] Then something changed that would make Roman coinage characterized by constantly changing designs and empower them as tools of political propaganda. The critical change was the introduction of secret ballots at political elections (*Lex Gabinia tabellaria*). This use of secret ballots forced politicians to use coinage to communicate their honor, family, and achievements to their city or province. Naturally, this expanded the types and range of imagery "far beyond what had previously been normal in Greek traditions."[26] Thus, coins became the equivalent of modern-day billboards for political self-promotion.

The Jewish Currency System

As a Roman province, Judaea used two contemporaneous currency systems: a Jewish provincial currency system and the imperial currency

21. Duncan-Jones, *Structure and Scale in the Roman Economy*, 45.
22. Ibid.
23. Duncan-Jones, *Money and Government in the Roman Empire*, 99.
24. Ibid., 102.
25. Williams, "Religion and Roman Coins," 144.
26. Ibid.

system. The two systems were not exactly parallel but must have functioned well enough to allow for international commerce.[27] Thus, it is not possible to separate Jewish coinage from Roman coinage completely.

Ancient Jewish coins were produced in Judaea in four non-contiguous periods that cover about 300 years.[28] The first period of production aligns with the Maccabean revolt (139–137 BCE). The second period roughly parallels the reign of Herod the Great (37–4 BCE). The Herodian period overlaps with a period characterized by Prefects and Procurators of Judaea (6–66 CE). The third period parallels the First Jewish Revolt against Rome (66–70 CE) and the fourth parallels the Second Revolt (132–135 CE). With respect to Jewish coins, we will focus on the first century, which includes coins from Herod the Great, Prefects and Procurators, and the First Jewish revolt.

Within the first century there were coins minted in and around Judaea by six parties: (1) Herod the Great, (2) his son, Herod Antipas, (3) his other son Herod Archelaus, (4) his grandson Herod Agrippa, (5) Roman Procurators or Equestrians responsible for fiscal administration and (6) rebels during the First Jewish Revolt.[29] As we proceed we will consider four major items that are relevant for understanding the Jewish currency system.

First, Jewish coinage came in a variety of fractions. One scholar explains: "The range of weights within the same type is often so great as to enable one to state the smallest specimen in terms of a fraction of the largest one, even though they are manifestly of the same denomination."[30] Small coinage based on fractions was especially important because it enabled merchants to make small transactions in the local markets. Coins of smaller denominations also rose in popularity when metal was scarce due to economic or war-time conditions. The wide use of small coinage likely led to the use of scales being used to weigh out the equivalent of larger amounts of monies. For example, Jesus' parable of the ten minas (Luke 19:11–27) relies upon the audience being familiar with the "mina" (μνᾶ), roughly the equivalent of one hundred drachmas or one hundred denarii. Likewise, the Gospel of Matthew exclusively refers to a "talent"

27. Sperber, "Palestinian Currency Systems During the Second Commonwealth," 275, also 280.

28. David Hendin and Nathan Bower, "Irregular Coins of Judaea, First Century BCE–First Century CE: New Insights from Comparisons of Stylistic, Physical, and Chemical Analysis," *AJN* Second Series 23 (2011): 36.

29. Romanoff, *Jewish Symbols*, 8.

30. Sperber, "Palestinian Currency Systems During the Second Commonwealth," 279.

(ταλάντον) fifteen times in the parable of the unmerciful servant (Matt 18:21–35) and the parable of the talents (Matt 25:14–30). Like the "mina," the "talent" was used to refer to a large sum of money—one "talent" being equal to about six thousand denarii.[31]

Second, the most commonly used Jewish coins were small copper denominations. The *prutah* stands out as a commonly used coinage available in fractions. The prutah was the smallest unit of currency available and it was available in half-prutah forms.[32] Two pruta made a *quadrans*.[33] There are at least 27 general types of prutah. During the first century, the *shekel* was worth 256 *prutot* and one prutah was worth a pomegranate—a fruit that was often freely available.[34] Jewish lead coins (*prutot*) appeared about 100 BCE and some were in usage around the first century CE.[35] The bronze prutah (or *pruta* or *perutah*; plural *prutot*) was one of the coins minted locally in Judaea and the word itself is Semitic in origin.[36] Although many were minted before the era of the New Testament, many would have continued to circulate well into the first century.[37] The prutah was also called a *lepton*. The word *leptos* (λεπτός) occurs only three times in the New Testament: Mark 12:41, Luke 12:59 and 21:2. The Koine Greek word *leptos* refers to something, small, thin, and light.[38] In the Septuagint, the word is used to describe scrawny cows in Genesis.[39] Clearly the word was appropriated by the marketplace and its connotations fit with the small copper prutot. The half-prutah would have been the smallest and most common copper coin in Judaea. There is no way absolutely to identify which prutah is the famous "widows mite" although some sellers today may claim this in order to increase sales.

31. Werner G. Marx, "Money Matters in Matthew," *BSac* 136 (1979): 156.

32. The "minute half-perutot all emanate from Caesarea, for all the coins of this type which we have been able to trace were found there" (Meshorer, *Jewish Coins of the Second Temple Period*, 89).

33. Sperber, "Mark 7:42 and Its Metrological Background," 180.

34. Hendin, "Current Viewpoints on Ancient Jewish Coinage," 262.

35. David Hendin, "Four New Jewish Lead Coins or Tokens," *INJ* 13 (1994–99): 63–65.

36. Sperber, "Palestinian Currency Systems During the Second Commonwealth," 282.

37. Hendin, "Current Viewpoints on Ancient Jewish Coinage," 262.

38. BDAG, 592, s.v. λεπτός.

39. English translation of LXX Gen 41:3: Robert J. V. Hiebert, trans., *A New English Translation of the Septuagint and the Other Greek Translations Traditionally Included Under That Title: Genesis* (Oxford: Oxford University Press, 2009), 34. Greek text: *Rahlfs Septuaginta: With Morphology*, Logos electronic ed. (Stuttgart: Deutsche Bibelgesellschaft, 1979), LXX Gen 41:3.

Third, smaller coins were irregularly produced and poorly made. As a whole, these small copper coins were "poorly made" and "off center."[40] But the irregular coinage makes up about 2% to 7% of the coinage from excavation data and coin hoards.[41] Some scholars have complained that "almost no excavation reports make distinctions between standard and irregular Jewish bronze issues."[42] The irregular coins are characterized by a cruder style and may be underweight. These might reflect war-time conditions that required temporary or mobile mints, the work of apprentices, quasi-legitimate copies, or ancient forgeries. Recent analysis indicates that this irregular (bad) coinage was characterized by longevity and consistency.[43] This points to the use of semi-official local Judaean minters that operated apart from the quality and control of the official mints (e.g. Jerusalem).[44]

Fourth, Jewish coinage was oriented around the shekel. Even though the small copper prutot were popular in the poor area of Judaea, the system was tied to the shekel. The Tyrian Shekel derives its name from the coinage of Tyre, a port city in modern day Lebanon. The mint in Tyre was a major source of coin production in the Levant from the fourth century BCE to the third century CE.[45] Some refer to this shekel as the "Tyrian standard" or the "holy shekel."[46] The shekel was a coin that appeared in half-shekel and quarter-shekel forms. It was also understood to be tetradrachm and part of the Greek system of coinage based on the drachma. The half-shekel was used for the yearly temple tax and was quite common, whereas the quarter-shekel seems to have been used much less.[47] Generally speaking, the shekel was worth about 256 copper prutot.[48]

Fifth, Jewish coinage was regularly mixed with Roman coinage. A good example of this that is relevant to the New Testament is the small copper *assarion*. The word assarion (ἀσσάριον) is the Greek form of the

40. Hendin and Bower, "Irregular Coins of Judaea, First Century BCE," 36.

41. Ibid.

42. Ibid.

43. Ibid., 38.

44. Ibid., 40.

45. Danny Syon, "The Bronze Coinage of Tyre: The First Years of Autonomy," *AJN* Second Series 20 (2008): 295.

46. Sperber, "Palestinian Currency Systems during the Second Commonwealth," 281.

47. Meshorer, *Jewish Coins of the Second Temple Period*, 89.

48. Hendin, "Current Viewpoints on Ancient Jewish Coinage," 262.

Latin word *asin* in the singular and *asses* in the plural.[49] The assarion was generally worth about 1/16 of a denarius. Some New Testament commentators cite the assarion as the smallest denomination of Roman coins.[50] This may be true, but bronze coinage was often broken down into even smaller amounts. Thus, the quadrans ("a quarter" of an assarion) served as the smallest low-value bronze coin available in the Roman Empire.[51] Like any currency, the value of it would fluctuate based on geographical and economic realities.

Sixth, Jewish coinage and Roman coinage in Judaea rarely pictured humans or animals. The Romans generally respected the Jewish aniconic beliefs that forbade images of humans and animals due to the Mosaic law and rabbinic customs. The Roman Procurators of Judaea and the Jews who were placed in positions of power rarely broke this rule. This was likely done out of a desire to keep the peace and avoid unnecessary uprisings against Roman authority. It was only after the Jewish revolt of 66–70 CE that coins with imperial portraits appear.[52]

Summary

This chapter sought to provide an entryway into understanding the Roman and Jewish currency systems of the first century. This was done by highlighting the poles of old and new, east and west, provincial and Empire-wide. Those interested in coinage that relates to the New Testament will have to understand both the Roman currency system and the Jewish currency system—and it may be more accurate to refer to currency *systems*. The currency systems are as complex as the social and cultural dynamics that characterized the people groups that are relevant for New Testament studies.

49. T. Mitchell, *The Bible in the British Museum: Interpreting the Evidence* (London: British Museum Press, 1988), 99.

50. The *assarion* "was the smallest of Roman coins" according to Craig A. Evans, *Luke*, UBCS (Grand Rapids: Baker, 1990), 200. Similarly, Darrell L. Bock, *Luke*, IVPNTC (Downers Grove: InterVarsity, 1994), 222.

51. "In the imperial series the quadrans replaced the sextans as the smallest denomination in c. 91/90 BC" (Howgego, *Ancient History from Coins*, 122).

52. Philip F. Esler, "God's Honour and Rome's Triumph: Responses to the Fall of Jerusalem in 70 CE in Three Jewish Apocalypses," in *Modelling Early Christianity: Social-Scientific Studies of the New Testament in Its Context*, ed. P. E. Esler (London: Routledge, 1995), 242.

Chapter 4

Coins as Context

The text of the New Testament directly references coins in several places. This means that coins are an integral part of the literary and historical context that must be considered in the process of interpretation.

Introduction

The goal of this chapter is to introduce the reader to the presence of coins in the text of the New Testament. With the exception of one reference to the denarius in Revelation (6:6), all of the references to coins in the New Testament occur in the four gospels (Matthew, Mark, Luke, and John). This does not mean that coinage is irrelevant to other New Testament books. The following chapters in this book have short sections at the end that suggests topics and questions for those who wish to probe connections further. This chapter proceeds by first highlighting three points of preliminary consideration for interpreting references to coins in the New Testament. It then goes on to define all of the terms for coins that appear in the New Testament. This section also includes references to extra-biblical texts and references that will aid in further research.

First, original languages are necessary to understand coins as context in the New Testament. One of the neglected topics of coins in the New Testament is the problem of translation. For example, one could accurately state that shekels do not appear in the New Testament. But a comparison of English translations reveals that the Greek word στατήρ is glossed in several ways in the scene in which a fish is caught with a coin in its mouth in Matt 17:27:

> And when you open its mouth, you will find a *coin* (NRSV)
>
> Open its mouth and you will find a *four-drachma coin* (NIV)
>
> And when you open its mouth, you will find a *four drachma coin* (NET)
>
> And when you open its mouth you will find a *shekel* (ESV)

The Greek word στατήρ in Matt 17:27 is surprisingly translated by a wide range of words. These variations reflect how the editors of bible translations seek to communicate words and concepts to modern readers. Most readers today would not know what a *stater* is and they might not even recognize that this was money if it was simply transliterated as "*stater*." Most translations do provide a footnote that explains when the word in English is significantly different from the source language. The truth is that important details may be lost in any translation, regardless of what languages are being used. The point should not be missed that those who are limited to research in English translations will likely experience confusion.

Second, consideration of the Synoptic problem is necessary to understand coins as context in the New Testament. It is one thing to talk about literary references to coins and yet another thing to talk about historical references to coins in the New Testament. The reason why literary occurrences should be differentiated from historical occurrences is because these are not always equivalent. What we possess today in canonical form are three gospel witnesses (Matthew, Mark, and Luke) that bear similarities that can be reasonably explained by literary dependence. They refer to the same stories and utilize similar sequences and wording, which indicates that one writer drew on other gospels as sources. Many scholars believe that Mark was the first written gospel and that other writers drew from it as a literary source. There are many theories, though it would be outside of the scope of this volume to discuss them in any detail here. What many scholars do agree upon is that the gospel writers emphasized or drew upon certain historical details in order to support their theological agenda. The sources may be harmonized but the unique voice of each gospel writer must be preserved. The goal of redaction criticism is to sort out why each gospel writer wrote what he did. The point here is that those who seek to study coins in the New Testament must be aware of these fundamental issues.

The need to consider the synoptic problem is evident in the following example. The Synoptics record three similar but diverse instructions for the Twelve apostles and their mission to the towns of Israel to announce the kingdom of God. These instructions include a statement about acquiring or carrying money for the journey:

> Acquire no gold (χρυσός) or silver (ἄργυρος) or copper (χαλκός) for your belts. (Matt 10:9 ESV)

> Take nothing for their journey except a staff…no money (χαλκός) in their belts. (Mark 6:8)

> Take nothing for your journey, no staff…nor money (ἀργύριον). (Luke 9:3)

One commentator observes, "In the prohibition of money Mark has copper (coins), Luke silver, and Matthew the full set: gold, silver, and copper. The sense is: not gold (rich provision), not silver (middling provision), and not even copper (modest provision)."[1] The unity and diversity in Jesus' instructions across the gospels has played an important part in the discussions over the nature of the voice of the historical Jesus and the order in which the Synoptics were penned. The predominant tool used to explore the relationships between various texts is redaction criticism. A comparison of these three passages above reveals that Matthew provides more details about Jesus' instructions whereas Mark and Luke use summarization. The three passages above illustrate the point that one historical event may be in view that utilizes several literary forms.

What complicates matters is that there are parallel New Testament texts where the wording is very similar but the references to coinage are different. For example, Matthew uses the quadrans, and Luke uses the lepton:

> Come to terms quickly with your accuser while you are going with him to court, lest your accuser hand you over to the judge, and the judge to the guard, and you be put in prison. Truly, I say to you, you will never get out until you have paid the last penny (κοδράντης). (Matt 5:25–26)

> And why do you not judge for yourselves what is right? As you go with your accuser before the magistrate, make an effort to settle with him on the way, lest he drag you to the judge, and the judge hand you over to the officer, and the officer put you in prison. I tell you, you will never get out until you have paid the very last penny (λεπτός). (Luke 12:57–59)

We cannot resolve the differences here, but the exegete must decide if these differences in the terminology used for the coins are the result of the Evangelist's hand or if they simply reflect variations in Jesus' own language. During Jesus' three years of teaching it is quite possible that he delivered similar parables and stories with minor variations. It is also quite possible that the Evangelists changed the coinage as an inconsequential detail that would relate to their implied audience.

1. John Nolland, *The Gospel of Matthew: A Commentary on the Greek Text*, NIGTC (Grand Rapids: Eerdmans, 2005), 418.

Third, consideration of the lack of specificity about coinage is necessary to understand coins as context in the New Testament. It is impossible to identify with certainty the references to coins in the New Testament. There are two reasons for this.

First, the references to coins only utilize terms for their denomination (e.g. drachma or denarius). But this terminology does not tell us which specific denarius is in view. Even when Jesus refers to Caesar's face being on a denarius (Mark 12:15–17), this does not mean it was the latest coin produced by the mint in Rome, Lugdunum, or another region. The fact is that coins circulated for years and often for decades. There is no way to know *which* Caesar was on the coin that Jesus referred to as each successive Caesar issued their own coinage. The Caesar on Jesus' denarius could have been Julius Caesar (reigned 48–44 BCE), Augustus Caesar (reigned 27 BCE to 14 CE), or Tiberius Caesar (reigned 14–37 CE). The fact that Jesus refers to this coinage as belonging to Caesar in the present tense suggests that it belonged to Tiberius Caesar.[2] This means that conclusions about coins and their imagery are tentative and should be focused on those symbols and inscriptions that were most common and most likely to have appeared within a given time frame and geographical area.

Second, the references to coins are sometimes general in nature because the author had other interests. For example, Judas Iscariot famously received thirty pieces of silver as a reward for betraying Jesus (Matt 26:15; 27:3–10). The word used in Matthew is *argurion* (ἀργύριον) and while this likely referred to the Tyrian shekel or tetradrachma, the text does not specify what coin it was. The lack of detail is due to the author's interest in creating salvation-historical allusions to the Old Testament text of Zech 11:12–13. This is important because the Septuagint version of Zech 11:12–13 also uses the same word *argurion* (ἀργύριον). We should not conclude that Matthew's lack of detail about the coinage reflects a disinterest in historical details, rather, it reflects *which* historical details he wanted to draw attention to in the narrative.

2. "If as is probable the denarius was a denarius of Tiberius himself, the reigning Caesar whose tribute and tribute money is under discussion, there is remarkably little choice and a highly probably 'identification'" (H. St J. Hart, "The Coin of 'Render unto Caesar,'" in *Jesus and the Politics of His Day* [Cambridge: Cambridge University Press, 1984], 243).

Types of Coins in the New Testament

This section will cover all of the values of coins referenced in the New Testament. There are nine different types or denominations of coins in the New Testament. Some lists might only refer to seven types of coins if they exclude those references that are general in nature and refer to sums or weights (e.g. *argurion* and *talenton*).[3]

1. *Assarion*

The Greek *assarion* (ἀσσάριον) is a Latin loanword from *assarius* and is translated as "penny" by the NRSV, ESV, and NIV.[4] It appears a total of two times in the New Testament and is not present in the Septuagint. The *assarion* appears in this saying of Jesus from the following synoptic texts:

> Are not five sparrows sold for two pennies (ἀσσάριον)? And not one of them is forgotten before God? (Luke 12:6)

> Are not two sparrows sold for a penny (ἀσσάριον)? And not one of them will fall to the ground apart from your Father. (Matt 10:29)

According to Jesus' teaching, the purchase of five sparrows for two assarion was the better deal. The *assarion* functioned in similar manner to the penny of today, not in terms of value, but as the building block for larger denominations.

2. *Lepton*

The word *leptos* (λεπτός) refers to a small copper Greek coin. The word occurs only three times in the New Testament: Mark 12:41, Luke 12:59; 21:2. The Koine Greek word *leptos* refers to something small, thin, and light.[5] The leptos was worth 1/8 of an assarion or half of a quadrans. Mark 12:42 explains to the reader that two lepta are equivalent to one quadrans. This might be important for a Roman context that had little exposure to Greek coinage.

3. Nanci DeBloois, "Coins in the New Testament," in *Masada and the World of the New Testament*, ed. John F. Hall and John W. Welch (Provo, UT: BYU Studies, 1997), 239.

4. BDAG, 144–45, s.v. ἀσσάριον.

5. BDAG, 592, s.v. λεπτός.

3. *Quadrans*

The word *quadrans* (κοδράντης) appears twice in the New Testament, most famously in the "widow's mite" scene in the Gospel of Mark:

> And he [Jesus] sat down opposite the treasury and watched the people putting money into the offering box. Many rich people put in large sums. And a poor widow came and put in two small copper coins (λεπτός), which make a penny (κοδράντης). (Mark 12:41–42)

A second reference to the quadrans (κοδράντης) appears in Matt 5:25–26 ("you will never get out [of jail] until you have paid the last κοδράντης"). Here the word functions as a reference to the "last coin" or most diminutive amount of money a person might possess.

4. *Denarius*

The *denarius* (δηνάριον) or denarii in the plural was the standard of the Greco-Roman world and was approximately equal to a day's wage. This valuation is reflected in Jesus' description of the kingdom of heaven being like a vineyard (Matt 20:1–16), with the workers in Jesus' teaching receiving one denarius for a day's work (Matt 20:2). Similarly, in Jesus' Parable of the Good Samaritan (Luke 10:25–37), the neighborly Samaritan gives the innkeeper two denarii to care for the injured man for several days. Each successive Caesar since Julius Caesar issued their own silver and gold denarii with their own likeness and corresponding inscriptions of their titles or deeds. The valuation of the denarius changed throughout the first century as various emperors changed the purity and amount of silver it contained, a process called debasement. This debasement was often done to divert silver to other government needs, often related to war. Workers may not have been paid in denarii but pay would have been equivalent to a denarius.[6] Even if the denarius was not readily available, they were common enough so that one could be found when Jesus requested that one be brought to him.

The denarius is the most common coin denomination in the New Testament, occurring sixteen times in fifteen verses (Matt 18:28; 20:2, 9, 10, 13; 22:19; Mark 6:37; 12:15; 14:5; Luke 7:41; 10:35; 20:24; John 6:7; 12:5; Rev 6:6 [×2]). The KJV translates the denarius with the misleading word "penny," referring to the modern British pence.[7] Some recent studies have challenged the historical accuracy of Jesus possessing a denarius. One commentator states "there seems to be little archaeological

6. Seo, *Luke's Jesus in the Roman Empire*, 58 n. 26.
7. DeBloois, "Coins in the New Testament," 241.

evidence that the denarius was circulating in the Syrian region at the time of Jesus."[8] However, this is a questionable conclusion on three accounts. First, the historical records and locations of coins found in the region were not systematically recorded until recent decades.[9] Second, the denarius was the day's wage for an agricultural worker, although this was not a static valuation.[10] Third, asking for the more common Tyrian shekel "would not have allowed Jesus to make his point" about Caesar.[11]

5. *Talent*

The *talent* (τάλαντον) features only twice in the New Testament (Matt 18:24; 25:14–30). The talent was a measure of weight used for the valuation of gold, silver, or copper in bullion. The word functions as a superlative for a great amount of money in Jesus' discourses. In Jesus' parable of the Unforgiving Servant (Matt 18:21–35), the servants of a king are described as having a debt of "ten thousand talents" (Matt 18:24). If the value of one talent was 6,000 drachmas or denarii, then this would be the modern equivalent of "millions of dollars" in debt.[12] In Matt 25:14–30, the talent is the central feature of the Parable of the Talents as a man goes on a journey and entrusts his servants with various amounts: one, two, and five talents. The man then returns from his journey and responds to the investments or lack of investments made by each servant. What is significant is that the word ἀργύριον is used to describe the talents. Jesus narrates the master who went on the journey as saying "Then you ought to have invested my money (ἀργύριον) with the bankers, and at my coming I should have received what was my own with interest" (Matt 18:27). This word ἀργύριον can be used generically to mean "money" or specifically to mean "silver." In this case, the word seems to connote money because there is interest to be gained on depositing it with bankers or money-changers. This means that a talent was a way to convey a large amount of money by weight but it was also understood as a term for currency.

8. Brian J. Incigneri, *The Gospel to the Romans: The Setting and Rhetoric of Mark's Gospel*, BIS 65 (Leiden: Brill, 2003), 195 n. 140. For similar critiques see Joel Markus, "The Jewish War: The *Sitz Im Leben* of Mark," *JBL* 111 (1992): 444 n. 18; Chancey, *Greco-Roman Culture and the Galilee of Jesus*, 175.

9. Pyung Soo Seo, *Luke's Jesus in the Roman Empire and the Emperor in the Gospel of Luke* (Eugene, OR: Wipf & Stock, 2015), 58.

10. *OGIS*, 2:629 (lines 153–56).

11. Chancey, *Greco-Roman Culture and the Galilee of Jesus*, 175.

12. BDAG, 988, s.v. τάλαντον.

6. *Mina*

The *mina* (μνᾶ, English plural *minas*, *minahs*, *minae*) appears only once in the New Testament, in Jesus' Parable of the Pounds or the Parable of the Ten Minas (Luke 19:11–27). In the Septuagint, the word appears ten times and at least three times in the Dead Sea Scrolls.[13] This parable in Luke is roughly equivalent to Matthew's Parable of the Talents. In both parables, the talent or mina function as superlatives for a large sum of money—far beyond what the average laborer would have possessed at once. Like the talent, the *mina* was used for weighing silver or gold bullion. The NRSV uses the word "pound" to translate the word "*mina*." The word "*mina*" is a Semitic loanword from the Akkadian word *Manû*.[14] In the Hellenistic context, it functioned as a monetary unity of 100 *drachmas*.

Like the talent in Matthew, Jesus has the master in the parable demand interest from the money changers or bank when a mina was deposited (Luke 19:23). This parallels the Parable of the Talents in Matt 18 because Jesus refers to minas as a financial unit although it also functioned as measure of weight. Josephus uses this word in his re-writing of the account of Absalom's handsome appearance and hair from 2 Sam 14. Josephus records the weight of Absalom's hair after one year of growth as being equal to 200 didrachmas or five minas (*Ant.* 7.189). Josephus also uses the word mina to refer to the weight of the beam of solid gold from the temple in Jerusalem that weighed 300 minas (*Ant.* 14.106). The pseudepigraphal *Testament of Joseph* describes the purchase of the patriarch Joseph as a slave for two minas (*T. Jos.* 16.4).[15] The Dead Sea Scroll 4Q159 notes that half a talent was equal to 30 minas, meaning that one talent was equal to 60 minas.[16] These texts demonstrate that the mina functioned in a very similar way to the talent—it could convey a large amount of money by weight but it was also understood as a term for currency.

7. *Stater*

The *stater* (στατήρ) is the most valuable coin mentioned in the New Testament and was worth approximately four drachmas in the first century.[17] Staters were minted by the Greeks in cities and regions such as Corinth,

13. 3 Kgdms 10:17; Esdras A 5:44; Esdras B 2:69; 1 Macc 14:24; 15:18; *3 Macc.* 1:4; Ezek 45:12; Bel 27; DSS 4Q159.

14. BDAG, s.v. μνᾶ, 654.

15. James H. Charlesworth, *The Old Testament Pseudepigrapha*, vol. 1 (New Haven: Yale University Press, 1983), 1:823.

16. Geza Vermes, *The Dead Sea Scrolls in English*, rev. and extended 4th ed. (Sheffield: Sheffield Academic, 1995), 357–58.

17. Von Reden, *Money in Classical Antiquity*, 150; DeBloois, "Coins in the New Testament," 242.

Tarsus, and Antioch in various forms since the fifth century BCE. They were minted in gold, silver, and electrum (an alloy of gold and silver). The origins of the stater remain obscure.[18] The stater was a weight unit and could be divided into 12 ounces (*uncia*). Some have suggested that the word "stater" was a translation of the Semitic word "shekel" and both words functioned as terms for similar amounts of weight (7.5–11.5 grams for shekels; 7.5–14 grams for staters).[19]

The word "stater" appears only once in the New Testament, in Matthew's narrative in which tax collectors ask Peter about Jesus' payment of the two-drachma tax for the temple in Jerusalem (Matt 17:24–27). The temple tax was based on texts such as Neh 10:32–33 and Exod 30:12–16 and required males over the age of twenty to pay half a shekel.[20] Jesus proceeds to explain that "sons" do not pay taxes or tolls. As the "son of God," Jesus is not obligated to pay the tax, but he pays to avoid giving "offense to them" (Matt 17:27). Jesus then prophetically directs Peter to catch a fish from the sea and they will find a single stater to pay the tax for himself and for Jesus. This is because the stater was worth two double drachmas (four drachmas or one tetradrachm) and thus able to satisfy the requirements for two people.

Some conclude that the word "stater" functioned as a colloquial term for a silver coin and that the coin Jesus is referring to was actually a tetradrachma.[21] In support of this conclusion is the fact that Antioch minted tetradrachmae in 30–13 BCE and the mint at Tyre produced the famed tetradrachme with the eagle on the reverse and the god Melqart on the obverse.[22] This means that the word "stater" could refer to Tyrian tetradrachma which was also called a shekel. Ultimately, we do not know exactly what was found in the fish's mouth.[23] Such parity explains why Jews appropriated staters to pay for the temple tax in Jerusalem. Jesus and Peter might have also paid together with one stater because the *didrachmon* (double drachma) was not commonly available.[24] Variations

18. William E. Metcalf, ed., *The Oxford Handbook of Greek and Roman Coinage* (Oxford: Oxford University Press, 2012), 40.

19. Ibid.

20. The DSS 4Q159 refers to the tax as "half" a shekel. Vermes, *The Dead Sea Scrolls*, 357–58. Josephus also refers to the tax as half a shekel (*Ant*. 18.312).

21. Harl states that the "principal stater" was the *tetradrachma* in *Coinage in the Roman Economy*, 98.

22. Ibid., 103.

23. Chancey states, "the exact meaning of stater in this passage is unclear" (*Greco-Roman Culture and the Galilee of Jesus*, 176 n. 51).

24. BDAG, 241–42, s.v. δίδραχμον. Similarly, see Robert H. Mounce, *Matthew*, UBCS (Grand Rapids: Baker, 2011), 172.

in the relative value of drachmas to shekels and staters might be accounted for by the regular fluctuations of value and rates of exchange that accompany any economy.

8. *Drachma*

The international standard currency of the Greek world was the *drachma* (δραχμή). The drachma could be divided into six *obols*, although these do not appear in the New Testament. As with many other terms related to coinage, it is closely related to words for weight and weighing. The *drachme* (δραχμή) was an Attic Greek word for the weight of 66½ grains and a *dragma* (δράγμα) meant "a handful."[25] The drachma appears only three times in the New Testament, all of them occurring in Jesus' short Parable of the Lost Coin:

> Or what woman, having ten silver coins (δραχμή), if she loses one coin (δραχμή), does not light a lamp and sweep the house and seek diligently until she finds it? And when she has found it, she calls together her friends and neighbors, saying, "Rejoice with me, for I have found the coin (δραχμή) that I had lost." Just so, I tell you, there is joy before the angels of God over one sinner who repents. (Luke 15:8–10)

According to Luke 15:1–2, the audience of this parable consisted of tax collectors, sinners, Pharisees, scribes and his disciples—all Hellenistic Jews. At this point, Jesus was passing between Samaria and Judea (Galilee) on his way to Jerusalem (Luke 17:11). According to Luke 19:1, he had also not yet made it to Jericho so Jesus was likely in the vicinity of, or east of the city of Ephraim at this point. This is significant because Jesus' parables were designed to appeal to a wide audience. Jesus certainly knew Aramaic but he also spoke Greek as well. For Jesus to have engaged with this wide variety of auditors in the cities around the Galilee, he would have needed conversational Koine Greek.[26] This means that the reference to a drachma was most likely not an interpolation by Luke, but an accurate historical record of Jesus' parable. This is surprising because if the drachma was not in circulation, the parable would have had little effect. What is more likely is that the drachma remained an important coinage for large and important purchases whereas small copper denominations such as the assarion and quadrans were used for most purchases

25. H. G. Liddell, *A Lexicon: Abridged from Liddell and Scott's Greek–English Lexicon* (Oak Harbor, WA: Logos Research Systems, 1996), 211.

26. G. Scott Gleaves, *Did Jesus Speak Greek? The Emerging Evidence of Greek Dominance in the First-Century Palestine* (Eugene, OR: Wipf & Stock, 2015), 18.

in the marketplace. This theory would account for why the woman in the parable would sweep the house to find the coin and then tell her neighbors about it. The whole parable turns on the historical audience of Jesus and the parable's audience (the woman's neighbors) knowing what a drachma was and how much it was worth.

9. *Didrachmon*

The *didrachma* (δίδραχμον) was an Attic Greek coin worth two drachma. This was just one of the denominations of Greek coinage that utilized multiples or fractions of the drachma. It appears only once in the New Testament, in Matthew's narrative in which tax collectors ask Peter about Jesus' payment of the two-drachma temple tax (Matt 17:24–27). Biblical commentators likely rely on the comment that the didrachma was not in circulation in the first century in the BDAG lexicon.[27] Josephus refers to the didrachma in his exposition on the weight of Absalom's hair and appearance from 2 Sam 14. As noted above, Josephus records the weight of Absalom's hair after one year of growth as being equal to 200 didrachmas or five minas (*Ant.* 7.189).

Summary

Coins are an important part of the literary and historical context of several books of the New Testament. Exegetes studying these passages will have to engage with the Synoptic problem and other considerations, such as original languages and the problem of specificity. Many of the conclusions about coins in the New Testament are going to be the result of conjecture and hypothesis. Future archaeological finds and historical work may yet improve our knowledge. The references to coins are as complex as the Hellenistic culture(s) surrounding Jesus and his first disciples. Those who pursue historical and grammatical exegesis of the New Testament will need to consider this difficult but rewarding area of research.

27. BDAG, 241–42, s.v. δίδραχμον.

Section I

The World in Front of the Coin

Chapter 5

Payment and Trust

Currency systems are built on a delicate web of public trust and confidence. The world in front of the coin (the people of the Empire) had to experience trust in several different ways in order for coins to function as currency.

Introduction

One of the major challenges of this volume is its attempt to describe coins as cultural texts in relation to the world in front of the coin—the entire Roman Empire. In order to account for the perlocutionary impact of the coins as cultural texts upon their audience(s), we must resort to broad categories—namely: trust, fear, and taxation. *This chapter will argue that a coin-based economy required people to participate in a web of trust, which was an important dimension of society in the first century.* Although the origins of coin-based currency systems likely began with value being based on the weight or intrinsic value of a metal object (disc, etc.), by the time of the first century, fiduciary or trust-based coinage was the norm. In the following chapter we will examine the natural corollary to this function and consider the role of fear. Trust is not only a recognized category for economic theory and numismatics, it is a universal human emotion that allows us to consider some of the sweeping complexities of the Roman Empire, including Judaea. In order to substantiate the argument that coins were evocative of trust, we will consider five points. First, we will describe the web-like relationships upon which currency relied. Second, we will examine how the substance and form of coinage contributed to trust. Third, we will briefly consider the role of money-changers. The fourth point is closely related to the third and covers weights and scales. The fifth and final section in this chapter makes some observations about community.

The Web of Trust

By the time of the first century, most currency systems were based on trust or fiduciary coinage. Perhaps the best image that captures the complex relationships at work is that of a web. The web of trust included the weight of the coin, the metal of the coin, the images on the coin, the government of Rome, the local cities, the buyers and the sellers.

In a fiduciary system of currency the weight of the coin's precious metal (copper, silver, gold) was important but not exclusively important. There is an inverse relationship between the weight of a coin and the state of the issuing authority. When the circumstances of the issuing authority moved toward instability and weakness, the importance of weight and metallic content went up. When the circumstances of the issuing authority moved toward stability and power, the importance of weight went down.

Although coinage in the first century should be considered fiduciary, there is an important tension that must be understood. On the one hand, if a coin is merely an object with a value dictated by the government, there should be little to no concern for the metallic content. On the other hand, if a coin is valued purely based on its metallic content, then its price will directly correspond to its weight. After all, the precious metal used to make coins had alternate possible uses such as weapons and jewelry.[1] As one scholar notes, "Roman coinage probably fell somewhere between these two extremes."[2]

There are many theories about the dynamics of power and public trust, but ancient discourses rarely discussed the philosophy behind monetary wealth. Rather, there was an emphasis on the practical (essence) rather than symbolic function.[3] When considering the Roman imperial currency system, it "was remarkably stable during the first two centuries CE."[4] This chapter will demonstrate the various ways in which trust was exercised by the people of the Roman Empire as they used coinage in everyday life.

The most important context for understanding trust for most of the people in the Roman Empire was the city or *polis*. While Caesar governed from Rome, and other authorities governed from the territorial level,

1. "The demand for gold and silver for prestige goods and decorative purposes may have helped to underpin the value of precious metal currencies, and to limit possible variations" (Howgego, *Ancient History from Coins*, 123).

2. Ibid., 128.

3. Leslie Kurke, *Coins, Bodies, Games, and Gold: The Politics of Meaning in Archaic Greece* (Princeton: Princeton University Press, 1999), 115.

4. David MacDonald, "The Worth of the Assarion," *Historia: Zeitschrift für Alte Geschichte* 38 (1989): 120.

the *polis* was the most immediate context for the general populace. The Greco-Roman *polis* was "the fundamental structure of social cohesion and identity."[5] When we refer to trust in the *polis*, we are not referring to an act that was explicit but rather to an act that was organic for the citizens. The city was simply the most important social structure for most Roman citizens. As a source of social cohesion, the city provided a natural web of trust within which fiduciary coinage could function.

The web of trust was also crucially important for coins to have communicative power. Speech-act theory helps us to understand that those who participated in the marketplace were also participating in the social discourse of which coins were a part. As people interacted with coins and the messages they bore, they could only engage these messages within a community or web in which some interaction took place. One scholar explains that if we are going to know what communication has occurred, "we must also know the conventions observed by a community where the words were spoken."[6] When we apply this truth to coinage, we understand that certain conventions must have been observed where the coins functioned as part of the cultural discourse between ruler and subjects. The social context or web of coins, Rome, local cities, buyers, and sellers all provided the necessary conventions in which coins functioned as cultural texts. Stated negatively, it is not possible to rip a coin out of any social context and suppose that its communicative powers were inherent in its images and inscriptions alone.

Substance and Form

Fiduciary coinage uses public trust to ascribe value. A coin's value is not based on the weight, but rather on the value that the public has agreed to or that the emperor has dictated. In the first century, coins would often be worth more than if they were melted down into a raw commodity. But the value of the coin was mostly based on the *forma publica* or markings rather than its *substantia*.[7] In other words, the symbols on the coin implicitly or explicitly guaranteed that the coin had value as a monetary instrument.[8] Thus, the use of silver rather than copper would only serve to *enhance* the public's trust. This meant that form was valued over

5. Lotz, "Coins of Asia Minor and Ephesians," 175.

6. Petrey, *Speech Acts and Literary Theory*, 9.

7. Reiser, "Numismatik und Neues Testament," 458.

8. Nathan T. Elkins, "Coins, Context, and an Iconographic Approach for the 21st Century," in Kaenel and Kemmers, eds., *Coins in Context I*, 25.

substance, although substance played a key role in determining value. One must avoid an either/or dichotomy here: both substance and form played important roles. Coins have value because they are greater than the sum of their parts. The trust that the public has in any given coinage is a result of combining substance (valuable metal) with a form (the mark, including images with inscriptions).[9]

When public confidence falters in the substance or form, value is usually lost.[10] The various wars and regional instability of the Roman Empire might account for the "predominately metallist approach to coinage" in the first century.[11] This metallist approach privileged the metallic content and purity of the coinage. This is also why emperors were "anxious to restore the fineness" of coinage whenever they could, especially with regard to the silver denarii.[12] Broadly speaking, if either the substance or form are lacking, the object will not function as currency. However, there are occasional unstamped or unmarked pieces of valuable metal that have been found in hoards, but these are not typical.

The Greeks used fiduciary coinage in some sense from the very beginning—ca. 600 BCE. The claim that ancient economies never used fiduciary coinage has been rejected.[13] There are two poles that must be considered whenever we talk about fiduciary coinage: the side of value based on attribution (face value) vs. the side of value based on bullion (weight value).

One of the ways that ancient moneyers sought to increase trust in their coinage was through notches around the edge of the coin. A coin with a serrated edge was thought to be more trustworthy because one could easily tell if the inside of the coin was of a different color or metal from the outside of the coin. This would supposedly ensure that the coin was made entirely of the same metal. Such measures were not always successful and ancient forgeries of serrated coins endured.

Fiduciary coinage was especially important in Judaea because the value of the common bronze coins in circulation were worth far less than their weight if melted. This would have also been true with denarii that had low amounts of silver in their alloy. The images and inscriptions on the

9. "What is required is the combination of substances (valuable metal) with form (the mark)" (Richard Seaford, *Money and the Early Greek Mind: Homer, Philosophy, Tragedy* [Cambridge: Cambridge University Press, 2004], 120).

10. MacDonald, "The Worth of the Assarion," 122.

11. Butcher and Ponting, "The Denarius in the First Century," 567.

12. Ibid.

13. Harris, *Monetary Systems of the Greeks and Romans*, 10.

coins were the modern day equivalent of the designation “legal tender” on a worthless piece of paper (a post-1971 US dollar bill that cannot be redeemed for silver).[14]

Money Changers

The world in front of the coin had to place their trust in the people who were experts in money exchange. This trust was offset to a large extent by verification systems—weights and scales—that will be discussed below. Despite the objectivity that scales brought to the process of money changing, there was always a human element involved that required trust.

Provincial and large city mints helped to stimulate the local economy through required exchanges. The cities with mints and their own coins gained honor and a sense of identity. These civic coins were often small bronze denominations designed for everyday transactions in the market-place. This function helped to simulate local and regional trade.[15] The charge for the required exchange amounted to a small tax.

Most people would have been aware that the exchange of money involved a small loss on the part of the person requiring the exchange. Money exchangers collected a fee called an *agio*.[16] The *agio* is the difference between the accounting or nominal value of money and the actual or street value of the money.

Money exchangers operated within a local monopoly. Local cities often monopolized the local exchange system in order to introduce their own coins and maintain their value.[17] This local system would be contempora-neous with the imperial system set by Rome. The bankers who controlled the exchange of money often had extensive control of the system. Because of this, debates between the bankers had to be resolved at the highest level. The Pergamum Banking Inscription is an example of the emperor Hadrian (76 to 138 CE) stepping in to resolve such a dispute.[18] Fragmentary evidence suggests that Hadrian occasionally granted local cities or

14. For a helpful discussion comparing fiat money vs. token money see Edward E. Cohen, “Elasticity of the Money Supply at Athens,” in *Monetary Systems of the Greeks and Romans*, ed. W. V. Harris (Oxford: Oxford University Press, 2008), 68.

15. Karsten Dahmen, *The Legend of Alexander the Great on Greek and Roman Coins* (Oxford: Routledge, 2007), 4.

16. For brief comments on the *agio* see Reiser, “Numismatik und Neues Testament,” 458.

17. MacDonald, “The Worth of the Assarion,” 122.

18. Ibid., 121.

territories such as Delphi, Stratonicea-Hadrianopolis, and Pergamum the ability to collect taxes that did not go to the central government.[19]

In many places throughout the Empire, experts on exchange would have to be trusted because of the banking techniques used. The Roman monetary system utilized terms for accounting value and real value. This means that certain references to money would have either been purely for the abstract purposes of record keeping or for referring to an actual coin. To make matters a bit more confusing, the same word could refer to both, although it would have been clear what was meant at the time. For example, let us consider the term "assarion." An inscription in Ephesus refers to "silver assaria" but this was only a unit of account, not a real coin.[20] In accounting value, one denarius equaled sixteen assaria, but because of the fees that money changers applied, this would never be the real or street value.

Weights and Scales

The weight of coins played an important part in first-century currency. Scales for weighing coins and bullion were an important part of the tools that facilitated commerce. Scales, like the money-changers themselves, required an element of trust to be established in the marketplace. One book on ancient scales states, "weights are like coins, a matter of continuity, trust, habit, and faith."[21]

Scales would have been necessary in the marketplace to distinguish between coins of the same denomination but different in size.[22] The more simple scales would have used two equally weighted pans that hung in balance. More complicated weight systems used a fulcrum or pivot point with a beam and were called a steelyard or "Roman balance."[23] Scales would have allowed coins to be weighed against known weights

19. Mary T. Boatwright, *Hadrian and the Cities of the Roman Empire* (Princeton: Princeton University Press, 2003), 90–91.

20. MacDonald, "The Worth of the Assarion," 120.

21. David Hendin, *Ancient Scale Weights and Pre-Coinage Currency of the Near East* (New York: Amphora, 2007), 9.

22. "It would have been impossible for a person in the market to distinguish on the spot, by hand, between a one gram and three gram coin of exactly the same design" (Hendin, "Current Viewpoints on Ancient Jewish Coinage," 261).

23. For detailed information on the "Roman balance" (*statera*) see Cesare Rossi, Flavio Russo, and Ferruccio Russo, *Ancient Engineers' Inventions: Precursors of the Present*, HMMS 8 (Naples: Springer, 2009), 8–9.

or other coins. Josephus makes reference to "uncoined silver" that was exchanged for gold coinage in his book *The Life of Flavius Josephus.*[24] This exchange was based on the weight of the uncoined money.

Amongst the population in Judaea, there was a long-standing association between payment and weight. The single Hebrew word *shaqal* could express "to pay" or "to weigh."[25] The Wisdom of Sirach (200–175 BCE) portrays the reader as finding favor for keeping honest weights and scales (Sir 41:4). The book of Proverbs expresses the negative side of this: "An abomination of Yahweh is a stone and a weight, and scales of falsehood are not good" (Prov 20:23). The obvious inference from these two texts is that scales could be manipulated so that more profit could be made. The use of scales and weights for currency exchange always required an element of trust.

Implications for Studying the New Testament

By necessity, the web of community-oriented trust required for any economic system to function is going to be quite broad. But there is another and much more narrow consideration of "community" that is helpful for describing the function of money in the first century. *The earliest Christians viewed themselves as belonging to a community that shared their material possessions (e.g. money) as though they were from the same family.*

This group of Jesus-followers is described as devoting themselves to "the apostles' teaching" (Acts 2:42). This "teaching" from the apostles was undoubtedly related to Jesus' earthly ministry and his appearances after the resurrection. When the apostles Peter and John taught in Solomon's Portico they called upon the people who heard to put their "faith" in Jesus' name. This vertically oriented trust in Jesus' name cannot be separated from the horizontal web of trust created in the community of disciples.

After these early disciples put their faith in Jesus, they began to meet together and share material possessions, including money. In Acts 2:42–47, the fledgling followers of "the Way" were selling their possessions and distributing the proceeds amongst those who were in need. This sharing of goods amongst the early Christian community was a response to the conditions of poverty and a response to their fledgling faith. This portrait of the early Christian community in Acts 2:42–47 is described

24. Josephus, *Life* 1.13. For commentary see *Flavius Josephus, Translation and Commentary: Vol. 9, Life of Josephus*, ed. Steve Mason, BJP 9 (Leiden: Brill, 2001), 61.

25. Stan Hudson, "Coins of the Bible," *BSP* 9 (1980): 85.

in entirely positive terms. For any group that is selling possessions and distributing money to those in need, it is difficult to imagine how this would not have resulted in many difficulties.

The pooling of wealth and sharing of possessions would likely result in coins being found by archeologists in hoards. Like the scene in Acts 2, other groups such as the Essenes seem to have created communal repositories for their monies.[26] This is likely the reason why not a single coin has been found in the Qumran caves that were used for pottery.

In sum, the world in front of the coin in the first century included a small but influential group of Jesus followers who began to sell their possessions for the benefit of those who were in need and who identified themselves as belonging to the "Way." This benefaction system did not move from the top down as in the rest of society but rather from the bottom up. When we consider this small group we see that trust in Jesus had a direct impact on economic realities for the first converts to follow Jesus.

Summary

This chapter has sought to explain that a web of trust was required if coins were to be used for payment throughout the Roman Empire. These relationships of trust were sometimes knit very tightly and sometimes characterized by "trust but verify." This web included social relationships, the substance and form of the coinage, money changers, and the instruments of weights and scales. Although it is well recognized that Paul's missionary journeys were facilitated by political stability and especially by the system of roads between major cities, it is not often recognized that such journeys relied upon a vast web of trust that enabled fiduciary coinage to provide easy payment for goods and services.

26. Philo (*Good Person* 12.86), Josephus (*War* 2.122). For a short discussion see Jodi Magness, *Stone and Dung, Oil and Spit: Jewish Daily Life in the Time of Jesus* (Grand Rapids: Eerdmans, 2011), 97.

Chapter 6

PAYMENT AND FEAR

While most of the first century enjoyed the peaceful fruits of the so-called *Pax Romana*, fear was an important factor in how coins were used, carried, and stored.

Introduction

One might argue that the universal human emotion of fear contributed to the success of coin-based money to begin with. One scholar notes that coinage was originally successful because it was "portable, imperishable, divisible, stable in value, and easily hidden."[1] The desire to hide one's valuables could only be driven by the emotion of fear. We may simply define "fear" as "the negative expectation of something in the future."[2] The category of fear is helpful because it is a universal and timeless human emotion that allows us to consider some of the sweeping complexities of the Roman Empire. Again, one of the major challenges of this volume is its attempt to describe coins as cultural texts in relation to the world in front of the coin.

Fear impacted everyone who participated in the economy and was no discerner of person or status. For example, those at the lower end of the social pyramid were often forced to hide coins due to fear of robbers. At the highest end we can cite the actions of Galba (emperor from 68 to 69 CE), who never travelled anywhere without a carriage containing 10,000 gold pieces (Suet., *Galba* 8).[3]

1. For an argument reflecting John Stuart Mill's analysis of Aristotle and the origins of coinage see von Reden, *Money in Classical Antiquity*, 2.

2. Matthew A. Elliott, *Faithful Feelings: Rethinking Emotion in the New Testament* (Grand Rapids: Kregel, 2006), 199.

3. David B. Hollander, "The Demand for Money in the Late Roman Republic," in Harris, ed., *The Monetary Systems of the Greeks and Romans*, 112.

There were three major factors that created fear amongst the general populace of the Roman Empire and especially amongst the populace of Judaea: (1) robbers, (2) war, (3) defilement, and (4) death. As we draw once again from our analytic for interpreting and exegeting culture, we note that cultural expressions can be used as a lens through which the world may be seen.[4] As we turn to each of these four causes of fear in the populace of the Roman Empire, we will see that coinage provided a way to pursue a degree of safety and security.

Coins, Robbers, and Fear

Robbers are routinely cited by commentaries and historians as a feature of countryside life in many areas of the Roman Empire.[5] Conceptually, the first century connected robbers and bandits with public murder, the taking of money, and the desire for power.[6] Some have even suggested that the fear of robbers and the dangers of rural life may have played a role in limiting demand for coin-based money.[7]

Several of Jesus' parables are designed to appeal to the widespread fear of robbers along the road (e.g. the parable of the Good Samaritan in Luke 10). The fact that Jesus was crucified on a cross between two robbers (Mark 15:27; Matt 27:38, 44) is an important indicator of how serious the problem was. Paul also referenced his experience with "robbers" in his list of dangerous situations in 2 Cor 11:26.

The identity and role of "robbers" within the Roman Empire has not been without difficulty. Some groups of so-called "robbers" were motivated by political and religious agendas that complicate descriptions and one-word glosses. Both Mark 15:27 and Matt 27:38 use the word *leistes* (ληστής) for the robbers that hung on crosses beside Jesus. In Latin, these were called *latrones* (*latro* in the singular).[8] One must also be aware that some

4. "We don't simply read cultural texts but we read through them. In short: the cultural texts we love best come to serve as the lens through which we view everything else and as the compass that orients us toward the good life" (Vanhoozer, *Everyday Theology*, 36).

5. For brief comments on the transportation of Paul's donation to the church in Jerusalem see David Garland, *1 Corinthians*, BECNT (Grand Rapids: Baker, 2003), 756–57.

6. Mark A. Brighton, *The Sicarii in Josephus's Judean War: Rhetorical Analysis and Historical Observations*, EJL 27 (Atlanta: Society of Biblical Literature, 2009), 79.

7. Hollander, "Demand for Money in the Late Roman Republic," 125.

8. For etymology and linguistic background on *latro* see Thomas Grünewald, *Bandits in the Roman Empire: Myth and Reality* (London: Routledge, 1999), 5.

literary constructs of robbers in ancient literature (much like those found in modern cinema) may not always reflect reality. The complexity of identifying robbers in the Roman Empire is evidenced by the fact that there are four categories of them: bandits, rebels, rivals, and avengers.[9] Recent scholarship on this matter has found that these categories are helpful but none is entirely distinct from the others. Thus, it is still possible to use "robbers" as a word that captures the unity of various first-century groups. As with other historical difficulties, care must be taken to develop the historical situation as much as is possible.

There is one reference to "Sicarii" (σικάριος) in the New Testament (Acts 21:38) that is relevant to the topic of robbers in the sense that readers today assume (it is not unreasonable to assume people brandishing daggers are robbers). The ESV translates this word "Sicarii" as "Assassins" because this group was known for their use of daggers and the speed of their executions.[10] The use of small concealable daggers is apparently what gave them the ability to strike anyone at any time. One of the more prominent victims was Jonathan the high priest.

The Romans did use the Latin word "sicae" for daggers, but this does not provide an easy explanation of who they were. The other appearance of this term is in the works of Josephus (*War* and *Antiquities*).[11] Some scholars have argued that Josephus portrays Sicarii as only operating in urban areas and not in the desert as Luke portrays. The problem with this reading is that Josephus had a tendency to embellish and twist facts for his rhetorical agendas. One must be careful against proof-texting him to prove matters related to Second Temple Judaism.[12] In addition, the context of the scene in Acts 21:37–40 is much more oriented to the issue of political revolt and uprising than robbery.[13]

9. "Classification of *latrones* according to their supposed personal characteristics produced two basic types: the 'common' and the 'noble' bandit. Classifications of *latrones* according to what they did produced four categories: 'bandits', 'rebels,' 'rivals' and 'avengers'" (ibid., 3).

10. For a discussion of the attack on Jonathan the high priest see Brighton, *The Sicarii in Josephus's Judean War*, 56.

11. For comments on Sicarii see Josephus' *Antiquities* (20.162–63, 185–87) and a parallel in *War* (2.254–57).

12. One should be "circumspect about accepting him as a reliable source for matters in first-century Judea" (Mark A. Brighton, "The Sicarii in Acts: A New Perspective," *JETS* 54 [2011]: 550).

13. "He [Paul] did not come to lead any civil revolt against the Judean leaders" (ibid., 558).

The term "Sicarii" was a term that could be applied to a range of people and groups. It likely had connotations of "terrorist" or political insurrection.[14] Josephus links banditry and political revolution (*War* 2.264–65). There is a certain paradox in the way that the Judean rebels "ironically threaten their compatriots with death if they choose voluntarily to be slaves" to Rome.[15]

Whatever the Sicarii were and however the term was meant, robbery of money and goods was not the issue that Paul was fearful of being associated with as he gives his defense in Acts 22. Other accounts of robbers are clearly more relevant for understanding how money was transported and carried.

The fact that money could be hidden and the sense of security that this entailed was especially important. The fear of robbers caused people to carry coins in unusual ways. One way to carry coins would have been with a money belt (ζώνη).[16] This method was evidently popular amongst Jews in Judaea based on Jesus' instructions to those going on a short journey around the region (Mark 6:8 // Matt 10:9). Money could also be carried in bags (βαλλάντιον) and Jesus charged the Seventy not to take one.[17] Another way to carry coins would have been to sew them into the folds of garments so that they would not clink or misshape the clothing.[18] Small purses of money were also tied around the neck, perhaps to keep it close to one's person.[19] Actions that communicate fear of robbery do not characterize every instance where money is transported, yet it is an important dimension to consider.

Coins, War, and Fear

Modern archaeological techniques rely heavily upon numismatic evidence to provide inscription-based evidence for dating a range of objects. The best numismatic evidence comes in the form of a hoard or stash of coins. These hoards provide archaeologists and researchers with several points of

14. According to Brighton, "Paul is no 'terrorist' or leader of 'Sicarii'" (ibid.).

15. Steve Mason, *Flavius Josephus: Translation and Commentary*. Vol. 1b, *Judean War 2*, ed. Steve Mason, BJP 1b (Leiden: Brill, 2008), 174.

16. BDAG, 431, s.v. ζώνη; *NIDNTT*, 3:120–21, s.v. ζώννυμι.

17. BDAG, 163, s.v. βαλλάντιον; *NIDNTT*, 1:142–43, s.v. βαλλάντιον.

18. Garland, *1 Corinthians*, 757.

19. Purses around the neck are considered in light of cleanliness issues in *b. Shabb.* 21. *The Babylonian Talmud, Volumes 1–10: Original Text, Edited, Corrected, Formulated, and Translated into English*, trans. Michael L. Rodkinson (Boston: The Talmud Society, 1918), 2:322.

data that can be used together. Coin hoards are the modern-day equivalent of hiding ones money "under the mattress." Where an increase in hoarding was present, there was likely an increase in perceived government instability.[20] When ancient coins hoards are found today, it is likely that the coins were deposited during a time of insecurity, not economic prosperity. One of the dominant reasons for government instability was the fear of war. Within the study of numismatics, hoards have become an important part of interpreting the world in front of the coin. One scholar explains: "Concentrations of coin hoards tend to reflect not prosperity or heavily monetized contexts, but rather the insecurity (particularly warfare) which resulted in owners not recovering their treasure."[21] The fear of war in the first century caused people to hoard coins in Roman contexts and in Jewish contexts.

In the Roman context, coin hoards often indicate war periods. Coin hoards could also reflect ransom for captives, booty from raids, diplomatic gifts, or large payments to Roman armies.[22] The presence of coin hoards has been especially important for piecing together the series of civil wars during the late Roman Republic. The forty years of Roman civil war helped set the stage for the end of the republic and the rise of an emperor by creating a precedent for civil war over social and economic policies. One scholar explains how the wars between the generals Marius and Sulla left their trace through coinage:

> The Social War and the struggle between Marius and Sulla were fought out in Italy itself, with widespread destruction in the areas affected; the losses involved, both human and financial, are graphically illustrated by the number of coin hoards found from these periods.[23]

This citation referring to the Social War in Rome (91 to 88 BCE) is just one illustration of how coin hoards are used to ascertain the effect of war upon the whole society.

Coin hoards were also indicative of war in the Jewish context. War or threats of war were an important element in the tensions of Judaea and perhaps other areas as well. The original audience who heard Jesus refer to "wars and rumors of wars" on the Mount of Olives would have

20. Kreitzer, *Striking New Images*, 24.

21. Howgego, *Ancient History from Coins*, 88.

22. Duncan-Jones, *Money and Government in the Roman Empire*, 93.

23. John Patterson, "Military Organization and Social Change in the Later Roman Republic," in *War and Society in the Roman World*, ed. J. Rich and G. Shipley (New York: Routledge, 1993), 101.

understood what he was referring to (Matt 24:6). In the first century, as in more ancient and modern times, fear of war resulted in hiding or hoarding coins.[24]

For the Jews living in Judaea, the fear of war became reality during the First Jewish Revolt. The result of Titus's triumph over the Jews is recorded in Josephus's first volume *The Jewish War* (written ca. 75 CE). Josephus records how the Jews who were left in the land were starving and subject to robbery. He also records how some Jews were able to smuggle money out of the area:

> As Josephus was speaking thus with a loud voice, the seditious would neither yield to what he said, nor did they deem it safe for them to alter their conduct; but as for the people, they had a great inclination to desert to the Romans; accordingly, some of them sold what they had, and even the most precious things that had been laid up as treasures by them, for a very small matter, and swallowed down pieces of gold, that they might not be found out by the robbers; and when they had escaped to the Romans, went to stool, and had wherewithal to provide plentifully for themselves; for Titus let a great number of them go away into the country, whither they pleased. (*War* 5.420–22)

The text above indicates that war and the danger of robbery forced some Jews to swallow gold coins in order to escape with financial means of survival.[25] This text also highlights how valuable a single gold coin could be. Gold coinage provided a means for transporting large amounts of value in a small form factor that could be hidden—or even swallowed if necessary—in a time of war.

Coins, Defilement, and Fear

For most Jews, coins had to be handled carefully because they could take on the quality of holiness and defilement. These qualities of holiness and defilement could be *externally* focused on physical objects or *internally* focused on the state of a person's inner being. With respect to the state of external objects, this was theoretically based upon the Mosaic law and mediated through rabbis, priests, scribes, synagogue leadership, and the Sanhedrin. Several New Testament texts demonstrate that an element of

24. "There is no time like a war for hiding coins" (Meshorer, *Jewish Coins of the Second Temple Period*, 93).

25. For a discussion that places this quote in the larger historical context see Richard A. Horsley, *Bandits, Prophets, and Messiahs: Popular Movements at the Time of Jesus* (Harrisburg: Trinity Press International, 1999), 124.

fear of defilement and concern about cultic holiness made a significant impact on how coinage was handled.

The narrative of Judas's payment for the betrayal of Jesus demonstrates that coinage was subject to laws of holiness and defilement:

> And throwing down the pieces of silver into the temple, he departed, and he went and hanged himself. But the chief priests, taking the pieces of silver, said, "It is not lawful to put them into the treasury, since it is blood money." So they took counsel and bought with them the potter's field as a burial place for strangers. (Matt 27:5–7)

The refusal of the chief priests and elders to take back the money paid to Judas is an example of the irreversibility of communicated defilement. In this scene, the money used to pay Judas Iscariot to betray Jesus could not be accepted into the temple because it had been used for sinful purposes. The "blood money" could not be purified and brought into the temple.

Jesus' concern was with the internal disposition of the heart toward greed. One scholar notes, "Jesus especially highlighted attachment to money as a source of defilement."[26] Jesus' teaching about money differed from *some* (we must respect the many variations of Judaism here) of the rabbis around him who emphasized concern for the external over the internal.

The concern for external defilement was horizontal or socially driven and took into consideration one's social status and exclusion from various cultic activities. The concern for internal defilement was vertically driven and concerned one's status before Yahweh. Neither are mutually exclusive of each other and Jesus' teaching about defilement seems simply to prioritize the internal, then move to the external. Whether focused on the external or internal, the New Testament demonstrates a sustained interest in how the use of money affected one's cleanliness or defilement. These cultic concerns were powerful enough to influence how money was spent or not spent.

Coins, Death, and Fear

The use of coins for payment for many in the Roman Empire did not stop at death. In some cases, coins literally functioned as lenses through which the dead "saw" their eternal destiny. Coins functioned as part of Hellenistic funerary liturgy that sought safety and comfort beyond the grave.

26. David A. deSilva, *Honor, Patronage, Kinship and Purity: Unlocking New Testament Culture* (Downers Grove: InterVarsity, 2000), 296.

Archaeological evidence has found coins in skulls from the first century. It is not certain whether there was a single coin placed in the mouth or two coins placed over the eyes.[27] These are referred to as the coin-in-mouth or the coin-on-eyes customs. There may also have been a tradition of placing the coin on top of the skull.[28] This use of coinage in ancient funerary and mortuary practice is evidence that even death and the fear of the uncertainty beyond death demanded a price.

Placing coins on the eyes or the mouth was predominately a custom of Roman religion in which money was placed with the body for the afterlife. This practice was also copied by the Phoenicians in the Persian period (fourth to fifth century BCE).[29] The coin would be payment for the ferry of Charon needed to reach the abode of the dead across the mythological river Styx (also known as the Stygian River). Thus, the coin is often referred to as "Charon's obol."[30]

The coin-on-eye tradition was likely motivated by fear of death. The writer of Hebrews addresses his audience of Hellenized Jews (likely in Rome) and speaks of "fear of death" as though it is a universal human condition (Heb 2:15). While the writer of Hebrews connects fear of death with "the devil," the pagan Roman citizens connected fear of death with the gods of the Pantheon. With more specific reference to Galatia one writer notes, "numismatic evidence show[s] that the gods were feared for their powers to punish humans."[31] It is likely that the citizens of Galatia were not alone in their fear of the gods. One scholar concludes that Romans "were not sure of survival after death."[32] While near-universal fear of the unknown beyond death is a relatively safe conclusion, one can only make *correlations* between funerary practice and doctrine. It is simply very difficult to draw direct lines of causality between beliefs about the afterlife and post-mortem rituals.[33]

27. Meacham, "Archaeological Evidence," 56–59.

28. Amos Kloner, *The Necropolis of Jerusalem in the Second Temple Period*, ISACR 8 (Leuven: Peeters, 2007), 131.

29. Samuel R. Wolff, "Mortuary Practices in the Persian Period of the Levant," *Near Eastern Archaeology* 65 (2002): 136.

30. Kloner, *The Necropolis of Jerusalem*, 131.

31. Aliou C. Niang, *Faith and Freedom in Galatia and Senegal: The Apostle Paul, Colonists and Sending Gods* (Leiden: Brill, 2009), 66.

32. Jon Davies, *Death, Burial, and Rebirth in the Religions of Antiquity*, RFCC (London: Routledge, 2003), 140.

33. "It has proved very difficult indeed to relate actual burial practices to death beliefs." Ibid., 7.

There is no evidence that the practice of placing coins on the eyes or mouth was widespread amongst Jews.[34] However, there is some evidence that it took place on rare occasions. As noted above, the placement of coins on the mouth or eyes has Hellenistic origins. The strong influence of Greco-Roman culture on Judaea resulted in some Jews, especially wealthier elites, following Hellenistic customs. Where Jews placed coins over the mouth of the deceased, other customs were likely being integrated.[35] For example, the use of ossuaries or burial urns also reflects Jewish cultural accommodation in the first century.

Even in the New Testament we see a range of Jewish burial traditions. The Sadducees, who did not believe in the afterlife, would have been less concerned than the Pharisees with maintaining the individual identities of bodies. Jesus' own body is placed in a "new tomb in which no one had yet been laid" (John 19:41). This indicates that not all burials were the same—as some corpses were presumably mixed with older bodies.[36]

The tradition of placing coins on the eyes at death may have originated with the fear of death in some, but eventually the tradition began to communicate other cultural meanings such as wealth and status. For some, the placement of coins on the mouth or eyes may have little to do with religious beliefs; rather, this practice might have communicated social status.[37] A tradition that may have begun with fear of death may have morphed into a tradition perpetuated by fear of shame associated with the inability to participate in expensive rituals.

Implications for Studying the New Testament

In addition to fear of war as was typical between nations, the emotion of fear was an important component in divine warfare or apocalyptic destruction. The book of Revelation uses the emotions of joy and fear to contrast the responses between God's people and those who reject the kingship of Jesus. Throughout Revelation are references to Babylon the Great which is the paradigm of the great Evil City seen throughout the

34. "The claim that placing coins over the eyes was a common Jewish burial practice during the Second Temple Period cannot be substantiated either by the archaeological or literary evidence" (Rachel Hachlili, *Jewish Funerary Customs, Practices and Rites in the Second Temple Period*, JSJSup 94 [Leiden: Brill, 2005], 443).

35. Magness, *Stone and Dung*, 154.

36. Davies, *Death, Burial and Rebirth*, 8.

37. Magness, *Stone and Dung*, 154.

Christian canon: Babel, Babylon, Rome, Jerusalem, and so on. Close to the center of what defines the paradigmatic Evil City in Revelation is her economic system.

The book of Revelation provides evidence that some first-century Christians feared their present economic system. The role of the economic system of the Evil City as a tool of Satan and his earthly powers appears prominently in the well-known references to the "mark of the beast" in Rev 13:16–17; 16:2; 19:20. Without this mark, it is impossible to buy, sell, or trade and participate in the fundamental dynamics of civilization. Economics is intertwined with Satan's current dominion in the world. One scholar concludes that this is all focused on the city of Rome: "Economic activity means participation in this political-military-religious power."[38] While there is undoubtedly a reference to Rome behind the label "Babylon the Great" (Rev 18:2), this initial historical referent does not exhaust the application to other great cities of the world who oppose God. What is significant about the "mark of the beast" is that it likely originated from the images found on coins.

The original "mark of the beast" likely developed from two sources related to coinage. One possibility is that these marks that appear on people's bodies were understood to be a development of the markings typically found on coins. In this way, the marks found on people's right hand or forehead (Rev 13:16) are the same markings that communicated Rome's idolatry and outrageous claims about being the source of salvation, peace, and hope for the entire world.

The second possibility is related to the first and may include what are known as countermarks.[39] A countermark is a small stamp added to coins after their production in order to establish their authenticity or approval for use. Without this small stamp, a coin may not be usable for any purchase—much like the requirement to provide the "mark of the beast." Markings on bodies and on coins are not mutually exclusive, as both played a role in the economic system.

The book of Revelation provides evidence that some first-century Christians anticipated an apocalyptic destruction of their economic system. We see evidence of this fear was primarily through literary and

38. Carter, *The Roman Empire and the New Testament*, 106.

39. "The symbol for the 'mark of the beast' originated within the numismatic environment of the first-century Roman world, and the historical referents for the 'mark' were special countermarks placed upon Roman imperial coins" (David M. May, "The Empire Strikes Back: The Mark of the Beast in Revelation," *RevExp* 106 [2009]: 84).

theological references in the Apocalypse of John (the book of Revelation). Revelation 18 portrays three different people groups who are consumed with the emotion of fear: kings, merchants, and sailors. The kings of the earth are described as living in "sexual immorality" and "luxury" (Rev 18:9). They "weep and wail" over the smoke of the destruction of Babylon the Great. The merchants and sailors "weep and mourn" (Rev 18:11, 18) because of the long list of goods that are no longer being traded and transported. The downfall of the Evil City is the equivalent to an apocalyptic event that affects the whole world through the end of her marketplace.

The stance of Revelation toward the Great Babylon or Evil City is radically separatist. To participate at all in her economic system is tantamount to apostasy from God. There is no room for cultural accommodation or redemptive activity with the city. Revelation calls for faithfulness to Christ, even if it means giving up on the normal means of "daily survival."[40]

Those who associated with the paradigmatic Evil City of Babylon the Great are those who participate in her economic system—they are the ones consumed with fear at her destruction by God. In contrast, those who have separated themselves from the Evil City and her economic system are directed by God himself to be filled with joy and "rejoice" at the judgment and destruction (Rev 18:20).

In sum, the book of Revelation provides two salient points for our study of coinage and the New Testament. First, the book of Revelation reveals that coins were powerful cultural texts whose marks (e.g. countermarks) had the capacity to grow into symbols of economic power well beyond their initial scope. Second, the book of Revelation reveals that apocalyptic scenes consisted of those consumed with fear at the prospect of economic ruin. This imagery would have initially encouraged those who viewed themselves as enmeshed in a diabolic and destructive economic system to stand firm in their faith.

Summary

This chapter demonstrated that coins provided an avenue for safety and security amidst the threats of robbers, war, and death. Some even swallowed gold coins to provide financial security while escaping the ravages of war. Jesus' concern for his disciples reflects our finding that coins were viewed as a source of stability and security. The Synoptics record Jesus warning against storing up treasures on earth because they

40. Carter, *The Roman Empire and the New Testament*, 109.

do not equate to storing up "treasures in heaven."[41] Robbers, war, and death all demanded one thing in the first century—money. This chapter has sought to unify the entire Roman Empire in the first century—a very difficult task! However, it is possible to understand the Roman Empire, in all of its ethnic and cultural diversity, as being unified by the use of coins as an important source of stability amidst chaos.

41. For Jesus' references to "treasures in heaven" see Matt 6:19; 19:21; Mark 10:21; Luke 18:22.

Chapter 7

Payment and Taxes

The Roman Empire saw little distinction between government and religion. In that context, paying taxes to any institution was an act that could have serious theological and social implications.

Introduction

This chapter will demonstrate that paying taxes was a communicative act with theological and social implications. Paying taxes in the first century was a great burden to a majority of the population. Taxation existed in the tension between Rome's desire for stability and its desire for revenue. This tension was particularly present in Judaea.

What complicates any study of coins from this time is the fact that in Judaea, there were "two competing taxation systems—the Jewish and the Roman."[1] Broadly speaking, the Roman taxation system consisted of three concentric circles: (1) Rome in the center, where all monies flowed, (2) taxed provinces, and (3) frontier provinces.[2] Generally speaking, Judaea was considered a taxed province. After the death of Herod the Great, Judaea applied to become a province, preferring Rome's taxes to the heavy-handedness of Herod (Josephus, *Ant.* 17.300–314).[3] The Jewish taxation system aided the Roman system by providing assessment and collection.[4]

1. Douglas Oakman, "Jesus and Agrarian Palestine: The Factor of Debt," in *The Social World of the New Testament*, ed. J. Neyrey and E. Stewart (Peabody, MA: Hendrickson, 2008), 71.

2. This three-ring model is based on Keith Hopkins, "Taxes and Trade in the Roman Empire: 200 BC to AD 400," *JRS* 70 (1980): 101.

3. Duncan-Jones, *Money and Government in the Roman Empire*, 6.

4. Oakman, "Jesus and Agrarian Palestine," 71.

Taxes were required by both the central government in Rome as well as the given city. On occasion, the emperor might allow a city to keep taxes in order to support local growth. This was likely the case when the emperor Hadrian wrote a letter (ca. 127 CE) allowing Stratonicea-Hadrianopolis to keep revenues from imperial land.[5] Taxation came from the city, from Rome, and from religious obligations including temple taxes and offerings. Those who collected taxes on behalf of Rome were called *publicani*.[6]

As we consider the communicative power of paying taxes in the first century, we will cover three broad scenarios with a particular spotlight on Judaea. First, we will observe how paying taxes could communicate cultic purity within the dynamics of Second Temple Judaism. Second, we will see how paying taxes could also be considered apostasy by certain sects of Judaism. Third, we will observe that the act of paying taxes could communicate submission to Rome.

Taxes and Cultic Purity

In the case of Jews living in and around Judaea, the issue of taxation involved the Mosaic law, the temple, and cultic purity. The payment of a temple tax was established by the Torah. The payment of taxes for the building and maintenance of the temple in Jerusalem was maintained throughout the pre-exilic and post-exilic eras. For Jews, payment of taxes was tightly bound to cultic purity and worship of Yahweh. This relationship was so close that one can argue that payment of the temple tax in the pre-70 CE era essentially functioned as a boundary marker, akin to the distinguishing marks of circumcision, dietary laws, and Sabbath regulations.[7]

According to the Law of Moses, those Jewish men and proselytes 20 years and older could pay a *voluntary* tax (priests, women, slaves, and minors excepted).[8] This tax consisted of a half-shekel for the sanctuary and a half-shekel as an offering to the Lord (Exod 30:11–16). After the return from Exile, the temple tax was changed to one-third of a shekel:

5. Boatwright, *Hadrian and the Cities of the Roman Empire*, 90.

6. Philip F. Esler, "Rome in Apocalyptic and Rabbinic Literature," in *The Gospel of Matthew in Its Roman Context* (London: T&T Clark, 2005), 13.

7. Mikael Tellbe, "The Temple Tax as a Pre-70 CE Identity Marker," in *The Formation of the Early Church*, ed. J. Ådna, WUNT 183 (Tübingen: Mohr Siebeck, 2005), 19.

8. Ibid., 20.

> We also take on ourselves the obligation to give yearly a third part of a shekel for the service of the house of our God: for the showbread, the regular grain offering, the regular burnt offering, the Sabbaths, the new moons, the appointed feasts, the holy things, and the sin offerings to make atonement for Israel, and for all the work of the house of our God. (Neh 10:32–33)

By paying one shekel to the temple (assuming the temple tax was a half-shekel), both requirements for the temple were met. Payment could also be made with two Attic *drachmae* or two Roman *denarii*.[9] The only explicit reference to the temple tax in the New Testament is Matt 17:24–27. In that passage, the tax is referred to as τὰ δίδραχμα (17:24), literally, the "the double drachma" and ὁ στατήρ (17:26).[10] The stater (ὁ στατήρ) was worth about four drachma or the equivalent to the Tyrian tetradrachma, also called the Tyrian shekel.[11]

Some have suggested that references to "one shekel" in Jewish literature does not mean a doubling of the temple tax but rather a "generic term."[12] What might account for this discrepancy is that there were competing interpretations amongst Jewish sects about how often a tax should be paid to the temple in Jerusalem.

This tax is clearly referenced in Matt 17:24–27 when the temple tax collectors inquire if Peter and Jesus pay the tax. The scene in Matthew's Gospel portrays the temple tax collectors as turning a voluntary tax into an involuntary one. Jesus provides the money only so as "not to give offense to them" (Matt 17:27). There was clearly a movement by those in control of the temple to put pressure on people to pay the tax.

Temple taxes at the Jerusalem temple had to be paid in silver coinage; specifically a shekel minted to imitate the silver coinage of Tyre. Although gold was at the head of the monetary system, silver was much more prevalent in Judaea. Because of the scarcity of gold, values were based on silver. The Jewish temple required pure silver for dues.[13] This is significant because silver coins were only struck in ancient Judaea during the "Persian period and the two revolts against Rome (CE 66–70) and (CE 132–135)."[14]

9. Ibid.
10. Ibid., 26.
11. Magness, *Stone and Dung*, 102.
12. Paul Foster, "Vespasian, Nerva, Jesus, and the *Fiscus Judaicus*," in *Israel's God and Rebecca's Children: Christology and Community in Early Judaism and Christianity*, ed. D. B. Capes, A. D. DeConick. H. K. Bond, and T. A. Miller (Waco: Baylor University Press, 2007), 306.
13. Hendin, "Current Viewpoints on Ancient Jewish Coinage," 259.
14. Ibid., 261.

Money exchanging was an important part of Jewish pilgrimage to the Jerusalem temple. One scholar explains: "pilgrims from all over the Greco-Roman world needed to exchange their foreign currency for the Tyrian coinage used in the temple."[15]

Cultic purity was sought even when the temple tax could not be paid. Those who could not make the trip to pay their taxes at the temple in Jerusalem may have been given special instructions as to where their money could be deposited. Payment for vows, offerings, and tithes that could not be made to the Jerusalem temple may have been cast into the Dead Sea (Salt Sea). This is supported by two lines of evidence. First, thousands of coins have been found in deposits that would have been close to the Dead Sea shoreline.[16] Second, there are several (post-70 CE) references to rabbinic literature that direct Jews who want to make Nazirite vows, sin offerings, freewill offerings, and so on, to cast coins into the Dead Sea.[17] This action would have stood in contrast to Deut 14:24–27, which directed Jews to spend tithes on a celebration:

> And if the way is too long for you, so that you are not able to carry the tithe, when the Lord your God blesses you, because the place is too far from you, which the Lord your God chooses, to set his name there, then you shall turn it into money and bind up the money in your hand and go to the place that the Lord your God chooses and spend the money for whatever you desire—oxen or sheep or wine or strong drink, whatever your appetite craves. And you shall eat there before the Lord your God and rejoice, you and your household. And you shall not neglect the Levite who is within your towns, for he has no portion or inheritance with you. (Deut 14:24–27)

It might be the case that those who deposited monies in the sea disregarded this text from Deuteronomy. Another possibility might be that the monies found in ancient shoreline deposits are from a sect who refused to participate in the Jerusalem temple cult. Yet another possible solution is that rabbinic traditions overshadowed the directions of Deut 14:24–27.

15. Curtis Mitch and Edward Sri, *The Gospel of Matthew*, CCSS (Grand Rapids: Baker, 2010), 269.

16. Magness, *Stone and Dung*, 104.

17. For a list of rabbinic quotations see ibid., 104–5. Magness points out that post-70 CE rabbinic quotations are often thought to originate in much earlier traditions. However, one must be careful about drawing strong conclusions based on later rabbinic writings.

The deep concern for cultic purity at the temple and the giving of tithes by the Jews was supposed to be characterized by joy and trust in Yahweh—the creator and redeemer of Israel. Understanding these demands from the Law of Moses will aid those who seek to understand archeological evidence and the New Testament. For most of the Jews in the early part of the first century, paying the temple tax was a way to express worship to Yahweh and possibly to maintain their social standing with the temple authorities.

Taxes and Apostasy

For some Jews in the first century, paying taxes to Rome was highly controversial and could communicate apostasy. *First, we see that paying taxes could communicate apostasy if it was believed that something sacred was being profaned.* The following text from Luke provides us with several historical clues about payment of taxes in a Hellenistic Jewish context:

> The scribes and the chief priests sought to lay hands on him at that very hour, for they perceived that he had told this parable against them, but they feared the people. So they watched him and sent spies, who pretended to be sincere, that they might catch him in something he said, so as to deliver him up to the authority and jurisdiction of the governor. So they asked him, "Teacher, we know that you speak and teach rightly, and show no partiality, but truly teach the way of God. Is it lawful for us to give tribute to Caesar, or not?" But he perceived their craftiness, and said to them, "Show me a denarius. Whose likeness and inscription does it have?" They said, "Caesar's." He said to them, "Then render to Caesar the things that are Caesar's, and to God the things that are God's." And they were not able in the presence of the people to catch him in what he said, but marveling at his answer they became silent. (Luke 20:19–26)

The trap that the scribes and chief priests set up for Jesus placed him in a no-win situation. If Jesus answers "no" to the question "is it lawful for Jews to give tribute to Caesar?," then he can be reported to the civic authorities as a rebel against Rome. If Jesus answers "yes," then he can be accused of breaking the Law of Moses by giving money to a man who claims to be divine, thus committing apostasy.

This scene provides strong historical evidence for the idea that coins ought to be read as cultural texts. It is the images on the coin and their communicative power that drives the confrontation between Jesus and his interlocutors. The New Testament bears witness to the fact that some people in the first century grappled with the implications of the messages sent by coins. These tiny cultural texts bore enough communicative power to justify killing a man—at least in the eyes of those who set this trap for Jesus.

Jesus' reply to the scribes and chief priests is based on the *denarius*, a coin which had a portrait of Caesar on the obverse. Jesus' answer draws a distinction between the things that are Caesar's and the things that are God's. For Jesus, taxation was simply Caesar receiving back what was already his. This is essentially a rejection of the ideological intentions of the Emperor while acknowledging that Jews could follow Yahweh as well as obey Caesar's demand for taxation.

Second, paying taxes could communicate apostasy if the temple was perceived as apostate. This was particularly true for the Qumran community as evidenced in the Dead Sea Scrolls. In some respects the coins found at Qumran are not unique, but they can indicate how taxes and tithes were used.[18] The presence of temple-tax collection at Qumran provides evidence that these sectarians viewed the collection of temple taxes in Jerusalem as problematic and perhaps even evidence of apostasy.

At least 1,234 coins have been discovered at the Qumran site, but no complete inventory has ever been published.[19] Some coins from the excavations of Rolland de Vaux have been reported as lost.[20] Others report that "a very large percentage of the coins found at Khirbet Qumran have disappeared."[21] Of the coins that have been found, many hypothesize that they were used for religious taxes or levies.[22]

About half of the coins found at Qumran were silver and the other half copper. In 1995–96, two Tyrian didrachmas were discovered there, one having a date of 25 CE.[23] Others include undated bronze coins minted by Herod around 30 to 37 BCE and a coin of the Procurators under Nero.[24]

18. "There is no reason to think that those coins found at Qumran are unique to Qumran" (E. C. Ulrich, "The Qumran Biblical Scrolls—The Scriptures of Late Second Temple Judaism," in *The Dead Sea Scrolls in Their Historical Context*, ed. T. Lim [London: T&T Clark, 2004], 80).

19. Murphy, *Wealth in the Dead Sea Scrolls*, 305.

20. Magness, *The Archaeology of Qumran*, 4.

21. Allan R. Petersen, "The Archaeology of Khirbet Qumran," in *Qumran Between the Old and New Testaments*, ed. F. H Cryer and T. L. Thompson, JSOTSup 290 (Sheffield: Sheffield Academic, 1998), 251.

22. For a discussion of using coins for dating archeological sites at Qumran see Magness, *The Archaeology of Qumran*, 56.

23. Murphy, *Wealth in the Dead Sea Scrolls*, 307 n. 53.

24. Magness, *The Archaeology of Qumran*, 56–57.

The silver coins were tetradrachmas and didrachmas from the Seleucid period (320 to 150 BCE) and the city of Tyre, as well as silver Roman denarii.[25] A hoard of 561 silver coins was placed in three pots and buried under the floor in one of the buildings.[26] This hoard contained Tyrian tetradrachmas (shekels) that were minted after 126 BCE, the most recent coin being minted in 9/8 BCE.[27] The copper coins were wide ranging in their origins and issues.

Because the Torah placed certain demands on Jews regarding taxation and the temple, the issue of taxation required considerable religious care. Documents found among the Dead Sea Scrolls indicate that the sect at Qumran viewed themselves as an alternative to the temple.[28] As an alternative to what could have been perceived as a corrupt and unclean temple in Jerusalem, the sect at Qumran had to collect the temple tithes and taxes. The document known as the Copper Scroll might be a record of these holdings, including "forty-two talents."[29] There are still many questions surrounding the nature of the Copper Scroll, but it does attest to the fact that taxes were collected even when the group was anticipating apocalyptic events or the end of the age.[30]

Another important source of evidence for understanding taxation in the Qumran community is the hoard of coins found in the Western sector (room L120). Arguably this hoard of coins was a "census collection or Temple tax."[31] This money could have been collected on behalf on the temple in Jerusalem or in place of the temple in Jerusalem.

In sum, the Dead Sea Scrolls and archeological artifacts from the Qumran community point to the conclusion that certain Jewish sectarians were driven by fear of apostasy to collect taxes that otherwise would have been given to the temple.

25. Murphy, *Wealth in the Dead Sea Scrolls*, 305.

26. Magness, *The Archaeology of Qumran*, 58.

27. Some of these silver coins from the hoard were countermarked from 9/8 BCE. Ibid.

28. Murphy, *Wealth in the Dead Sea Scrolls*, 289, also 305.

29. Ibid., 289.

30. "It attests to the exaction of religious levies and to the ongoing collection of these taxes even in uncertain political circumstances" (ibid., 290).

31. Ibid.

Taxes and Submission

After the Jews were defeated in the "First Jewish Revolt" of 66–73 CE, the Roman government of Vespasian instituted the humiliating tax called the *fiscus Judaicus*.[32] This act transformed the Jewish temple tax into a revenue stream for Roman projects. In order to memorialize the victory and spread the news of it, a series of coins was minted by the Flavian dynasty called the *Iudaea Capta* coins. *Besides providing income, payment of this tax by Jews was designed to communicate submission to Rome.*

The *Iudaea Capta* series was composed of imperial and provincial coinage. This series included variations of the gold aureus, the sestertius, and the denarius. The intention to humiliate the Jews was dramatically portrayed by the famous *Iudaea Capta* coin that featured a Roman centurion with a spear standing over a subjugated Jewess that personified the nation. In a coin by Titus, the god Nike appears with a foot on a helm.[33] To add insult to injury, this tax was used to rebuild the temple of Jupiter Capitolinus (The Temple of Jupiter Optimus Maximus) on Capitoline Hill in Rome.[34] There were, of course, pragmatic reasons for this tax. Vespasian wanted a steady stream of income to finance projects aimed at rebuilding Rome as it recovered from civil war.[35] Josephus records that Caesar "also laid a tribute upon the Jews wheresoever they were and enjoined every one of them to bring two drachmae every year into the Capitol, as they used to pay the same to the Temple at Jerusalem" (*War* 7.218). This was not all; the *fiscus Judaicus* was required of both sexes (child or adult), whereas the previous temple tax was due from Jewish males only.[36]

This tax effectively communicated two ideas within the social sphere: honor and shame. The picture of a subjugated Jew clearly degraded the Jews and elevated Rome, its generals, and its gods.[37]

32. For an argument on the parity and the political nature of paying taxes in Jerusalem before and after 70 CE see E. J. Carter, "Toll and Tribute: A Political Reading of Matthew 17:24–27," *JSNT* 25 (2003): 413–31.

33. Hendin 743–74. Vagi, *Coinage and History of Roman Empire*, 2:318.

34. Carter, *The Roman Empire and The New Testament*, 67.

35. Foster, "Vespasian, Nerva, Jesus, and the *Fiscus Judaicus*," 305.

36. Esler, "God's Honour and Rome's Triumph," 240.

37. Ibid., 237; Esler, "Rome in Apocalyptic and Rabbinic Literature," 12.

A large bronze sestertius of Vespasian portraying a captive Jew sitting on the ground to the right of a palm tree (ca. 71 CE). The text reads "IVDAEA CAPTA SC." (RIC 159, BMC 533). Photo credit: David Hendin.

The *Iudaea Capta* coin is regularly cited as an example of subjugation because of the depiction of the standing Roman soldier juxtaposed with a captive Jew. The coin memorialized not just Roman victory but Jewish defeat. For the Jews, it had the potential to force those who used it to re-live continuously this devastating event. One author explains, "we should see these coins as a primary means whereby the Flavians developed a discourse to communicate an imperial ideology in connection with their defeat of the Jews and the establishment of their line."[38]

The *fiscus Judaicus* continued from Vespasian to the reign of his second son, the Emperor Domitian. The Roman historian Suetonius reports that during this administration, the tax was collected from the people with severity.[39] However, Suetonius also reports that those who concealed that they were Jews did not pay the tax.[40] After the assassination of Domitian, the Emperor Nerva issued a new coin (a sestertius) that proclaimed the cancellation of the humiliating tax. The new coin issued read: *Fisci Iudaici Calumnia Sublata* (the humiliation of the *fiscus Judaicus* has been cancelled).

One must be careful when using the category of taxes to study the first-century Jewish context. Taxes were paid to ruling parties such as Rome, but they were also paid to the temple as an act of worship. While this act of worship may have been a financial hardship for the destitute, such an act could be a cultic demonstration of one's faith in Yahweh (Mark 12:41–44; Luke 21:1–4). This worship was not to be equated to

38. Esler, "God's Honour and Rome's Triumph," 240.

39. Suet., *Dom.* 12.2.

40. Marius Heemstra, *Fiscus Judaicus and the Parting of the Ways*, WUNT 277 (Tübingen: Mohr Siebeck, 2010), 2.

paying taxes to an impersonal bureaucracy. As one considers each text in its proper context, one must be careful not to use the category of taxes to overshadow the equally or even more important category of worship.

Lastly, we see that the *fiscus Judaicus* provides strong historical evidence of coinage being used to communicate a political message to an entire province. The use of a later coin by the Emperor Nerva (ruling from 96 to 98 CE) to undo the tax of Vespasian highlights the centrality of coinage in providing wide dissemination of political messages to the regional populace.

The *fiscus Judaicus* tax is an important topic for studying earliest Christianity because it may be related to the "parting of the ways" between Jews and Christians. The topic of the "parting of the ways" is related to the historical emergence of earliest Christianity as an independent form of religious thought and life that was "essentially different from all the national peculiarities of Judaism."[41] It was because the earliest Christians were so identified with the Jewish community in the eyes of the Romans that "mixed Christian communities (consisting of Jews and non-Jews) were at a great risk of falling into the hands of the *fiscus Judaicus*."[42] However, those who denied Judaism in name and practice would not pay the tax. Thus, one can conclude that "Christians who did not pay the tax were clearly not Jews."[43] Under the emperor Domitian, there may have been some official distinction between Jewish and Gentile Christians, but this may have been ignored under his successor Nerva. Some sought to hide their Jewish identity to avoid the tax, and Domitian utilized government agents to identify these people.[44] The tax would have given an incentive for some groups, especially proselytes, to identify themselves as non-Jews to evade the tax. It was under the emperor Nerva that this tax may have contributed to a stronger distinction between Jews and Christians as separate religious groups.

Implications for Studying the New Testament

The topic of taxes is wide ranging and this chapter has only provided a cursory overview. The communicative act of paying taxes is relevant for several issues related to the New Testament. The fact that paying taxes

41. J. D. G. Dunn, "Preface," in *Jews and Christians: The Parting of the Ways: A.D. 70 to 135*, ed. J. D. G. Dunn, WUNT 66 (Grand Rapids: Eerdmans, 1999), vii.

42. Heemstra, *Fiscus Judaicus and the Parting of the Ways*, 66.

43. Tellbe, "The Temple Tax as a Pre-70 CE Identity Marker," 25.

44. Ibid.

was a communicative act meant that there were all sorts of religious and social implications for the taxpayers, depending on the context. These often fell within the broad concerns of purity, apostasy, and submission to the state. First, the payment of taxes was not simply a matter of civic duty for most Jews. Rather, payment of taxes was integral to the cult of Yahweh worship under the Mosaic covenant and an expression of faith. Second, the payment of taxes is important for studying the historical context surrounding Jesus' ministry and his interaction with Roman authorities and Jewish opponents. Third, the *fiscus Judaicus* demonstrates that paying certain kinds of taxes could imply one's identity (Jew or non-Jew in this case). The Roman interest in subjugating Jews after the fall of Jerusalem in 70 CE through taxes may explain the persecution of Christians as found in the book of Revelation (ch. 5), the Letter to the Hebrews (ch. 6), and the Gospel of John (ch. 7).[45]

Summary

This section has focused on the world in front on the coin: the Roman Empire as it existed in and around the first century. There are few things that characterized all of the people groups and cultures that lived in the geographical context as diverse as modern-day France and the Levant. But there were at least two things that unified them: death *and taxes*. We have argued the point *that paying taxes was a communicative act with theological and social implications*. Indeed, the act of paying or withholding taxes in the first century could communicate all kinds of things to all kinds of people. Paying taxes to Rome had the potential to communicate that a Jew was an apostate to his own people. Jesus' instructions to pay taxes to Caesar while simultaneously paying what was owed to God allowed him to avert an explosive situation. After considering the dynamics between purity, apostasy, and submission, it is not difficult to conclude that paying or withholding taxes was a powerful communicative act in the first century. Whether one is focusing on the pre-70 temple tax or the post-70 Roman tax (*fiscus Judaicus*), the paying of taxes was bound up with issues of power, politics, purity, and submission.

45. Heemstra, *Fiscus Judaicus and the Parting of the Ways*, 66.

Section II

The World of the Coin: Propaganda

Chapter 8

Propaganda and Inscriptions

There are three languages that are used for the inscriptions on coins in the world of the New Testament: Paleo-Hebrew, Greek, and Latin. These languages functioned as the primary means for communication through inscriptions.

Introduction

The study of inscriptions is often referred to as *epigraphy*. Over half a million ancient Greek and Latin inscriptions are extant today.[1] Before discussing the interpretation of coinage we must avoid the error of interpreting coins outside of historical contexts. The temptation for many in numismatics has been to begin their study with the coin as an exclusive source of history, without due consideration of archaeological contexts.[2] That being said, coins are often considered epigraphic evidence for re-constructing ancient history. When seeking to interpret ancient coins, it is important to consider the inscriptions (also called "legends") together with the imagery. Other sources of epigraphic evidence include papyri, stamps, seals, and tablets. Inscriptions on coins played an important symbolic role and often functioned as a way to communicate ideological concerns.[3] *In other words, it is possible that an inscription on a coin could function as a symbol as well as a text to be read.*

The argument in this chapter is an attempt to explain how to account for the following paradox: a majority of the population of the Empire could not read inscriptions on coins (or elsewhere) and yet a majority of

1. McLean, *Introduction to Greek Epigraphy*, 21.

2. Krmnicek, "Das Konzept der Objektbiographie in der antiken Numismatik," 52.

3. "Inscriptions had a strong symbolic meaning in antiquity (witness, for example, the many addresses to divine beings and the curse tablets), and despite saying what was meant (for the ancients) they are a poor reflection of common literacy" (Botha, *Orality and Literacy*, 45).

coins used inscriptions. One author tries to account for this paradox by suggesting that some people "would have discovered at least the general sense of those inscriptions' meanings."[4] Certainly some meaning could be discovered contextually from the interplay between symbol (iconography) and inscription. What is being suggested in this chapter is that this interplay would have turned *inscriptions into iconography*, particularly for those who were illiterate or semi-literate.[5] The ability of inscriptions to function this way rests on the foundation that "language is not a neutral tool of communication between people."[6]

Although the New Testament specialist will likely be focused on Koine Greek and perhaps classical Hebrew, the coins from the first-century context of the New Testament draw heavily from Latin. Languages such as Latin usually fall outside the typical research language curriculum for students of biblical studies. Even where Greek is present, the inscriptions are often cryptic and difficult to read. This is precisely where scholarship from the domains of classics and numismatics can provide the most help. Other relevant languages outside the scope of this book include Nabataean and Phoenician from the regions around the Levant.

In this chapter we will first describe how inscriptions could function as symbols in their own right and then we will cover the three languages that appear on coins minted in the Roman Empire in the first century: Paleo-Hebrew, Greek, and Latin. We will see that the use of Paleo-Hebrew on coins could communicate Jewish nationalism and a desire to return to an independently ruled theocracy. The use of Greek on coins could communicate that what was written was intended for mass consumption across the Empire. The use of Latin could communicate that what was written had the official or semi-official support of Rome. Each one of these languages will be examined separately due to the fact that only a few coins were minted that featured more than one language. The last section in this chapter will explore how inscriptions and their symbolic function relates to the New Testament.

4. Chancey, "City Coins and Roman Power in Palestine," 104.

5. Referring to inscriptions on a carved staircase, Rhodes states: "Recently some scholars have stressed their symbolic function" (P. J. Rhodes, "The Non-literary Written Sources," in *A Companion to the Classical Greek World*, ed. K. H. Kinzl, BCAW [Oxford: Blackwell, 2010], 50).

6. Kathy Ehrensperger, "Speaking Greek Under Rome: Paul, the Power of Language and the Language of Power," *Neot* 46 (2012): 15.

Coin Inscriptions and Symbolism

There are three points that will help us to understand inscriptions on coins. Each of these three points draws connections between the way that inscriptions on coins were both symbols in their own right and texts to be read.

First, scholars must be careful not to equate the presence of inscriptions with literacy. The debate about literacy in Judaea and the Mediterranean as a whole continues.[7] Coins offered limited space for legible text, and abbreviations were often used.[8] In the first century, this small abbreviated text may have been readable only by a very small number of people. Some have suggested that the literacy rate of the Roman Empire was around ten percent.[9] For some people, the abbreviations could only function as a symbol because they could not be understood in any other way. This may not be how they were intended to function, but it reflects the reality that readers of coins may only have been able to identify the type of language present and not the actual meaning of the words. Although coins provided a medium for rulers and powerful figures to speak to the world, it was not always the case that large portions of society were actually listening. In addition, the fact that coins were widely used as tools of propaganda makes them suspect for indicating the education of the culture in question.[10] This means that coins *might* reflect the nature of a very narrow and specific audience, making them difficult sources for generalized literacy data. As far as evidence of literacy goes, coins "may imply literacy—but do not necessarily."[11] Also, having only a rudimentary command of a (written

7. Botha, *Orality and Literacy*, passim. A recent study that concludes that literacy in Judaea was relatively low is that by Catherine Hezser, *Jewish Literacy in Roman Palestine*, TSAJ 81 (Tübingen: Mohr Siebeck, 2001), 496. For a challenge to the consensus about low literacy, see Brian J. Wright, "Ancient Literacy in New Testament Research: Incorporating a Few More Lines of Enquiry," *TrinJ* 36 (2015): 1–29.

8. Larry W. Hurtado, *The Earliest Christian Artifacts: Manuscripts and Christian Origins* (Grand Rapids: Eerdmans, 2006), 99.

9. William V. Harris, *Ancient Literacy* (Cambridge, MA: Harvard University Press, 1989), 22.

10. Royce M. Victor excludes coins from his study of education and literacy because "rulers often used the coins as instruments of political propaganda" in *Colonial Education and Class Formation in Early Judaism: A Postcolonial Reading*, LSTS (London: T&T Clark, 2010), 90.

11. Chris Keith, *Jesus' Literacy: Scribal Culture and the Teacher from Galilee*, LNTS (London: T&T Clark, 2011), 75.

or spoken) language typically suffices for commercial purposes (buying, selling, and trading).[12]

Second, it is well-documented that some languages in antiquity functioned as sacred. Sacred languages become symbols of divinity and possibly ethnocentrism. In the case of Jews, the Hebrew language itself could symbolize national election vis-à-vis the nations. The very presence of sacred languages, regardless of textual meaning, will communicate religious overtones. When a sacred language appears on coinage, the cultural exegete must interpret its presence along with its text. As we will see, the very language chosen by the minters (city, province, or imperial) communicated something to someone.

Third, only a few coins from the first century were minted with inscriptions in more than one language. One of the rare examples comes from Alexander Jannaeus who minted coins with Greek on one side and Hebrew on the other.[13] Similarly, Herod the Great minted coins for use in Judaea with Greek-only inscriptions.[14] This is germane to the topic of the historical Jesus.[15] Coins such as these indicate that some Jews were bi-lingual and able to use both Greek and Aramaic. For example, Herod the Great minted coins for use in Judaea with Greek-only inscriptions.

In sum, these four points help to frame the argument that inscriptions could function symbolically. Even though the authors and minters of coins may have intended their inscriptions to be legible, the reality was that a majority of the Roman Empire was illiterate or semi-literate. Coins were an easy way to communicate in such a society.[16] One of the reasons for this may be that the mere presence of one type of language or another could communicate something to someone about something. In order to pursue this argument in more detail we will examine inscriptions in Paleo-Hebrew, Greek, and Latin.

Coin Inscriptions and Paleo-Hebrew

The presence of Paleo-Hebrew on coins may be a strong example of inscription functioning as *symbol* as well as something to be *read*. This

12. Miguel P. Fernández, *An Introductory Grammar of Rabbinic Hebrew*, trans. J. Elwolde (Leiden: Brill, 1997), 3.

13. Victor, *Colonial Education and Class Formation in Early Judaism*, 89.

14. Ibid., 90.

15. G. Scott Gleaves, *Did Jesus Speak Greek? The Emerging Evidence of Greek Dominance in First-Century Palestine* (Eugene, OR: Pickwick, 2015), xii.

16. Morten H. Jensen, *Herod Antipas in Galilee*, 2nd ed., WUNT 215 (Tübingen: Mohr Siebeck, 2010), 187.

language called Paleo-Hebrew has also been called (1) square script, (2) Syrian script, or (3) Aramaic script.[17] Most of the coins that have Paleo-Hebrew are small and made of bronze. They will often show little wear although most were poorly minted.[18]

During the revolt of 66–70 CE, also known as the "First Jewish–Roman war," the Jews minted their own coins with a Paleo-Hebrew script that had not been widely used since before the fall of the Judean monarchy.[19] The use of Paleo-Hebrew script in conjunction with the act of minting coins was a demonstrable act of Jewish independence from Roman rule.[20] The Paleo-Hebrew script also helps to identify which coins were minted in or around Jerusalem.[21] The use of Paleo-Hebrew on coinage during the first revolt parallels examples found on documents. Whereas most Jewish legal documents prior to the war were written in Aramaic, evidence suggests that the new era of freedom may have been marked by a sudden change to Hebrew.[22] There are four points of argumentation that support the conclusion that Paleo-Hebrew functioned as both a symbol and as script to be read.

A half-shekel of the First Jewish War, minted in Jerusalem, year 1 (ca. 66/7 CE). A chalice is figured on the left image with the inscription "Half Shekel." On the right are three pomegranates on a stem. The Paleo-Hebrew inscription on the right reads "Jerusalem the Holy." (Hendin 656.) Photo credit: David Hendin.

17. On the Aramaisms of Jesus see Ben Witherington III, *Jesus, Paul and the End of the World* (Downers Grove: InterVarsity, 1992), 86.

18. Magness, *Stone and Dung*, 104.

19. "The last time the script was widely used in Judea was before the fall of the Judean monarchy" (Bennie H. Reynolds III, *Between Symbolism and Realism: The Use of Symbolic and Non-Symbolic Language in Ancient Jewish Apocalypses 333–63 B.C.E.*, JAJSup [Göttingen: Vandenhoeck & Ruprecht, 2012], 354).

20. Martin Goodman, "Coinage and Identity: The Jewish Evidence," in Howgego, Heuchert, and Burnett, eds., *Coinage and Identity in the Roman Provinces*, 165

21. Ariel, "Identifying the Mints, Minters, and Meanings," 373.

22. James S. McLaren, "Going to War Against Rome: The Motivation of the Jewish Rebels," in Popović, ed., *The Jewish Revolt Against Rome*, 129–53 (143).

First, some Jews may have viewed the Hebrew language itself as God-given or as a holy tongue (*leshon hakodesh*).[23] In this view, Hebrew is the language of Torah and carries a special status. The Hebrew Bible itself claims to be the "very words of God."[24] At the very least, the Hebrew language was the language of God's people and their scripture—it was a symbol of national and religious identity. By choosing to use Paleo-Hebrew, the Jews who minted the coins were communicating something ideological and political: their "new" government was nothing less than the continuation of God's chosen nation.[25] It is likely that some Jews in the first century (or earlier) believed that Hebrew was the original divine language directly given by Yahweh to humanity and spoken by Adam. For example, the residents of Qumran did not use Greek as their dominant language and only three percent of their texts are written in Greek.[26] The Hebrew language alone was the "sacred tongue" of humanity and thus superior to all other languages that were formed as a result of the judgment of the Tower of Babel.[27]

Second, the Hebrew Bible identifies the Hebrew language as part of the distinction between Israel and its neighbors. To lose the language of Hebrew placed national and spiritual identities at stake. This objection to the use of non-Israelite language was specifically based on the relationship between language, identity, self-expression, and the Torah.[28] Some have pointed to the book of Nehemiah as providing evidence of the "connection between language and identity."[29]

> In those days also I saw the Jews who had married women of Ashdod, Ammon, and Moab. And half of their children spoke the language of Ashdod, and they could not speak the language of Judah, but only the language of each people. And I confronted them and cursed them and beat some of

23. David Patterson, *Hebrew Language and Jewish Thought* (London: Routledge-Curzon, 2005), 7.

24. Timothy M. Law, *When God Spoke Greek: The Septuagint and the Making of the Christian Bible* (Oxford: Oxford University Press, 2013), 35.

25. William M. Schniedewind notes that the choice of a Paleo-Hebrew script was "motivated by underlying ideologies" in *A Social History of Hebrew: Its Origins Through the Rabbinic Period*, ABYRL (New Haven: Yale University Press, 2013), 12.

26. Victor, *Colonial Education and Class Formation in Early Judaism*, 89.

27. For a discussion and citations from ancient sources see James L. Kugel, *Traditions of the Bible: A Guide to the Bible as it was at the Start of the Common Era* (Cambridge, MA: Harvard University Press, 2009), 235–36.

28. Derek Kidner, *Ezra and Nehemiah: An Introduction and Commentary*, TOTC 12 (Downers Grove: InterVarsity, 1979), 144.

29. Schniedewind, *A Social History of Hebrew*, 81.

> them and pulled out their hair. And I made them take an oath in the name of God, saying, "You shall not give your daughters to their sons, or take their daughters for your sons or for yourselves." (Neh 13:13–25)

Third, the Babylonian exile placed the Hebrew language in danger of being replaced by Aramaic. The Jews who returned from Exile in Babylon did not speak Hebrew, but Aramaic. This reinforced the idea that Hebrew was crucial to the identity of Jews. By the time of the first century, many Jews spoke Greek as well. One author states, "While there is evidence of continued use of Hebrew and Aramaic during this period, most Jews will have fully adopted Koine Greek."[30] When first-century Jews in Judaea were able to mint their own coins, they used a language that was anachronistic and had not been spoken or written for several hundred years.

Fourth, the use of Paleo-Hebrew in the first-century was an intentional symbol of Israel's relatively recent past. The paleo-script of the first century CE was appearing on coins in the fourth century BCE.[31] These are often referred to as Yehud coins. These are the coins of the periods when Judaea was under the control of the Babylonian and Persian Empires. Yehud coins of the Persian period were likely struck in Gaza.[32] The significance of Yehud coins is that they used the Hebrew language as a symbol of Jewish identity and nationalism. This use of inscription-as-symbol also occurred during the Hasmonean revolt and may give insight into the era of the New Testament. Those first-century Jewish coins that used Paleo-Hebrew imitated the so-called Yehud coins from 400 to 260 BCE that used the language as a symbol of "nationalistic pride and religious tradition."[33]

To summarize: the use of Paleo-Hebrew inscriptions on coins was most likely a way to symbolize and communicate ideas as intertwined as Jewish nationalism, identity, and divine election. One scholar concludes that the use of Paleo-Hebrew inscriptions on coins was a way to demonstrate "national pride and religious tradition."[34] It may also have been the

30. Law, *When God Spoke Greek*, 16.

31. Oded Lipschits and David Vanderhooft, "Yehud Stamp Impressions in the Fourth Century BC: A Time of Administrative Consolidation?," in *Judah and the Judeans in the Fourth Century BCE*, ed. O. Lipschits, G. N. Knoppers, and R. Albertz (Winona Lake: Eisenbrauns, 2007), 78.

32. Hendin, "Current Viewpoints on Ancient Jewish Coinage," 257.

33. David Hendin, *Cultural Change: Jewish, Christian, and Islamic Coins of the Holy Land* (New York: American Numismatic Society, 2011), 20.

34. The use of Paleo-Hebrew inscriptions on coins was a way to demonstrate "national pride and religious tradition" (Hendin, "Current Viewpoints on Ancient Jewish Coinage," 256).

case that Aramaic and Greek were viewed as "the scripts that Gentiles used."[35] Another scholar demurs: "It is impossible to say whether the use of Paleo-Hebrew reflects a special political or ideological intent."[36] What is important to note is that we do not possess ancillary literary evidence that allows us to be definitive on the matter.

Coin Inscriptions and Koine Greek

The presence of Greek language on coinage typically communicates that it was minted for local use.[37] Greek was especially used on provincial coinage to indicate the year in which a coin was struck.[38] It was only into the Hellenistic period that Greek letters were used to indicate a sequence of years.[39] Like the use of Paleo-Hebrew inscriptions on coins, the use of Greek language on coins may have functioned more as a symbol than a legible text. In other words, simply because Greek inscriptions occur on coinage does not mean that Greek was necessarily spoken by the people who used the coins (and it does not mean that the population would have a high rate of literacy in Greek).[40] Koine Greek was a language with both empire-wide and regional qualities.

Koine Greek was the common language of Judaea. When the Romans wanted to communicate clearly their domination of Judaea after the capture of Jerusalem in 70 CE, they produced a series of coins known as the Iudaea Capta coins, described in some detail above. Some of the coins in this series used Greek instead of Latin legends and inscriptions. One of the coins from this series depicts the military commander Titus and a "Winged Victory affixing a shield to a palm tree with the words IOUDAIAS EALOKUIAS" or "Judaea captured."[41] The use of Greek by

35. As suggested by Stephan J. Pfann, "Scripts and Scribal Practice," in *The Eerdmans Dictionary of Early Judaism*, ed. J. J. Collins and D. C. Harlow (Grand Rapids: Eerdmans, 2010), 1205.

36. Jürgen K. Zangenberg, "Archaeology, Papyri, and Inscriptions," in *Early Judaism: A Comprehensive Overview*, ed. J. J. Collins and D. C. Harlow (Grand Rapids: Eerdmans), 345.

37. Kreitzer, *Striking New Images*, 50.

38. Vagi, *Coinage and History of the Roman Empire*, 2:118.

39. Rhodes, "The Non-Literary Written Sources," 56.

40. "Greek letters engraved for governmental purposes tell us very little about what the masses spoke" (Chancey, *Greco-Roman Culture and the Galilee of Jesus*, 143).

41. Esler, "God's Honour and Rome's Triumph," 242.

Jews went beyond Judaea and Greek was the dominant language used by Jews who lived in Asia Minor.[42]

Koine Greek was the common language of trade across the Empire. We have mentioned the matter of literacy and the difficulty of relating it to numismatic evidence. Simply because most Jews in Judaea understood some Koine Greek, it does not mean that this was their only spoken language.[43] Aramaic would have been the dominant language used by Jews in Judaea, especially in rural areas where Greek influences would have been weaker. It is not difficult to imagine that Aramaic-speaking Jews who came across Greek inscriptions on coins would have associated the inscriptions with urban life. Despite pockets of resistance to Hellenistic influence, Koine Greek was the "common" language of the Empire (lingua franca) and allowed traders to interface easily. As one writer points out, the apostle Paul could write a letter in Greek to the church in Rome without any problem.[44] The Septuagint itself, in all of its many forms, also testifies to the importance of the Greek language on Jews.

Koine Greek inscriptions on coins differ somewhat from the script that most students become familiar with while learning the Koine Greek of the New Testament. The standard inscriptions on Greek coins use uppercase letters instead of lower case letters. Unlike Latin, Greek abbreviations never caught on because the Greeks utilized context to provide understanding.[45] The key point here is that Greek relied upon localized context and customs to be understood. It was a language that, when used, would have been recognized but not necessarily understood. This is particularly true for abbreviations and names.

Koine Greek inscriptions on coins point to their status as public documents that honored Caesar. With respect to grammar, inscriptions mostly use the genitive form (such as "of Herod the Great") or the

42. "Aus Kleinasien sind ca. 250 Inschriften bekannt, die man mit einigem Recht als 'jüdisch' bezeichnen kann. Mehr als 95% von ihnen sind in griechischer Sprache geschrieben." W. Ameling, "Die Jüdische Diaspora Kleinasiens und der 'Epigraphic Habit'," in *Jewish Identity in the Greco-Roman World*, ed. J. Frey et al., AJEC 71 (Leiden: Brill, 2007), 255.

43. "One cannot jump to the conclusion that most Jews of this time were monolingual, speaking only Greek" (Victor, *Colonial Education and Class Formation in Early Judaism*, 90).

44. Law, *When God Spoke Greek*, 15.

45. McLean, *Introduction to Greek Epigraphy*, 49.

nominative form (such as "Herod the King").[46] Where dative coin legends appear, this might communicate that the coins were "dedicated *to* and made *for* the emperor."[47] The nominative might simply name the imperial person or imply that he or she was ultimately (not directly) responsible for the coin.[48]

To summarize, the use of Koine Greek on coins relied heavily on local customs and context to facilitate meaning, even while being utilized as the universal language of trade. One scholar explains that "anyone wanting to reach a wider public in the Roman world would need Greek."[49] Greek functioned as a universal language that lacked the same associations with governmental authority that Latin had. Those who minted coins using Greek would have wanted that to be used widely and those who used such coinage may not have been able to decipher every abbreviation or word completely.

Coin Inscriptions and Latin

It is our argument that even when Latin inscriptions on coins could not be read linguistically they would have functioned symbolically. Those who were illiterate or semi-literate would have created associations between the presence of the language and Roman authority. This would have been particularly true for coinage. On the one hand, the Latin abbreviations on coins utilized a fixed standard throughout the Roman world. On the other hand, the political, social, and cultural diversity of the Empire made this system impractical and subject to misunderstanding.[50]

Latin inscriptions of some kind were widely used on coinage in the first-century context of the Roman Empire. The most common symbol used across the Roman Empire was the letters "SC," which stood for *Senatus Consulto* (by decree of the senate). This symbol appeared on the reverse side of most coinage in the Roman Empire. This Latin phraseology appears in the *Res Gestae Divi Augusti* (*The Deeds of Divine*

46. Meshorer, *Jewish Coins of the Second Temple Period*, 64; Ariel and Fontanille, *The Coins of Herod*, 121.

47. Williams, "The Republican Identity of Roman Imperial Coinage," 68.

48. Williams asserts that "coins cannot be made both for and by the emperor." But this does take into account the fact that an imperial figure could be considered the ultimate author and not the direct author (ibid.).

49. Alan Millard, "Latin in First-Century Palestine," in *Solving Riddles and Untying Knots: Biblical, Epigraphic and Semitic Studies in Honor of Jonas C. Greenfield*, ed. A. Berlin et al. (Winona Lake: Eisenbrauns, 1995), 451.

50. McLean, *Introduction to Roman Epigraphy*, 49.

Augustus) as a common way to refer to the approval of the Roman senate.[51] Initially, this symbol referred to the fact that the Senate was tasked with approving small change (copper and bronze) while the emperor approved gold and silver.

Titus as Caesar (69–79 CE), Dupondius, ca. 77–8 CE, Lugdunum (Lyon) mint, RIC 1252. Note how the reverse prominently indicates "SC" on either side of Felicitas who is standing to the left, holding a caduceus with her right hand and a cornucopia with her left.

Latin inscriptions on coins generally communicated that it was minted for Empire-wide circulation and held an official or semi-official status.[52] Latin has been described as the "official language of the ruling power."[53] It was the standard language on coins in the Roman Empire and the official language of the Roman army.[54] The first century Greek essayist and biographer Plutarch (45–120 CE) comments that Latin was recognized as a universal language (*Mor.* 1010D). All of Corinth's coins were minted with Latin inscriptions until 67 CE.[55] The "elite in Rome" viewed the Latin language "as a symbol of their citizenship and political institutions."[56] In the context of the first-century, it seems best to situate language by

51. Alison E. Cooley, *Res Gestae Divi Augusti: Texts, Translation, and Commentary* (Cambridge: Cambridge University Press, 2009), 62.

52. Kreitzer, *Striking New Images*, 50.

53. Millard, "Latin in First-Century Palestine," 451.

54. A point highlighted by D. A. Carson in his discussion of the trilingual placard on the cross of Jesus in John 19:19–22 (*The Gospel According to John*, PNTC [Grand Rapids: InterVarsity, 1991], 610).

55. Winter, *After Paul Left Corinth*, 11; Robert S. Dutch, *The Educated Elite in 1 Corinthians: Education and Community Conflict in Graeco-Roman Context*, JSNTSup 271 (London: T&T Clark, 2005), 50.

56. Alison E. Cooley, *The Cambridge Manual of Latin Epigraphy* (Cambridge: Cambridge University Press, 2012), 302.

acknowledging the complexity of bilingualism within the Roman world.[57] Sometimes the presence of Latin communicated the power or Rome and sometimes it did not. In the case of coinage, the presence of Latin was intended to communicate official or semi-official status.[58]

Latin inscriptions were used for legal functions in contexts other than coinage. The most famous example of Latin in the New Testament is the record found in John 19:19–22 of the sign that was posted on Jesus' cross in Aramaic, Greek, and Latin (each translated as: Jesus, king of the Jews). This likely reflected the fact that emperors such as Tiberius required legal declarations to be made in Latin, not Greek. The Emperor Claudius had a Greek-speaking judge removed from his seat and stripped him of his citizenship because he did not know Latin.[59] Another supporting piece of evidence is that Greek's often borrowed Latin abbreviations for official titles.[60] This suggests that the use of Latin itself was associated with governmental power.

Latin inscriptions would not have been universally understood across the Empire. Although Latin appears on many coins within Judaea, it is doubtful that many could read it.[61] Many Latin inscriptions on coins would have been indecipherable to most of the inhabitants of the Roman Empire due to their length and cryptic abbreviations.[62] It is true that many Roman coins used inscriptions to explain very small and complex imagery. These inscriptions would have identified some families by their initials or names.[63] Without these inscriptions the symbolism of the images would have only been understood by a very small group of educated elites.[64] Even those who could read Latin for the purpose of engaging in marketplace transactions might not have been able to read or interpret obscure words, abbreviations, or initials.

57. For an argument that early Christianity was largely bilingual see Udo Schnelle, "Das frühe Christentum und die Bildung," *NTS* 41 (2015): 113–43.

58. Kathy Ehrensperger comments, "there is abundant evidence of bi- and multilingualism at all social levels" ("Speaking Greek Under Rome," 14).

59. Nicholas Ostler, *Ad Infinitum: A Biography of Latin* (New York: Walker & Co., 2007), 15.

60. McLean, *Introduction to Greek Epigraphy*, 50.

61. Chancey, *Greco-Roman Culture and the Galilee of Jesus*, 144.

62. Zanker, *The Power of Images*, 14.

63. Evans, *The Art of Persuasion*, 17.

64. "The complexity and obscurity of the images led to coin inscriptions being used to explain, clarify, or extend meanings in a way which had never happened before" (Howgego, *Ancient History from Coins*, 75).

In this section we have simply sought to apply a rather non-controversial thesis to coinage: even when Latin inscriptions could not be read, they would have been functioned broadly as symbols of Roman authority. The thesis is stated by one scholar thus: "inscriptions that were inextricably linked with Roman authority were written in Latin."[65] When applied to coinage it is easy to see how even the most obscure Latin words and initials could have communicative power.

Implications for Studying the New Testament

The use of divine names written in Greek by early Christian scribes ties inscriptions on coins to the study of the New Testament. The question has arisen as to whether the use of "sacred names" (*nomina sacra*) by scribes and manuscript copyists are imitations of the divine abbreviations found on coins.[66] The answer to this question is likely "no." The *nomina sacra* are "abbreviates, contractions or suspensions" that reflect words that were thought to deserve special treatment.[67] These symbols were used to save time and space when writing. An example would be θυ—the *nomina sacra* form of the genitive of θεος ("god"). Amongst early Christians, the names Ιησους, Κυριος, θεος, and Χριστος served as *nomina sacra*.[68] It is difficult to ascertain the historical origins of this practice but some have suggested that the evidence points to a Christian innovation.[69] This might be true when focusing on the use of symbols for names. However, this chapter has established the wide use of inscriptions of all kinds as a type of symbol, particularly on coinage. Scholars acknowledge that coins and "abbreviated or shortened forms may have had some influence upon Christian development of *nomina sacra*."[70] However, the motivation for shortened forms on coins is to save space or include long words whereas the motivation for shortened forms in Christian manuscripts does not appear to have been driven by these motivations.[71] Although the use of

65. Cooley, *The Cambridge Manual of Latin Epigraphy*, 302.

66. Stanley Porter, "What Do We Know and How Do We Know It? Reconstructing Early Christianity from Its Manuscripts," in *Christian Origins and Greco-Roman Culture: Social and Literary Contexts for the New Testament*, ed. S. E. Porter and A. W. Pitts, TENT 9 (Leiden: Brill, 2013), 65.

67. Ibid.

68. Hurtado, *The Earliest Christian Artifacts*, 120.

69. Ibid.

70. Porter, "What Do We Know and How Do We Know It?," 64–65.

71. For more discussion see James R. Edwards, "A *Nomen Sacrum* in the Sardis Synagogue," *JBL* 128 (2009): 813–21.

shorthand for divine names may have been drawn from the shortening of Yahweh's name, resulting in the Tetragrammaton, the widespread use of Latin abbreviations on coinage may have fostered a cultural acceptance and recognition of early Christian symbols. What is most significant is that Jesus' name and God's name were treated by early Christians in the same way, reflecting an early form of proto-Trinitarian worship.[72]

Summary

The student of the New Testament is likely used to approaching text as *text* rather than text as *symbol*. This, of course, is an over-simplification but it is an important reminder that both aspects must be considered when interpreting coins. Coins are one of the few ancient media sources where images and writing functioned together to create "a strong symbolic power."[73] The broad argument of this chapter sought to reconcile the paradox of text amongst a largely illiterate or semi-literate population. One way to account for some of this paradox is to view *inscriptions as iconography*.

The thesis in this chapter found that Paleo-Hebrew inscriptions on coins functioned naturally as symbols because the language itself was tightly related to national identity by divine revelation. The same cannot be said for Greek or Latin. However, both Greek and Latin had unique relationships to the culture of the Mediterranean. The presence of any language on coinage is not necessarily the marker of power discourse, but the possibility should be considered. The very presence of the Greek language on a coin could communicate universality or paradoxically provinciality while Latin carried the authority of Rome.[74] In a world in which literacy was very low in some areas, the simple ability to recognize languages would have allowed coins to function as important cultural texts.

72. "It is remarkable for early Christians to have treated Jesus' name and key epithets for God in the same, apparently reverential, manner" (Hurtado, *The Earliest Christian Artifacts*, 121).

73. Mireille Corbier, "Writing in Roman Public Space," in *Written Space in the Latin West: 200 BC to AD 300*, ed. G. Sears, P. Keegan, and R. Laurence (London: Bloomsbury, 2013), 18.

74. My conclusions about the associations with various languages bears some similarities to Patterson who notes, "When [Hebrew] Scripture was rendered into Greek, it was turned over to the philosophical language of Athens. When it was rendered into Latin, it was surrendered to the political language of Rome. Both amounted to a betrayal of the holy tongue and the holy teaching. Both finally led to a devastating sense of alienation among the Jews" (*Hebrew Language and Jewish Thought*, 20).

Chapter 9

Propaganda and Dating

Here we continue the broad argument that inscriptions on coins functioned as tools of propaganda to the masses of the Roman Empire. This chapter specifically addresses the use of dates on coins to communicate the status of rulers and nations.

Introduction

The central idea of this chapter is that the dates on coins communicated frameworks for understanding time that was tied to rulers and political eras. When coins feature dates (and some do not), this was an attempt to communicate that the inauguration of a given reign was the beginning of a new era. As such, many coins used year one to mark the beginning of a kingdom or reign. The way in which rulers used coins to promote the key dates in their respective reigns is evidence that coins served as cultural texts through which time itself could be manipulated.

It is difficult actually to imagine that those who lived in the first-century Mediterranean and across the Roman Empire conceived of historical time without the use of our delineation of BCE and CE.[1] There was no standard numerical dating system. In reality, the Roman Empire's use of time and calendars was both complex and simplistic, thus defying easy characterization.[2] This poses unique challenges for dating coins but also opens up the question of the nature of time and how it was conceived in the ancient world.

Many historians and numismatic specialists focus most of their energies on using the dates on coins to establish its chronology. This is for good reason. The whole task of interpreting any given coin should integrate as much as possible with external data. One numismatic expert concludes: "It must be remembered that for any particular coin the interpretation may

1. Denis Feeney, *Caesar's Calendar: Ancient Time and the Beginnings of History*, SCL 65 (Berkeley: University of California Press, 2007), 7, similarly 156.

2. Ibid., 2.

be very different depending on the date assigned to it and that therefore the date of a coin must always be determined as closely as possible on external grounds before interpretation is attempted."[3]

While we do not deny the significance of historical chronology, this focus may obscure the communicative act of dating and its power to promote political propaganda.

The presence of dates on coins in the first century is strong evidence that those in power sought to use coins as a lens through which the people would see the world. Those in power used coins to structure or re-structure the world and how it was perceived. The very ability to set years and establish eras also reflected the identity of those in power, whether in Rome, a province, or city. One numismatist notes: "the structuring of time itself could be a marker of identity."[4] With respect to explicit dates appearing on coins from the first century, these are most common to coins issued by Rome although several Jewish coins have dates as well. In this chapter we will examine how Roman and Jewish elites sought to use coins as tools of propaganda by utilizing dating systems.

An important historical reality to note at the beginning of this chapter is that the inhabitants of the first-century Roman Empire were accustomed to living with several contemporaneous frameworks for time. As one historian explains: "In any society individuals are liable to inhabit different frames of time, often simultaneously—cyclical or recurrent, linear, seasonal, social, historical."[5] One example of contemporaneous frameworks is the idea that Rome could be dated based on the foundation of the city or the foundation of the Republic.[6]

Despite the desire of those in power to use coins to establish the dates, memorials, and victories of their reign, this communicative power was likely dampened by the reality of *familiarity*. One author states this problem of familiarity succinctly: "the inhabitants of the empire would have been carrying around collections of coins of various ages and may not have noticed the latest legends appearing on the new ones."[7] In other words, the inhabitants of the Empire may have been so inundated with claims about ages and eras that they may have ignored such claims. This problem moves us away from the world of the coin or the illocutionary force of the coin and toward the reception of the coin or its perlocutionary effect.

3. Crawford, *Roman Republican Coinage*, 2:726.
4. Howgego, "Coinage and Identity in the Roman Provinces," 7.
5. Feeney, *Caesar's Calendar*, 3.
6. Ibid., 175.
7. Esler, "God's Honour and Rome's Triumph," 240.

While it is possible that dates on coins may have simply lost their voice amidst the competing voices, we can point to the historical evidence that coins did have some effect upon their audiences. Again we can point to the fact that the hairstyles of Livia (the wife of Augustus) on coins were widely copied.[8] One scholar concludes, "Coin types were no doubt often 'misunderstood,'" but there is no doubt they had an impact.[9] We might also point out that having some minimal agreement about how time was ordered was an important part of Rome's homogenization efforts. Another scholar notes, "For Rome to become a world empire it was essential that the Romans become part of the time schemes of the Greeks, and the work that went on to make this happen was collaborative work."[10] These historical considerations temper any assertion that dates on coins were completely ignored. We agree with the conclusion that some coins with legends defining new eras and reigns were ignored, but other coins served to provide some sort of chronology.

Roman Coinage and Dates

Those new to the study of numismatics might assume that if one wants to determine the date of coin, they should simply look at what date is featured on the coin. But this straightforward approach is impossible because the regnal system of dating. Determining the date of a Roman coin starts with identifying the emperor appearing on the coin. This might require a comparative study with other Roman coins. Some Roman coins have inscriptions that provide names or titles. What complicates this process is that some emperors had the same name. Furthermore, some Roman coins used a template and sought to copy coins that resembled rulers such as Alexander the Great. The dates on Roman coins cannot be separated from the image and identity of the Ruler appearing on the coin. The establishment of dates and times was bound up with imperial authority.

Dates on Roman coinage during the first century were based on the Julian calendar. The calendar underwent "radical changes" as part of the transformation from Republic to Principate during the reign of Julius Caesar.[11] Today, this is known as the Julian calendar. The reform of the Roman calendar took effect on 1 January 45 BCE and instituted a solar calendar consisting of 365 ¼ days.[12] The year was divided into month,

8. Howgego, *Ancient History from Coins*, 74.
9. Ibid.
10. Feeney, *Caesar's Calendar*, 5.
11. Ibid., 6.
12. Ibid., 152.

some having 31 days and some having 29. Some dates in the Republican calendar, typically at the end of a month, did not even transfer into this Julian system. This system melded astronomy and seasons into an accurate calendar that combined "civil and natural time."[13] This new system of organizing time was a "watershed" moment for Ancient Rome and "eventually the whole modern world."[14]

Dates on Roman coinage during the first century used a regnal system.[15] A regnal system of dating used the first day of ascension to the throne as the anchor point for future dates. The exception proves the rule and only one coin (from 121 CE) is dated based on the founding of Rome.[16] The accession to the throne would be "year one."[17] These numbers are ordinal numbers, meaning that each number is adjectival (e.g., the first year of Augustus). Thus these dates do not reflect our modern dating system but rather that of the then current ruler or emperor. Because of this close relationship between time and kingdoms, the dates on coins are difficult to understand without reference to the other symbols, images, and inscriptions on the coin.[18] Even the presence of names on coins can make it difficult to discern what the year represents as it is not always clear if the name or abbreviation refers to the ruler or minter.

Dates on Roman coinage used letters for numbers.[19] One might ask, how can words be numbers? Linguistically, the phenomenon of using letters and words for numbers has been explained thus: "Words—verbal entities—can be employed as elements of a number sequence: they do not refer to numbers, they serve as numbers (they serve as the tools in our number assignments."[20] Besides numerical indicators, the following markers might also appear on Roman coinage to indicate the date or year:

13. Ibid., 193.

14. Ibid.

15. "Few Greek coins bear explicit dates, although some of the eras in use in the Hellenistic period appear on coinage, notably on the coinage of the kings of Syria which are regularly dated by the Seleucid era beginning in 312 BC" (Burnett, *Coins*, 21). Similarly, Meshorer, *Jewish Coins of the Second Temple Period*, 74.

16. "Only one coin survives that gives a date A.U.C. a Hadrianic coin from 121 C.E., marked as minted in the '874th birth year of the city' (ann[o] DCCCLXXIIII nat[ali] urbis). This appears to be the only imperial coin that bears any date other than a regnal year" (Feeney, *Caesar's Calendar*, 140).

17. Vagi, *Coinage and History of the Roman Empire*, 2:117–18.

18. Howgego, "Coinage and Identity in the Roman Provinces," 7.

19. For a chart of Greek dates see Wayne G. Sayles, *Ancient Coin Collecting IV: Roman Provincial Coins* (Iola: Krause, 1998), 149.

20. Heike Wiese, *Numbers, Language, and the Human Mind* (Cambridge: Cambridge University Press, 2003), 5.

(1) imperial acclamation, (2) renewal of Tribunician power, (3) consulship, (4) honorary tiles for military victories, and (5) vows.[21]

Dates on Roman coinage were tied to the cult of the anniversary. Times and dates could be established through images as well as dates inscribed on coins. This chapter has focused primarily on inscriptions but it is important to state that these were inseparable from memorialized events on the calendar. One scholar states: "The calendar also provided a platform for connection between past and present in the form of anniversaries, linking significant days and events across time."[22] Caesar's calendar reforms reinforced the importance of anniversaries because the Julian calendar allowed an anniversary to occur on the same day every year.[23] Coins struck by Augustus featured astrological signs such as Capricorn. This particular image may have "been intended to allude to the whole horoscope through a significant part of it."[24] His birthday was almost to the day the autumn equinox and his conception aligned with the winter solstice. Throughout his reign, Augustus used these two facts to shore up evidence for his divine election by the gods.[25]

Dates on Roman coins may not have been understood in the same way across the Empire. Any attempt at a universally understood expression of time faced major intellectual, organizational, and cultural challenges.[26] The inhabitants of different cities and different regions would have used different historical events to structure reality.

Jewish Coinage and Dates

Jewish coinage can be roughly divided up into the two categories of Herodian coinage and the First Great Revolt coinage (66–73 CE). The former coinage was minted in submission to Rome and the latter was minted in rebellion against Rome. Of the Herodian lineage, the use of dates on coins by Herod the Great stands out. According to one theory, all of Herod's coins were dated after he realigned himself with Octavian

21. Vagi, *Coinage and History of the Roman Empire*, 2:117–18.

22. Feeney, *Caesar's Calendar*, 6.

23. Ibid., 157.

24. Robert Hannah, *Greek and Roman Calendars: Constructions of Time in the Classical World* (London: Duckworth, 2005), 127.

25. Ibid., 129.

26. "In the atomized time world of the ancient Mediterranean, expressing dates in a format that would make sense to inhabitants of more than one city presented an intellectual and organizational challenge of a high order" (Feeney, *Caesar's Calendar*, 10).

following the emperor's victory over Antony at Actium.[27] This may indicate that Herod viewed the use of dates on coins as one way to communicate his connection to Rome and the emperor. This section focuses on the revolt coinage because of its distinctive use of dating.

There are many gaps in our knowledge of the first revolt coins, to be sure. We are not sure exactly who minted them or what faction of the Jewish rebellion controlled their production, and it is even questioned whether they were minted in Jerusalem.[28] What we do know is that the dates stamped on some coins were part of a larger desire to communicate the fact that the Jews believed that a new era of independence had begun.

The coinage of the first Jewish revolt used dates to reflect their independence from Rome. The first Jewish revolt against Rome allowed Jews to mint their own coinage for the first time since Mattathias Antigonus (40–37 BCE) minted bronze prutah at the end of the Hasmonean dynasty. The coins minted during the first four years of the revolt state: "Year 1 of the Redemption of Israel," "Year 2 of the Freedom of the Israel," "Year 3 of the Freedom of Zion," and "year 4."[29] The coins of the fourth year are different and may reflect a separate mint or separate minting authority.[30] The first silver shekel of the First Jewish Revolt read "Shekel of Israel" with the date "year 1."[31]

Jewish revolt coins, like their Roman counterparts, used letters for numbers. The coins minted during this time are all variants of the silver shekel or the bronze prutot. The years are enumerated with Hebrew letters (א = 1, ב = 2, ג = 3, ד = 4, ה = 5). These sometimes appear on the obverse and sometimes on the reverse. The letter שׁ (*šîn*) is also sometimes used to denote the word "year."[32] What is perhaps more significant is that these Hebrew letters were written in Paleo-Hebrew script, which was not used in popular writing.[33] While many numismatists use the script and its minor variations to look for patterns related to minting, they do not always note the communicative properties of such symbolism. Some have noted that despite all of the fighting between rival groups of Jewish rebels, a well-designed coinage was struck by a provisional government of some kind.

27. Ariel and Fontanille, *The Coins of Herod*, 187.

28. Ariel, "Identifying the Mints, Minters, and Meanings," 375, also 382.

29. Hendin 1363, similarly: 1360, 1360b.

30. Robert Deutsch, "Coinage of the First Jewish Revolt Against Rome: Iconography, Minting Authority, Metallurgy," in Popović, ed., *The Jewish Revolt Against Rome*, 368.

31. Ibid., 361.

32. Ariel, "Identifying the Mints, Minters, and Meanings," 378.

33. Ibid., 379.

The silver shekels produced during this time might have been minted by priests who used silver items taken from the temple treasury.[34] What this might also suggest is that coins were viewed as such an important tool for social cohesion and unification that rival groups were willing to overlook their differences.

Dates on Jewish revolt coins do not reflect a disregard for the Mosaic law. The Jewish cultic calendar was integral to the festivals, fasts, and worship of the Mosaic law. The reason why the establishment of years on coinage does not affect the festivals and related worship is that these were based on changes in harvest seasons. The Hebrew bible does express concern about changes in the calendar. In the apocalyptic vision of the fourth beast in Daniel, the one who "shall speak words against the Most High" is also the one who "shall think to change the times and the law" (Dan 7:25). One commentator on Daniel explains that the comment on the changing of the "times" was focused on the "suppression of traditional Jewish observances."[35] The 364-day solar calendar is mentioned in both *1 Enoch* and *Jubilees* and was observed by the Qumran community.[36] The text of *Jub.* 23 suggests that an "evil generation" has forgotten "feasts and months and Sabbaths and jubilees."[37] This concern with the maintenance of the calendar endured till the writing of the *Damascus Rule* or the *Cairo Damascus* (CD) document, a document from the Dead Sea Scrolls that communicates the importance of the Sabbaths and festivals around the third century BCE (CD 3:14).[38]

There are no programmatic or prescriptive statements about calendars in the Hebrew bible.[39] Descriptively speaking, the Hebrew bible mentions twelve months in ordinal numbers (first to twelfth).[40] While the agricultural cycle ended with the harvest in the autumn, the new year began in the spring. Passages from Exodus, Leviticus, and Numbers all use spring to mark the first month of the year.[41] Because Jewish revolt coins make

34. Ibid., 386.

35. J. J. Collins, *Daniel: A Commentary on the Book of Daniel*, Hermeneia (Minneapolis: Augsburg, 1993), 322.

36. J. J. Collins, *The Apocalyptic Imagination: An Introduction to Jewish Apocalyptic Literature*, 2nd ed. (Grand Rapids: Eerdmans, 1998), 79.

37. Ibid., 82.

38. Ibid., 77.

39. James C. VanderKam, *Calendars in the Dead Sea Scrolls: Measuring Time* (London: Routledge, 1998), 6.

40. Ibid.

41. See Exod 12:2, Lev 23, and Num 28–29. VanderKam, *Calendars in the Dead Sea Scrolls*, 10.

no claim as to when the year begins or ends, they do not disregard any Mosaic law. The key idea is that Jews would not have viewed dates on their coinage as "changing the times."

Implications for Studying the New Testament

One of the most challenging questions that biblical scholars face is the multiple eschatological schemas presented in the New Testament. Here we return to this key explanation of the wider phenomenon in the first century: "In any society individuals are liable to inhabit different frames of time, often simultaneously—cyclical or recurrent, linear, seasonal, social, historical."[42] What this text and the data from coinage confirms, is that a majority of people in the first century were familiar with contemporaneously inhabiting various frameworks of time.

The New Testament, along with the testimony of numismatic evidence, points to the fact that there was no single dominant grid for chronology, but rather a "medley of diverse tools for orientation in time."[43] Some schemas were appropriated by apocalyptic historiography to present the whole of history in compact fashion.

This phenomenon is evident within the New Testament as one finds a variety of frameworks for understanding time—for example, an inaugurated eschatology schema of now-and-not-yet embedded in the "lost and found" parables of Luke 15.[44] In the Gospel of Matthew, one finds that narrative uses theology to "schematize history."[45] In the book of Hebrews, the writer defines the present time in 1:2 as "these last days" (ἐσχάτου τῶν ἡμερῶν τούτων). The book of Revelation (12:14) refers to the eschatological "woman" being nourished in the wilderness for "a time, and times, and half a time." Within the Old Testament, one sees schemas wherein a thousand years are equal to a day (Ps 90:4) or Jeremiah's seventy years.[46] The pseudepigraphal text of *2 Baruch* refers to twelve periods before the final judgment (*2 Bar*. 27).[47] Theological systems have typically focused on one schema of time to the exclusion of all others. This approach often

42. Feeney, *Caesar's Calendar*, 3.

43. Ibid., 147.

44. N. T. Wright, *The Resurrection of the Son of God: Christian Origins and the Question of God* (London: SPCK, 2003), 438. Also see David H. Wenkel, "When the Apostles Became Kings: Ruling and Judging the Twelve Tribes of Israel," *BTB* 42 (2012): 115.

45. Donald Senior, *The Gospel of Matthew* (Nashville: Abingdon, 1997), 13.

46. Stone, *Ancient Judaism*, 85.

47. Ibid.

has difficulty integrating all of the epochal events and redemptive contours presented by the existence of other schemas within the canon of scripture. The study of coins and the dates and schemas of history provided by their inscriptions and images remains a field that awaits further integration with the study of the New Testament.

Summary

When coins feature dates, they were an attempt to communicate how long a ruler had been in power. Whereas most numismatists focus on using dates on coins for the purpose of establishing historical chronology, we have focused on the use of dates on coins as a tool of propaganda. The world of the coin often sought to define and demarcate eras and reigns, establishing them as signposts for understanding time itself. The whole point of producing a framework for time, whether an era, anniversary, epoch, or reign, was to assign meaning to the past and functionally to coordinate events and activities in the future.[48]

48. Feeney refers to the imposition of "meaningful shape" upon time (*Caesar's Calendar*, 147); on the pragmatic function of the calendar in ancient Judaism see p. 194.

Chapter 10

Propaganda and Roman Images

This chapter provides an introduction to the role of Roman images on coins as cultural texts and tools of propaganda that encouraged patron–client relationships.

Introduction

"The patron–client relationship was the most important, non-familial relationship in Roman society."[1] This quotation forms the foundation for the central thesis in this chapter: *the images on Roman coins in the first century encouraged participation in a patron–client relationship*. This central argument provides one way in which to organize and summarize the vast amount of imagery that appeared on Greco-Roman coins of the first century. The images on coins may be studied from the perspective of representation art, beauty, and aesthetics. But these images were also powerful tools of communication and propaganda in an economy where giving money was an integral part of the relationship between patrons and clients. One scholar concludes that "the nature of patron–client relationships ensured constant distortion of what we might expect to be market interaction."[2]

As noted previously, the significance and meaning of images cannot be divorced from their accompanying inscriptions. This chapter on Roman images and the following chapter on Jewish images reflects an artificial dichotomy that is only meant to simplify a complex topic.

Those who are seeking to bridge the study of the New Testament with the study of ancient Roman coins will need to understand the difference between *imperial* coins and *provincial* coins. These two terms are used by numismatics to classify coinage following the death of Julius Caesar

1. Kevin MacGeough, *The Romans: New Perspectives* (Santa Barbara: ABC-CLIO, 2004), 113.

2. Oakes, "Methodological Issues in Using Economic Evidence," 11.

in 44 BCE. Imperial coins are defined as those coins minted directly under imperial authority, mostly at Rome, for Empire-wide distribution. Provincial coins are defined as those coins minted for use in a single province of the Empire; they are often identified by references to the name of a significant city.

There is no way to catalog, identify, and interpret every image that appeared on coins in the Roman Empire in the first century without requiring a massive tome or database.[3] As a result, we will only seek to analyze those images which are very common or relevant to New Testament studies. With each cultic symbol, one might ask if the image appears as a result of (1) continuity, (2) revival, or (3) invention.[4] Again, the purpose of this volume is to provide a bridge for those in biblical studies who are seeking to integrate numismatics.

The patron–client relationship had two parties. Under the Roman Republic, only a patrician was allowed to be a "patron." Eventually this restriction was opened up to any wealthy citizen.[5] The client was bound to his patron in a voluntary relationship that may have been practically and financially involuntary. Entering a patron–client relationship would have been necessary for many people who wanted access to land, food, or money. Despite our focus on this relationship, we do not want to press everything into this mold and ignore other important dynamics such as the gift-exchange relationship.

There is another important qualification to make: not all images are created equal. Some abbreviations on coins may have even been intentionally ambiguous.[6] Consequently, not all images would have possessed the same communicative power. Some coins would have had more or less communicative force. In politically explosive contexts such as Judaea (especially Jerusalem), it has been suggested that some images were designed to be ambiguous so that neither Jews nor non-Jews would have been offended by the images on the coin.[7] This seems to be the case with Herod the Great (37–4 BCE). One scholar found that "the symbols on the

3. Reiser, "Numismatik und Neues Testament," 461.

4. Howgego, "Coinage and Identity in the Roman Provinces," 3.

5. MacGeough, *The Romans*, 113.

6. "Perhaps the possibility of using ambiguous abbreviations was employed as well. Some Romans were aware of such ambiguity, occasionally even intended" (Hekster, "Coins and Messages," 30).

7. "One gains the impression that Herod [the Great] tried to have on his coins symbols which could be interpreted ambiguously and which both Jews and non-Jews could construe as they wished" (Meshorer, *Jewish Coins of the Second Temple Period*, 65–66).

coins of Herod provide ample scope for divergent views on problems of symbolism which may well continue for a long time."[8]

Attempts at political neutrality can also be interpreted as attempts to establish the status quo. Nevertheless, in our attempt to relate symbols to patron–client relationships, we do not want to over-reach by ignoring attempts at neutrality. Some images on coins will remain a mystery, not because we lack the right historical data, but perhaps because the authors intentionally sought images that communicated ideas that were non-offensive, politically neutered, and religiously sterilized. That being stated, these neutral images do not make up the majority of the images on first-century coins.

Some have argued that Roman iconography on coins was "unimaginative," reflecting Emperors who were uninterested in exploiting "the propaganda potential of the coinage to the full."[9] The alleged support for this claim is that symbolic, religious, and mythological imagery was "conventional."[10] The first problem with this argument is that it is too far reaching to claim that all conventional imagery is not propaganda. On the contrary, it was the combination of antiquity and ubiquity that made for strong argumentation in the first century. It was those images that had an appeal to antiquity that were recognized by the widest array of people that used the communicative power of coinage to its full extent. In this chapter we will cover the two large themes of military victory and Roman religion to see the communicative power of conventional imagery to encourage the patron–client relationship.

Patronage and Military Victory

In the section above we introduced the three most common denominations of coins in the first century. We will now examine how *coins communicated patronage through images of military victory*. Military victory was interpreted as a divinely given sign that Caesar was chosen by the gods. Some have suggested that this is why images of piety are combined with images of victory.[11] These images will include: (1) the eagle, (2) the laurel wreath, and (3) the four-horse chariot. There are, of course, many more

8. Ibid., 66.

9. Duncan-Jones, *Money and Government in the Roman Empire*, 97.

10. Ibid.

11. David Nystrom, "We Have No King but Caesar: Roman Imperial Ideology and the Imperial Cult," in *Jesus Is Lord, Caesar Is Not: Evaluating Empire in New Testament Studies*, ed. S. McKnight and J. B. Modica (Downers Grove: InterVarsity, 2013), 29.

types of images present on coins in the first century. These three images will provide the reader with an introduction to some of the images that were most common.

1. *The Eagle*

Because coins were used to communicate military power, announce victories, and honor military leaders, they are naturally full of military images. Some of the most common images include the eagle (Latin, *aquilae*) that appeared on banners and/or poles that preceded every Roman legion into battle.[12] The eagle is associated with and is sometimes depicted as clutching a bolt of lightning or bolt of thunder.[13] This in turn is associated with the Roman god Jupiter, another indication of the tight connection between religion and military life in the Roman Empire. Those who were military victors were often depicted as having the striking power of devastating lighting from the heavens.

This image of a Roman legionary eagle on a pole would have been used in conquests and exercises alongside other military standards. This image appears on the silver denarius of the moneyer Cn. Nerius at Rome in 48 BCE (BMC 3950).

The symbol of the Eagle was so prominent and connected with Rome that it appears in *4 Ezra* 11–12 as the symbol that updates the four-empire scheme of Dan 7.[14] The symbol of the eagle is important for the interpretation of Jesus' apocalyptic statements in the Synoptics about the Son of Man:

12. See Josephus, *War* 3.6.2 and comments by Kreitzer, *Striking New Images*, 30.
13. Kreitzer, *Striking New Images*, 66.
14. Ibid., 57.

> There will be two women grinding together. One will be taken and the other left. And they said to him, "Where, Lord?" He said to them, "Where the corpse is, there the vultures [or eagles] will gather." (Luke 17:35–37)

> For as the lightning comes from the east and shines as far as the west, so will be the coming of the Son of Man. Wherever the corpse is, there the vultures [or eagles] will gather. (Matt 24:27–28)

This rather cryptic statement of Jesus lends itself to a wide array of interpretations.[15] There is also little to be gained by parsing the plural noun ἀετός as an eagle versus a vulture (or other type of bird), as these distinctions would not *always* have been made in the original setting. It is also worth noting that both vultures and eagles will eat carrion.[16] One of the most interesting and persuasive interpretations has this saying of Jesus referring to Jerusalem and the Temple as the corpse and the Roman army as the eagles.[17] Whatever interpretation one arrives at, the eagle symbolism on Roman coinage is part of a matrix of options that should be carefully considered. Where Rome is indeed understood to be intimately connected with the eagle, this would reinforce the idea that Rome was the dominant patron of military safety, peace, and victory.

2. *Laurel Wreath*

The laurel wreath "is a symbol of victory."[18] As such, the laurel wreath appears around items, portraits, and a wide range of scenes. For example, the laurel wreath appears on the head of Julius Caesar on coins from Thessalonica that proclaim him as "god" (THEOS).[19] On another coin, laurel crowns are held in the hands of winged victories.[20] Traditionally, these crowns were given for military victories, funeral decorations, festivals, and other achievements of excellence. What is significant for our argument is that Augustus "repurposed" this traditional Roman religious

15. "People will be able to miss the Parousia no more than the vultures overlook a dead animal" (Ulrich Luz, *Matthew 21–28: A Commentary*, Hermeneia [Minneapolis: Augsburg Fortress, 2005], 199).

16. Contra Nolland, who argues that ἀετός must be a vulture because meat is in view, in *The Gospel of Matthew*, 981.

17. Kreitzer, *Striking New Images*, 57–68.

18. Ibid., 78.

19. See RPC 1555. For comments on Paul's use of Father and Lord in contrast with the emperor's claim to divinity see Ben Witherington III, *1 and 2 Thessalonians: A Socio-Rhetorical Commentary* (Grand Rapids: Eerdmans, 2006), 184.

20. Kreitzer, *Striking New Images*, 87.

symbol so that it referred to a single individual—the emperor. This act of Augustus "set the pattern for successive later emperors, whose coins regularly refer to the symbols of the four great priestly colleges, representing the emperor's continuing leading role in Roman public religion."[21] Thus, the laurel wreath became a symbol of the emperor and his status as benefactor of the Empire.

The laurel wreath is an important element for the many New Testament texts that refer to crowns. Some texts refer to a "crown of glory" (1 Pet 5:4) or a "crown of boasting" (1 Thess 2:19). These and other references in the New Testament may be understood as standing in contrast to the laurel wreath that would eventually wither and fade.[22] Some argue that Paul's references to a crown (*stephanos*) were to the laurel wreath rather that a gold diadem (*diadēma*).[23] At least one positive use of the laurel wreath imagery is likely found as the background imagery in 1 Cor 9:24 ("Do you not know that in a race all the runners run, but only one receives the prize?").

New Testament allusions to glory and boasting draw heavily from the laurel wreath tradition. Those in power who would have themselves portrayed on coins with laurel wreaths would have been communicating military or political success and their worthiness to be viewed as a patron worthy of glory and honor.

3. *Quadriga or Four-Horse Chariot*

The quadriga was a two-wheeled chariot driven by four horses controlled by a standing charioteer. The charioteer is sometimes Victory or the god Jupiter. The quadriga was featured on coins across a wide span of time and geography and was most likely a symbol of victory. The actual Arch of Titus depicts Titus driving a quadriga, led by the goddess Roma and the goddess Victoria (Victory).[24] The Roman use of the quadriga may be in the background of 2 Cor 2:14. The "divine throne-chariot" theme is also important for the Jewish tradition, although it does not directly appear on

21. Williams, "Religion and Romans Coins," 151.

22. "A laurel wreath can soon wither, public acclaim can be short-lived, and a royal crown lost" (Norman Hillyer, *1 & 2 Peter, Jude*, UBCS [Grand Rapids: Baker, 2011], 143).

23. Leon Morris, *1 and 2 Thessalonians: An Introduction and Commentary* (Downers Grove: InterVarsity, 1984), 67.

24. Daniel P. Bailey, "Arch of Titus," in Collins and Harlow, eds., *The Eerdmans Dictionary of Early Judaism*, 375.

coins during the first century.[25] The quadriga appears on coins that use military images to elevate the status of Roman power and lower the status of others.

Perhaps the most remarkable of all these coins is an *aureus* minted at Lugdunum which contains an image depicting both Vespasian in his triumphal chariot (*quadriga*) and a bound Judaean captive. In the one image we have the two intertwined rituals—of Roman status elevation and Judaean status degradation.[26] To speak of status elevation and degradation for Judaea is equivalent to a national patron–client relationship with Rome. Again, the images of military victory were tightly connected to the patron–client relationship pyramid.

Patronage and Roman Religion

The images on coins almost always had religious implications. One of the challenges of New Testament scholarship is that contemporary Western culture prizes the separation between Church and State. In the first century, there was no difference between religion and politics in Judaea or the surrounding Roman Empire. This section will introduce the following types of images: (1) mythological gods, (2) Roman temples, and (3) portraits.

1. *Mythological Gods*

Images from Roman authorities often referenced characters from the Pantheon of gods (such as Hermes or Mercury). About 84 percent of the denarius reverse types featured gods and their personifications between 69 and 235 CE.[27] The religious nature of coins must be carefully set in context. For many in the Empire, religious devotion or references to gods was both religious and political. For example, many generals would select a god who would serve as their patron. Whereas Greek coins rarely featured the accoutrements of Roman cultic practice or sacrifice, these appear regularly on Roman coinage.[28]

25. James M. Scott, *2 Corinthians*, UBCS (Grand Rapids: Baker, 2011), 62.

26. John K. Riches and David C. Sim, eds., *The Gospel of Matthew in Its Roman Imperial Context*, LNTS 276 (London: T&T Clark, 2005), 16.

27. Ibid., 155.

28. Ibid., 150.

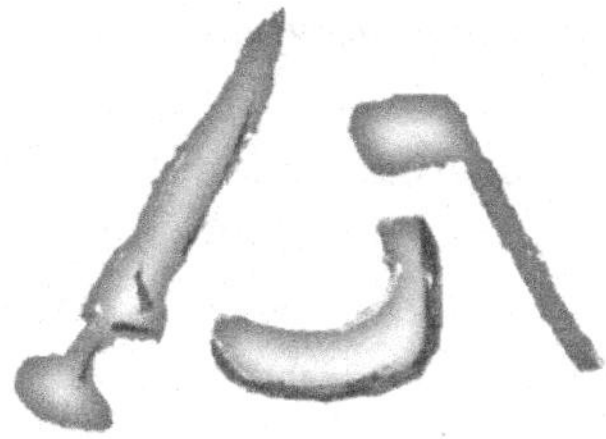

The cultic tools of a *secespita* (knife), *sim-pulum* (drinking ladle), and *secures* (ceremonial axe) appear on the denarii of the emperor Galba. These were used for animal sacrifices. See Crawford 406/1.

The movement toward using coins for partisan politics began in the second century BCE.[29] Coins provided rulers of provinces and cities the opportunity to communicate what they had accomplished. This might also have included images linking their family ancestry with gods of the Roman pantheon.

The presence of personifications of mythological gods from the Roman and Greek pantheon are numerous on coins. These personifications falls into the two categories of the emperor's virtues and the Empire's virtues.[30] The emperor's virtues were personified as the following gods: Aequitas (fairness), Clementia (mercy), Liberalitas (generosity), Pietas (religiosity), and so on. The Empire's virtues were personified as the following gods: Salus (safety), Spes (hope), Securitas (security), Felicitas (prosperity), Hilaritas (joyfulness), and so on. These gods may or may not have received cultic worship and some seem to have "no life apart from their imagery on coins and elsewhere."[31]

Local deities were also integrated into the pantheon. In Alexandria, under the rules of Augustus and Claudius, the Roman images of Zeus may have provided a template for coins depicting the cult surrounding the Nile River and its god.[32] These images of the god Nile were connected to economic and agricultural prosperity. What may be surprising is that

29. John Pollini, *From Republic to Empire: Rhetoric, Religion, and Power in the Visual Culture of Ancient Rome*, OSCC 48 (Norman: University of Oklahoma Press, 2012), 72.

30. The following two lists of gods are taken wholly from Williams, "Religion and Roman Coins," 156.

31. Ibid.

32. Sarah K. Pearce, "Philo on the Nile," in Frey et al., eds., *Jewish Identity in the Greco-Roman World*, 151.

"there is little evidence of system in the selection of which individual gods to depict" and the logic of their associated symbols and titles is "fairly arbitrary."[33]

Our goal here is to make broad and sweeping conclusions that will provide a foundation for seeing coins as cultural texts with communicative power. The presence of mythological gods on coinage communicated that a patron–client relationship remained at the center of Roman life. For example, the god Hermes appears on lead coins from the early Roman Near East and likely functions as a patron of merchants.[34] One historian concludes: "in ordinary life, they [the gods] did not behave as absolute masters and tyrants, but as fellow-citizens and benevolent patrons."[35]

2. Roman Temples

Temples are featured on many coins from the Roman Empire, although some scholars may have overstated their importance. The imperial coinage minted during the reign of Vespasian (69–79 CE) utilized architecture on 34 of 818 types.[36] The appearance of temples on coins began in the late second century BCE and became a distinctly Roman feature, as opposed to Greek coinage.[37] The styles of temples on coins can be described by referencing the number of columns. A four column image is described as a "tetrastyle" temple and a six column image as a "hexastyle" temple. Coins from Corinth include both styles.[38] The wide and spacious columns represented on coins help explain how a Christian could observe another "reclining for a meal in the idol temple" (ἐν εἰδωλείῳ κατακείμενον) (1 Cor 8:10).[39] Although the architecture depicted on these coins remains a popular topic, these buildings had religious significance: the temple communicated the emperor's devoutness as well as "communal religious identity."[40]

In the East, temples of Greco-Roman gods dominated the commercial and civic activities of the city. The emperor at any given time may have been associated with some temple so that some aspect of divinity was connected with him. This is referred to as the "imperial cult." During the

33. Williams, "Religion and Roman Coins," 155.

34. Hoover, "A New Hellenistic Lead Issue," 52.

35. John Scheid, *An Introduction to Roman Religion*, trans. J. Lloyd (Bloomington: Indiana University Press, 2003), 147.

36. Williams, "Religion and Roman Coins," 148.

37. Ibid., 147.

38. Winter, "The Enigma of Imperial Cultic Activities and Paul in Corinth," 65.

39. Ibid.

40. Williams, "Religion and Roman Coins," 148.

reign of Octavian, the cultic worship solidified around the emperor and his family. This was ensured by denying the establishment of new ruler cults.[41] As a result, the provincial temples became associated with the imperial cult. For example, a coin from Corinth portrays Nero standing in the middle of four columns.[42] The presence of temples on coins communicated the importance of emperor worship, Roman mythological religion, communal identity, euergetism, and politics.

This strong association between the temples with respective god(s) and communal identity appears in the riot scene in Ephesus (Acts 19:23–41). After Paul had preached to the city, the craftsmen of silver idols responded by stirring up the city and chanting "Great is Artemis of the Ephesians" (Acts 19:28). The chanting reveals how strongly the people connect the goddess Artemis with their city.[43] The image of a temple on coinage projected a world in which Caesar was restorer or founder of a building that gave cities and their people their identity and sometimes their livelihood.

3. *Human Portraits*

As we introduce the human portrait motif, we begin with this startling fact: "Until 44 BC no living person had ever appeared on Roman coinage."[44] This aversion to glorifying a human that characterized the Republic did not survive the turn to Empire. The widespread presence of human portraits on coins is perhaps one of the most obvious visible differences between the Roman Republic and the Roman Empire.[45] By the time of the Early Roman Period (63 BCE to 125 CE), one of the dominant faces on coins is Caesar. These portraits often use the template of Alexander the Great (356–323 BCE) with the goal of transferring some of his glory onto contemporaries of the first century.

Broadly speaking, the most important reason why human portraits appear on coinage from the first century is because people could make a judgment about the present character and the future of the person. This ancient process of evaluating people's nature based on their physical qualities is called "physiognomy" and has historical roots in the ancient

41. Steven J. Friesen, *Imperial Cults and the Apocalypse of John: Reading Revelation in the Ruins* (Oxford: Oxford University Press, 2001), 29.

42. Bruce W. Winter, "The Enigma of Imperial Cultic Activities and Paul in Corinth," in *Greco-Roman Culture and the New Testament*, ed. D. E. Aune and F. E. Brenk, NovTSup 143 (Leiden: Brill, 2012), 65.

43. Williams, "Religion and Roman Coins," 148.

44. Kreitzer, *Striking New Images*, 82.

45. Howgego, *Ancient History from Coins*, 74.

Near East.[46] By ascertaining the physical qualities of rulers (e.g. the shape of the forehead or nose), conclusions could be drawn about the moral qualities of the person.

Alexander the Great is featured or referenced on so many coins hundreds of years after his birth that an entire volume could be devoted to this theme. Alexander was viewed by the Roman Empire with such esteem in the first century that emperors wanted to be seen in his likeness. Alexander was the "pupil of Aristotle"—the archetype of the ideal philosopher-warrior-king. This esteem for Alexander tied in with the penchant for deification or apotheosis of dead Roman emperors.

One example of an emperor who likened himself to Alexander the Great on coinage was Augustus. One scholar has argued that Alexander's image was a "symbolic figure of cosmic rulers."[47] Augustus's use of Alexander's image communicated that he and his power was divine-like. The important point here is that when individual portraits began to appear on coins, the individual ruler was inextricably tied to the power of the state and its benefaction.[48]

The use of human portraits on coins that resembled Alexander the Great are part of a larger theme of retrospective Roman eschatology in which the past was the ideal golden age that the present could aspire to.[49] The Romans looked back on Alexander, his conquests, and his empire as a golden age that they wanted to echo. This golden age also happened to be characterized by a formal patronage system that was "openly spoken of in Athens."[50]

Implications for Studying the New Testament

Coins are important for studying the New Testament because they powerfully illustrate the fact that the patron–client relationship was one of the dominant social contexts in which the early Christian concept of grace (*charis*) developed. In order to understand grace, we must begin with the foundational idea that the heart of patronage was the concept of reciprocity.

46. Documents from the first millennium (BCE) indicate that "attributes of human physiognomy and behavior were studied not as events to be understood for their own sake, but for their cryptic power to signify." William W. Hallo and K. Lawson Younger, *The Context of Scripture*, 3 vols. (Leiden: Brill, 1997), 1:422.

47. Kreitzer, *Striking New Images*, 78.

48. Howgego, *Ancient History from Coins*, 63–64.

49. N. T. Wright, *Simply Jesus: Who He Was, What He Did, Why It Matters* (London: SPCK, 2011), 32.

50. deSilva, *Honor, Patronage, Kinship and Purity*, 103.

One scholar argues that reciprocity "encapsulated the entire ethos of the relationships" in the patron–client relationship.[51] The reciprocity flowed in both directions. The benefactor would bestow gifts upon the recipient out of their grace. These gifts could be peace, prosperity, land, or money.

The images of military victory and Roman religion contain a surplus of images that project a world in which Caesar was the ultimate benefactor of the Empire. Other high-ranking officials and honorable people sought the title of benefactor as well. The title of "Benefactor" (*Euergetes*) was bestowed on Xenophon, the physician of Claudius, by the people of Cos around 53 CE for his service to the island.[52] As a result of receiving these gifts, the recipient was bound to show deference, loyalty, and gratitude toward the giver. These acts were obligatory, although they were unspoken and unwritten laws: gifts require the response of gratitude. This was the social context within which the gospel of God's grace grew. This is important because the gospel was news of free gifts, it was news that God gave his Son as a free gift for all people, both Jew and Gentile, so that they could have eternal life, know forgiveness of sins, and become co-heirs with Christ by faith.

The Christian Gospel appropriates the common language of grace (*charis*) utilized by the relationships of patronage and friendship networks. This utilization included elements of continuity and discontinuity. With respect to continuity, Paul's letter to Philemon relies heavily on the "dynamics of reciprocity."[53] In this letter, Paul is the benefactor who has bestowed previous gifts on Philemon. When requesting Philemon release Onesimus the slave to Paul, he writes, "Yes, brother, I want some benefit from you in the Lord. Refresh my heart in Christ" (Phlm 20). With respect to discontinuity, we see how Jesus singles out "kings of the Gentiles… who are called benefactors" (Luke 22:25). The greatest leaders in the kingdom of God are those who are the most child-like and servant-like. Thus, Jesus seeks to turn the whole system of benefaction upside-down. By defining grace in this way, those who follow Jesus should give, but expect nothing in return, much less a formal title of honor. In addition, the early Christians understood grace as a gift from God, a "vital third party" that is often left out of patron–client analyses.[54] The role of God alters

51. Ibid., 104.

52. The title "Benefactor" appears on a marble inscription from the city of Cos (Adolf Deissmann and Lionel Richard Mortimer Strachan, *Light from the Ancient East the New Testament Illustrated by Recently Discovered Texts of the Graeco-Roman World* [London: Hodder & Stoughton, 1910], 248).

53. deSilva, *Honor, Patronage, Kinship & Purity*, 124.

54. Briones, *Paul's Financial Policy*, 18.

the rules of patron exchange because humans are all dependent upon God for this gift.[55] Thus, the identity of all humans as dependents and having equality before God alters the existing social frameworks of patronage and friendship. This stands in stark contrast with the prevailing message of patronage found on many Roman coins of the first century.

The Roman imperial coins of the first century utilized images that reinforced the idea that Caesar was the ultimate Benefactor, the source of peace, prosperity, and victory. Some coins referenced benefaction explicitly while some coins suggested it by depicting Caesar as divine. The Christian message of God's grace engaged this message in complex ways, both utilizing it and overturning it.

Summary

This chapter sought to introduce the reader to the plethora of images on first-century Roman coins by focusing on their encouragement of client–patron relationships. We began by noting the widely accepted conclusion about the impact of patron–client relationships on the first-century economy. We then sought to introduce some of the major categories of images used to communicate power relationships. Broadly speaking, Roman coins have images of military victories, pagan gods, and portraits of the hierarchy of the imperial cult. All of these images supported and encouraged the idea that the inhabitants of the Empire lived in a reality characterized by a pyramid of patronage, beginning with the emperor. All of the peace, prosperity, order, and success was tied to the favor of the gods acquired through piety and the might of the Roman army.

55. Ibid., 130.

Chapter 11

PROPAGANDA AND JEWISH IMAGES

This chapter will introduce Jewish coinage in the first century and consider how its imagery reflected the propaganda, tensions, and sometimes mixtures of Judaism and Hellenism.

Introduction

As we transition from the wide context of the Roman Empire and focus on the narrow strip of land called Judaea, we begin with a quote: "The individual inhabitants of the Roman Empire lived in vertical relationships of dependency."[1] This quote reminds us of the context of dependency and patronage that the Jews lived under, particularly in the geographical region of Judaea.[2] This geographical qualification is important because Jews lived in almost every part of the Roman Empire.[3] When the Jews were able to mint their own coins through rebellion, their images generally communicated autonomy and Jewish religious and ethnic boundary markers.

By the time of Jesus, coins had been around the region for about 500 years. The entire region of Judaea was firmly established as a "coined economy."[4] Studying this area of history is challenging because it was

1. Peter Lampe, "Paul, Patrons, and Clients," in *Paul in the Greco-Roman World: A Handbook*, ed. J. P. Sampley (Harrisburg: Trinity Press International, 2003), 488.

2. Our geographical focus on Judaea (Palestine) reflects the fact that Jewish symbols did not appear upon or influence any coinage outside of this area. One exception is that Noah's ark appears on the coins of Apamea, Phrygia (modern Dinar, Turkey). But Howgego suggests that this reflects appropriation of this narrative into the local pagan myths ("Coinage and Identity in the Roman Provinces," 3).

3. "Juden lebten zu Beginn der Kaiserzeit in fast allen Teilen des römischen Reiches" (Ameling, "Die Jüdische Diaspora Kleinasiens und der 'Epigraphic Habit'," 254).

4. Haim Gitler, "Coins," in Collins and Harlow, eds., *The Eerdmans Dictionary of Early Judaism*, 479–80.

a mix of cultures and sometimes a mix of monetary systems. To make matters even more difficult, there may have been two different monetary systems operating, albeit at slightly different times.[5]

One of the acute problems accompanying the study of symbols or iconography of ancient Jewish coins is that almost any image such as an ear of corn would likely have religious connotations.[6] It is not easy to create a taxonomy that will incorporate all of the various coins of the first century let alone their various symbols. Our study will approach this difficulty by focusing on how symbols and images were used as propaganda. By exploring how coins were used as communicative tools and cultural texts, we can highlight the unifying themes across the various coins.[7]

Another acute problem with Jewish iconography is that some images were intentionally ambiguous. Judaea and especially Jerusalem was a politically charged context. The provincial rulers responsible for peace seem to favor coinage that did not incite local tensions. It has been suggested that some images were designed to be ambiguous so that neither Jews nor non-Jews would have been offended by the images on the coin.[8] This seems to be the case with Herod the Great and his son Herod Antipas. For example, Herod Antipas chose the symbol of a large reed on his bronze coinage. This symbol was politically expedient because it was a shared image for the Jordan River that connected the communities of Galilee and Peraea.[9] This ambiguous image may be the imagery behind Jesus' reference to a "reed shaken by the wind" (Matt 11:7).[10] The point of this is that not every iconography on Jewish coins will be easily interpreted or categorized—and that ambiguity may be intentional.

5. Daniel Sperber, "Mark 7:42 and Its Metrological Background: A Study in Ancient Syriac Versions," *NovT* 9 (1967), 182.

6. Howgego, "Coinage and Identity in the Roman Provinces," 2.

7. For a dated work that sought to find a "unifying principle amidst the varied types, or symbols" see Romanoff, *Jewish Symbols*, xi.

8. "One gains the impression that Herod [the Great] tried to have on his coins symbols which could be interpreted ambiguously and which both Jews and non-Jews could construe as they wished" (Meshorer, *Jewish Coins of the Second Temple Period*, 65–66).

9. "Herodes Antipas mußte nach einem Emblem suchen, das beide Landesteile verband" [translation: "Herod Antipas had to go search for an emblem that combined both parts of the country"] (Gerd Theissen, *Lokalkolorit und Zeitgeschichte in den Evangelien. Ein Beitrag zur Geschichte der synoptischen Tradition*, NTOA 8 [Göttingen: Vandenhoeck & Ruprecht, 1989], 33).

10. Ibid., 34.

A previous attempt to unify Jewish themes on ancient coinage focused on the poles of *emancipation* and *domination*: "By the presence or absence of foreign artistic models on the Jewish coins, one may trace the course of Jewish emancipation from Hellenism or subservience to foreign domination."[11] This approach is helpful in that it allows one to thematically unify coinage across hundreds of years. However, it is not specific enough for those wanting to investigate the historical particulars of the first century. Moreover, this quote reflects a much older and less nuanced perspective on the relationship between Second Temple Judaism and Hellenism.[12]

A better approach to Jewish coins near the first century is spectrum based and seeks to nuance the tensions between Judaism and Hellenism. At the ends of this spectrum are the poles of *Jewish independence* and *patronage to Rome*. Those Jewish coins near the former pole encouraged the populace of Judaea to see the world through the lens of autonomy and the maintenance of unique socio-religious characteristics or identity markers. Those coins toward the latter pole encouraged the populace to see the world through the lens of patronage toward Rome. After we establish a basic framework for understanding Jewish coins in a Hellenistic context, we will introduce the questions and controversies by highlighting key questions raised by coinage.

The Hellenistic Context

Images on coins often reflect the double identity or the *mixing* of cultures in the Hellenistic milieu. One side of the coin may relate to one part of the culture and the reverse may relate to another part of the culture. For example, on one coin the Persian goddess appears as Artemis beside a deer and the reverse has her in Persian dress.[13] Coins can help interpreters of the New Testament draw historically informed conclusions about the social world of the first century. Specifically, coins allow one to make conclusions about how well known certain symbols and images had become.[14]

11. Romanoff, *Jewish Symbols*, x.

12. For example, Romanoff considered some eras reflective of "*pure* Jewish symbolism" (ibid., 7). Emphasis mine.

13. Frederick E. Brenk, "Hierosolyma: The Greek Name of Jerusalem," *Glotta* 87 (2011): 3.

14. Kreitzer uses numismatic evidence to find out how well known and how widespread was military triumph imagery (*Striking New Images*, 128).

The images on Jewish coins may reflect *rejection* of Hellenistic cultural assimilation. The rejection of Greco-Roman images by Jews reflects the fact that images were often a source of conflict and cultural polarization. With few exceptions, there were no images of animals or humans on their coins. The most notable exception of the eagle appearing on the coinage of Herod the Great is discussed below. The most obvious difficulty for Jews would have been the presence of the deified emperor or other gods of the Pantheon on Roman coins.

There are also images that reflect *acceptance* of cultural pluralism. The Jews of the first century lived under Roman rule and this rule was evidenced even on coins minted by Jewish rulers. The iconography or symbolism on coins of Herod the Great are closely aligned with patterns from the rule of Augustus.[15]

The coins of Judaea reflect both acceptance and rejection of the Hellenistic influences that permeated and surrounded them. One might even say that coinage reflects the fact that some Jews would have been simultaneously living in two different cultural worlds, using two systems of coinage.

As noted above, the Mosaic law provided Jews with an entire worldview as well as specific references to precious metals that informed how coinage was received and handled.[16] The Mosaic law strictly forbids the use of images:

> You shall not make for yourself a carved image, or any likeness of anything that is in heaven above, or that is in the earth beneath, or that is in the water under the earth. (Exod 20:4)

> You shall not make idols for yourselves or erect an image or pillar, and you shall not set up a figured stone in your land to bow down to it, for I am the Lord your God. (Lev 26:1)

> You shall not make for yourself a carved image, or any likeness of anything that is in heaven above, or that is on the earth beneath, or that is in the water under the earth. (Deut 5:8)

This strong repetition created a reluctance to use images of humans and animals on any sort of media, including coins. There has been some scholarly discussion as to how strictly these verses were interpreted

15. "Some of the symbols, however, are more closely aligned to Augustan imagery than Roman republican iconography" (Ariel, "The Coins of Herod the Great," 119).

16. For comments on the Decalogue and its ban on images as Jewish context for coinage see Jensen, *Herod Antipas in Galilee*, 188.

and applied by various Jewish sects.[17] When coins were minted under the Hasmonean dynasty (ca. 140 to ca. 116 BCE), "human and animal imagery was strictly avoided."[18] This sets up the background for our introduction to key questions about first-century Jewish coinage.

Animal Imagery

Simply because the Mosaic law forbade images in worship that does not mean that all Jews interpreted the law in the same way or that it was actually applied. Thus, the first question significant for numismatics and the world of the New Testament is: *How scandalous was animal imagery in the Judaean context* (particularly in a pre-70 CE context)?

Herod the Great is the only Jewish leader to mint a coin with a living being on it: a bronze lepton with an eagle on it.[19] The coins minted under Herod the Great were all bronze prutah, its larger variants (prutot), and lepton. Generally speaking, Jewish coins minted under Herod the Great displayed images that were politically neutral or imitations of Roman coins. It is possible that Herod did not care about the response of his subjects. If we consider the historical witness of the Gospel of Matthew as evidence that he was willing to kill Jewish babies at a whim, this cannot be ruled out.[20]

Figure 15. Eagle standing right on a half-prutah of Herod the Great; cornucopia on obv. Minted ca. 13 BCE in Jerusalem (Meshorer 66; Hendin 1190). An approximate sketch of the eagle is on the right.

17. Ariel and Fontanille, *The Coins of Herod*, 116.
18. Zangenberg, "Archaeology, Papyri, and Inscriptions," 332.
19. Hendin 1190.
20. Contra Donald T. Ariel and Jean-Philippe Fontanille who state, "But the idea that Herod did not care, or was cavalier in his behavior, cannot be corroborated" (*The Coins of Herod: A Modern Analysis and Die Classification*, AJC 79 [Leiden: Brill, 2012], 119).

In favor of this eagle being scandalous are the following points. First, this coin of Herod the Great is the only coin minted in Jerusalem that bore a picture of an animal until the second century CE.[21] The eagle was not only a living creature, forbidden by the Mosaic law, it echoed the common theme of the Roman eagle. The image of the eagle would have been well known from Roman standards and banners carried by the military. Another possible explanation for this highly unusual move is that Herod was trying to justify his placement of an eagle on the gate of the Jerusalem Temple. Some have tried to draw conclusions about the meaning of this symbol from the fact that the eagle on Herod's coinage has its wings folded, but the evidence is not conclusive.[22]

The other side of this debate highlights evidence that animal images were almost always scandalous (even if they should have been according to the Mosaic law). One could conclude that Herod was simply imitating the commonly accepted Shekel of Tyre that featured an eagle and the god Melqart. This was the official coinage accepted in the Jerusalem temple.

Messianic Ambition

Many coins communicate some kind of political ambition. But what kind of ambition was this? This question is especially pertinent in the Jewish context. We might further ask: Were the communications focused on fulfilling the ideals of power as defined by a Roman worldview or were they focused on fulfilling Jewish ideals? Coins raise the vitally important question for interdisciplinary ties to the New Testament: What constitutes evidence of *messianic* ambition? Here we might define "messianic ambition" as actions or words that publicly communicate that a prophet, priest, or king is fulfilling Israel's destiny as God's chosen people by saving or delivering them.[23] In this section we focus on the figure of Herod Antipas to explore how important this topic is.

When Herod the Great died, his kingdom was divided among his three sons: Antipas, Archelaus, and Philip. Herod Antipas became the tetrarch of Galilee and Peraea. The coins minted under him are rather scarce and typically in poor condition because they were produced with a bronze content subject to corrosion. As a result the features are often difficult to discern. His coins were minted in the city of Tiberias, which he founded,

21. Ariel and Fontanille, *The Coins of Herod*, 117.

22. Ibid., 118.

23. Michael F. Bird, *Are You the One Who Is to Come? The Historical Jesus and the Messianic Question* (Grand Rapids: Baker, 2009), 33.

named after Emperor Tiberius as well as Sepphoris.[24] His coins include bronze prutot in 1/8, 1/4, and 1/2 denominations and a bronze dupondius.

The coins communicating that Herod Antipas's rule was characterized by fertility and production include depictions of a bunch of dates,[25] a palm branch,[26] and perhaps a variant with an upright reed. The palm branch was a symbol of production and abundance.[27] The theme of honor is explicit rather than subtle as is common of most city-coinage.[28] Some coins feature explicit references to the name Caligula, "Gaius Caesar Germanicus" (ΓΆΙΩ ΚΆΙCΆΡΙ ΓΕΡΜΆΝΙΚΩ), surrounded by a wreath.[29] Such deference could be described as reflecting *auctoritas* (deference to authority) and *dignitas* (social honor).[30] But how should such symbols be construed?

The case for interpreting these symbols as reflective of messianic ambition has been more or less asserted, even if it has not been proven. In this view, the palm branch is reflective of the fertility of the land of Israel and the Roman laurel wreath establishes connections to the Emperor Tiberius and his pyramid of patronage.[31]

Another view finds that these symbols are indicative of Herod Antipas's simple desire for power and honor through economic prosperity in the land of Judaea. This is not necessarily mutually exclusive to messianic ambitions but it is difficult to see how the symbol of the palm branch can bear so much interpretive weight. Even those who argue for the presence of Antipas's messianic ambition on his coinage admit that they "carried a cleverly mixed message."[32]

In further support for the latter view we might point out that Antipas was raised in Rome from the age of ten and his mother was a Samaritan

24. David Hendin, "A New Coin Type of Herod Antipas," *INJ* 15 (2003–2006): 56–61.

25. Hendin 1217.

26. Hendin 1203, 1212.

27. Romanoff, *Jewish Symbols*, 16.

28. City-coinage share similar traits, including a portrait of the emperor on the obverse and localized imagery on the reverse (Sigismund, "Small Change?," 317).

29. Hendin 1217.

30. Richard A. Horsley and Neil A. Silberman, *The Message and the Kingdom: How Jesus and Paul Ignited a Revolution and Transformed the Ancient World* (repr., Minneapolis: Augsburg Fortress, 2002 [1997]), 22.

31. Ibid. This view is also noted by Morton H. Jensen, "Message and Minting," in Zangenberg, Attridge, and Martin, eds., *Religion, Ethnicity, and Identity in Ancient Galilee*, 278.

32. Ibid.

named Malthace. Even his building projects in Judaea, such as the rebuilding of the city of Sepphoris, were driven by Roman ideals. His upbringing likely urged him to develop a worldview dominated by Roman ideas of kingship rather than Jewish themes of an anointed Davidic-type kingship. There is no doubt that Antipas was ambitious, but his desire for kingship appears to bear little interest in fulfilling the role of Messiah or Jewish prophetic motifs.

The coins of Herod Antipas help to sharpen the messianic question and the communication of ambition to the inhabitants of Judaea. The same question we applied to Antipas could be applied to other Herodian rulers as well to probe the nature of their rule and their political ambitions. For example, when Simon bar Giora took control of Jerusalem just before 70 CE, he minted coins "celebrating the redemption of Zion."[33] This is significant because Simon bar Giora is described by Josephus as having messianic qualities such as proclaiming liberty for slaves (*War* 4.508). When and where these symbols on coins were understood as messianic, they offer clues about the historical context of Jesus' own messianic claims.

Military Power and Economic Prosperity

Herod Archelaus inherited the southern part of his father's kingdom as Ethnarch of Samaria, Judea, and Idumea. Coins from the reign of Herod Archelaus were minted in Jerusalem. All of the coins were bronze prutot. His coins were dominated by three themes: fertility/production, military strength, and peace. The symbols on his coins lead us to another question for interpreting Jewish coinage: *When do symbols communicate military power and when do they communicate economic prosperity*?

The coinage of Herod Archelaus had images of fertility, including grapes on a vine with leaves[34] and double cornucopia.[35] It also had strong military themes including a military helmet,[36] and a war galley (war ship) featuring oars and the aphlaston (the ram and helm of the ship).[37] The images of peace are depicted by the caduceus or wing-topped staff with two snakes around it.[38] This symbolized the messenger staff of truce and neutrality. Of course, this peace was established by Rome and thus had military undertones to it.

33. Bird, *Are You the One Who Is to Come?*, 51.
34. RPC I 4917.
35. RPC I 4914; 4915.
36. RPC I 4917.
37. RPC I 4915.
38. Hendin 1192.

One view of these images is that they are focused on communicating the presence and support of the Roman military. In the context of other images on Archelaus's coinage, it is highly doubtful that the images of grapes were intended to communicate anything more than economic prosperity. Although grapes did appear on the Jerusalem Temple and could be described as "sacred" in their symbolic weight, this is not likely part of Archelaus's intended meaning. The use of military symbols alongside symbols of peace would have communicated that any rebellion in Samaria, Judaea, and Idumea would not be tolerated.

Another view is that all of the military imagery was primarily meant to support economic prosperity. For example, it is quite possible that the image of the war ship may be intended to communicate economic superiority through sea trade. One scholar suggests, "The intense use of maritime symbols is generally regarded as Archelaos' way of communicating his superiority in both political and economic respects."[39]

The coinage of Herod Archelaus is dominated by images of patronage to Rome. There is very little evidence that Herod Archelaus intended his coins to communicate anything distinctly Jewish. Despite the symbols communicating the power of the Roman military, he did not depict any animals or human figures, perhaps reflecting a certain sensitivity for popular religious concerns. This interpretation is supported by the fact that he was so unpopular with the people that he was exiled to Gaul by Caesar Augustus. This unpopularity might direct us to the view that his coinage communicated support of the Roman military rather than economic prosperity.

The coinage of Herod Archelaus points us to the complex nature of Roman "peace." It points to the significance of images that communicate military power and those that communicate peace. This peace did support economic prosperity but it also came at a price. This means that even those symbols on coins that communicated peace could also communicate death to anyone who dared to challenge the puppet rulers backed by Rome.

Agriculture and Jewish Identity

"The underlying motif" of the coins from the "First Revolt" of the Jews against Rome are "symbols connected with fertility."[40] This conclusion can be misleading if one does not answer how fertility in the land is

39. Jensen, "Message and Minting," 289.
40. Romanoff, *Jewish Symbols*, 9.

related to Jewish identity. *In this section we will explore this question and see that agricultural fertility was very close to the core of Jewish identity because it was bound up with Yahweh's covenantal promises.*

The "Four Species" theme appears especially on Jewish coins from the First Jewish Revolt (66–70 CE). This theme consists of various arrangements of four plants used in the festival of Sukkot (the Feast of Booths or Tabernacles that commemorated the years of living in the desert after the Exodus). The Four Species were absolutely necessary for a celebration of Sukkot that was faithful to the Law of Moses. The Four Species are: (1) the myrtle, (2) the willow, (3) the palm branch (*lulav*), and (4) citron fruit (*etrog* or *ethrog*).[41] This theme appears amongst other trends on Jewish coinage related to the façade of the Temple in Jerusalem and Temple vessels.[42]

The *etrog* (citrus fruit) appears to the left of the lulav on the example of a Bar Kochba revolt coin from c. CE 135. An enlarged version of these items appears to the right of the coin.

The meaning behind the images of the chalice and the pomegranates on the shekels minted by the Jews rebelling against Rome is still unknown.[43] The pomegranate was a symbol of fertility throughout the ancient Near East. A thumb-sized pomegranate decoration is the only known surviving relic from Solomon's Temple. We should also note that symbols of pomegranates could be the berries of the myrtle tree.[44]

The symbols on Jewish coins provide insight into the lives of the commoners (the people of the Land). They were an agricultural people who were concerned with crop production and fertility.[45] When images

41. Ariel, "Identifying the Mints, Minters, and Meanings," 376.
42. "Art," *EDEJ*, 386.
43. Kreitzer, *Striking New Images*, 19; Goodman, "Coinage and Identity," 165.
44. Meshorer, *Jewish Coins of the Second Temple Period*, 91.
45. Romanoff, *Jewish Symbols*, 5.

of production such as grapes and pomegranates appeared on coins, they featured images that resonated with the people of the Land and established Jewish identity. The following text from the Pentateuch establishes the connection between productivity in the Promised Land and the identity of Jews as being blessed by Yahweh:

> For the Lord your God is bringing you into a good land, a land of brooks of water, of fountains and springs, flowing out in the valleys and hills, a land of wheat and barley, of vines and fig trees and pomegranates, a land of olive trees and honey, a land in which you will eat bread without scarcity, in which you will lack nothing, a land whose stones are iron, and out of whose hills you can dig copper. And you shall eat and be full, and you shall bless the Lord your God for the good land he has given you. (Deut 8:7–10)

This passage refers specifically to seven types of produce known as the "Seven Species," comprising two grains and five fruits that reflected God's blessing. These in turn became connected to the two festivals of Pentecost and the Feast of Booths.

Where symbols of these are present, there is little doubt that the dominant idea being communicated is abundance and economic stability. However, it is reasonable to ask whether this specific promise in Deuteronomy or a related concept is being communicated particularly in the absence of other interests in Jewish scripture, theology, and identity markers. Furthermore, where there is evidence that a given ruler is significantly invested in the Roman worldview one should ask if the images of abundance are a reflection of a desire to be a patron. If that is the case, the ruler would be taking the place of Yahweh, not supporting acknowledgement of him or fulfillment of his promises.

Second, while it is true that the messianic idea did not appear *explicitly* on Jewish coinage, the appearance of produce related to the "Seven Species" of Deuteronomy may have evoked connections with festivals that were related to messianic expectations. For example, according to John 7:37 Jesus stood up on the last day of the Feast of Booths and declared that he was its fulfillment. Did rulers such as Herod Antipas really have messianic ambitions? Or, did they have general ambitions to power and success that happened to take on the occasional Jewish flair?

Implications for Studying the New Testament

The world of the coin in the context of Judaea is an important part of the historical matrix in which Jesus' own messianic claims should be considered. This is all the more true if the Jewish rulers in the first century were also making competing claims and communicating these through coinage. The "messianic question" of historical-critical New Testament scholarship revolves around whether or not Jesus believed himself to be the Messiah.[46] One recent monograph goes to great lengths to demonstrate just how many historical-critical scholars of the historical Jesus deny that he regarded himself as the Messiah.[47] The Jewish coins of the first century may provide further data about how some rulers displayed some elements of messianic self-understanding.[48] Correspondingly, such Jewish coins would have elicited some responses in the population about what a messianic figure might do or say.

Summary

This chapter sought to introduce ancient Jewish coinage as cultural texts that communicated propaganda. We began by using the polar relationship of Jewish independence and patronage to frame the context in an accessible way. Then we highlighted the spectrum of Jewish interaction with Hellenism that covered everything from acceptance to rejection of Greco-Roman values, ideas, and worldviews. A series of critical questions for those who want to engage in interdisciplinary work between numismatics and New Testament studies were put forward: How scandalous was animal imagery? Is there evidence of messianic ambition? Are the symbols ones of military power or economic prosperity? How is agricultural fertility related to Jewish identity? These questions are not designed to be exhaustive by any means. Rather, the discussion around these questions opens up vistas for understanding the way in which coins functioned as a means for propaganda in the tumultuous world of Jerusalem, Judaea, and its wider environs.

46. Bird, *Are You the One Who Is to Come?*, 24.
47. For a list of quotations on this see ibid., 25.
48. I borrow the term "messianic self-understanding" from ibid., 29.

Chapter 12

PROPAGANDA AND METALLURGY

One of the theories that emerged from the domain of Classical Studies is that precious metals possessed a language all their own in archaic Greek culture. This chapter will seek to develop this theory and apply it to the first century.

Introduction

The raw material used to make coins reflected a cultural hierarchy of metals.[1] The historian Pliny (23–79 CE) explains that this is because gold was recognized to increase in purity when tested with fire.[2] This hierarchy of purity was appropriated by both Jewish and Roman writers, and it provided an established set of cultural signs for communication. The power of precious metals to become cultural signifiers has been widely received in Classical Studies, but has not received any attention by those seeking to understand the historical milieu of the first century and Christian origins. This chapter will seek to fill this void by examining the language of metals in the first century CE and arguing that *the language of metals in the first century often communicated purity or lack thereof.*

We will present this argument in three steps. First, we will examine the theory of the language of metals. Second, we will look at the elements that constituted the hierarchy of metals. Third, we will see how first-century writers relevant to the study of the New Testament used the language of metals.

1. Kurke, *Coins, Bodies, Games, and Gold*, 49.

2. For a quotation of Pliny (*NH* 33.59–60) in Latin with English translation see Kurke, *Coins, Bodies, Games, and Gold*, 50 n. 22. For further notes on Seneca and Pliny the Elder see Paul J. Achtemeier, *1 Peter: A Commentary on First Peter*, Hermeneia (Minneapolis: Fortress, 1996), 101 nn. 34, 33.

Before presenting the argument of this chapter, it will aid the reader to clarify some words and concepts. Greek words may refer to a specific type of coinage or to money in general. The Greek word for copper (χαλκός) could refer to copper coins specifically or money in general.[3] The parallelism between Mark 6:8 and Matt 10:9 demonstrates that the word for copper had a semantic range that included the generic sense of "money." The Septuagint also uses it in the general sense of "money" (LXX Jer 6:35). It is important to note that the Greek word for silver (ἀργύριον) could also be used generically or for silver coins in particular.[4] The quality of silver in coins varied from place to place and from time to time. Silver appears many times in the New Testament and, as mentioned above, is found in the instructions to the Twelve in Matt 10:9. In the parallel text from Luke 9:3 silver is referred to more generically as "money" (ἀργύριον). One of the salient points to take away from these semantics is that context is always key to understanding words in primary sources that refer to money or coinage.

The Theory of the Language of Metals

In order to understand the language of metals, we will draw a brief historical arc beginning with Archaic Greece (600–500 BCE) and ending with the first century. The "language of metals" that arose in archaic Greece (ca. 600 BCE) is well outside the scope of our timeframe but it is helpful to describe for historical background. According to this theory, ideological use of coinage reflected tensions between the aristocratic and populist demographics.[5] It has been argued that Greek aristocrats originally favored gift exchange over and against the use of coins.

As coinage arose in archaic Greek culture (ca. 600 BCE) it likely caused controversy amongst the cultural elites who were accustomed to gift giving. Those at the bottom of the cultural hierarchy could not afford to give gifts and therefore they were reliant upon those above them. Coinage brought an element of equality to society as it allowed all layers of social strata to participate in the marketplace.

3. D. H. Wheaton, "Money: In the New Testament," in *The New Bible Dictionary*, ed. R. W. Wood and I. H. Marshall, 3rd ed. (Downers Grove: InterVarsity, 1996), 780–82.

4. BDAG, 128, s.v. ἀργύριον.

5. Leslie Kurke, "Herodotus and the Language of Metals," *Helios* 22 (1995): 35–64.

The aristocratic poetic texts of archaic Greece used references to precious metals to convey social boundary markers. The language of metals was used by Plato to “articulate hierarchies or divisions” in the *Republic*.[6] For example, gold was associated with aristocracy and the cultural elite.

This thesis is not without its critics and evidence tends to point to the fact that early coinage was embraced by a wide range of social classes.[7] Even if this theory about the origins of coinage in Greece is true, it would not necessarily be applicable in the same way several hundred years later in the first century. The theory of the language of metals must consider the vast cultural changes that took place over time.[8]

One suggestion has already been put forth as to how the language of metals changed as Greek culture transitioned from the archaic traditions to the Hellenistic era (ca. 323–146 BCE). Arguably, an “epochal shift” occurred in the Hellenistic period that allowed the individual to use “reason and self-mastery” to define him or herself.[9] Of course, the *polis* remained central to defining the life of the citizen, but the growing interest in the individual remains an important development.[10] However this argument is assessed, it is difficult to deny that the language of metals evolved over time.

Whatever the “language of metals” was in the early formation of Greek society, it had changed by the first century CE. The question that remains unanswered is what form the language of metals took in the culture of the Roman era, in the context of the first century. The central argument about the metallic content in coins and their use as signifiers in society is this: *the language of metals in the first century communicated purity or lack thereof.*

6. Mary Ebbott, *Imagining Illegitimacy in Classical Greek Literature* (Lanham: Lexington, 2003), 96.

7. Thomas Figueira, “Review of *Coins, Bodies, Games, and Gold*,” *AJP* 121 (2000): 642–46. For a more wide-ranging interaction with this theory see Lin Foxhall, *Olive Cultivation in Ancient Greece: Seeking the Ancient Economy* (Oxford: Oxford University Press, 2007), 29–30.

8. “Just as coinage develops over time, so do the poetics that use coin imagery” (Ebbott, *Imagining Illegitimacy in Classical Greek Literature*, 96).

9. Kurke, *Coins, Bodies, Games, and Gold*, 330.

10. “I do not mean to imply that the Greek (democratic) polis disappeared in the Hellenistic and Roman periods; on the contrary, it is clear that the polis system endured tenaciously. I want simply to highlight a development within Hellenistic philosophy that differentiates it from the thought of Plato and Aristotle” (ibid., 331 n. 63).

The Use of the Language of Metals

The repetition of references to purity and refinement in first-century literature demonstrates a connection between metals and purity.[11] The more purity that a metal could achieve through refinement, the more valuable it was. This process of refinement was not nearly as scientific or thorough as it is today.[12] Nevertheless, the Romans understood that they were able to achieve 100% purity in elements such as silver. Gold was the metal that could achieve the highest level of purity and this meant gold was the most valuable metal.

By the time of the first century, the process of refining metals to increase purity had a long social and literary history. The refining of precious metals like gold was often referenced in Greek drama and poetry. This was, no doubt, reinforced amongst Jewish communities by references to refining gold and silver in the Hebrew Scriptures (Job 28:1; Ps 12:6; Zech 13:9; Mal 3:3).[13] The hierarchy of metals was a three to five tier system for viewing the relative value of precious metals. The three-tier system consisted of gold, silver, and copper, whereas the five-tier system consisted of gold, silver, copper, tin, and lead.

Jerusalem's Jewish temple was regulated according to the Law of Moses by a principle of relative sanctity. A hierarchy of metals and materials was used to communicate an increase in holiness as one moved from the outside of the temple toward the Holy of Holies. One scholar explains:

> The same principle of relative sanctity can be seen in the metals used in particular sections of the tabernacle. The pillars of the *pārōket* veil are overlaid with gold, with golden hooks and silver bases. Further out, the pillars of the outer veil are similar with their gold overlay and golden hooks, but have bronze, not silver, bases. Only the inner furniture of the tabernacle and its vessels are specifically to be made of, or overlaid with, "pure gold" ([Exod] 25:11, 17, 24, 29, 31, 36, 38; 30:3; 37:2, 6, 11, 16, 22, 26). Gold is not found in the court, while bronze, the least precious of the metals mentioned in Exodus, cannot be found in the Holy of Holies. Again, the preciousness of the materials corresponds to their proximity to the Holy of Holies.[14]

11. For references to metal purification in the New Testament see Rev 1:15 and 3:18.

12. The silver used in some denarii of the first century was "100% pure in Romans terms" (Butcher and Ponting, "The Denarius in the First Century," 557).

13. For more references to refinement of metals and purity see the non-canonical Jewish texts: Sir 2:5; Wis 3:4–6; Jdt 8:25–27, and the Shepherd of Hermas, *Vis.* 4.3, 4 (Achtemeier, *1 Peter*, 102 n. 36).

14. W. Ross Blackburn, *The God Who Makes Himself Known: The Missionary Heart of the Book of Exodus*, NSBT 28 (Downers Grove: InterVarsity, 2012), 128.

According to this arrangement of metals from Exodus, gold is at the top of the hierarchy while bronze is at the bottom. Because gold was the most valuable and pure, it represents the highest state of righteousness and therefore reflects the character of Yahweh. Copper or bronze is never an offering that Yahweh accepts.

Another reason why there was a language of metals is the fact that the Roman monetary system was based on a gold standard.[15] Gold coins weighed significantly less than silver coins and likely functioned as a "slowly circulating store of value."[16] From the several references to gold coins in the New Testament, it seems that gold coins were used in Judaea for actual payments.[17] The gold coins present in Judaea during the first century likely originated in Rome. They were in use in the Jewish towns of Judaea during the time of Jesus' ministry. Among the many references to gold in the New Testament, several refer implicitly or explicitly to gold coins.

There are two areas of evidence that point to the conclusion that the language of metals in the first century often communicated purity or lack thereof: (1) non-canonical texts, and (2) New Testament canonical texts.

Non-Canonical Texts

By analyzing some first-century non-canonical texts we will demonstrate that *a hierarchy of metals was operative behind references to coinages in the first century*. In this section we will look at Pseudo-Philo, Josephus, and Plutarch.

Pseudo-Philo. In the example from Pseudo-Philo (likely written post-70 CE), the order is reversed so that copper or another lower value metal is first with silver and gold at the end of the list. In the following quote, Murphy explains how Pseudo-Philo is drawing on the hierarchy of metals from the narratives of Genesis to depict idolatry:

> Genesis says that Tubal-cain "made all kinds of bronze and iron tools." The narrator of the Biblical Antiquities goes further: "This is the Tubal who showed men techniques in using lead and tin and iron and bronze and silver and gold. And then those inhabiting the earth began to make statues and to

15. MacDonald "The Worth of the Assarion," 122 n. 13.

16. W. V. Harris, ed., *The Monetary Systems of the Greeks and Romans* (Oxford: Oxford University Press, 2008), 9.

17. Kreitzer states that "silver and gold denominations" prevailed but it is not clear what specific geographic region he is referring to (*Striking New Images*, 17).

> adore them" (*LAB* 2:9). Idolatry is the fundamental sin in Pseudo-Philo; this passage places its beginnings very early in history and generalizes it through the stock phrase "those inhabiting the earth."[18]

The author of Pseudo-Philo likely wants to add the hierarchy of metals to this list because he believes that the more valuable metals represent greater temptations. Gold was the most valuable; it represents the greatest temptation.

Josephus. The writings of Josephus indicate his familiarity with the hierarchy of metals present in the Hebrew Scriptures (Septuagint). In this quotation, Josephus refers to a certain type of high quality brass that had beauty like gold:

> He also made a brazen altar, whose length was twenty cubits, and its breadth the same, and its height ten, for the burnt offerings. He also made all its vessels of brass, the pots, and the shovels, and the basins; and besides these, the snuffers and the tongs, and all its other vessels, he made of brass, and such brass as was in splendor and beauty like gold. (Josephus, *Ant*. 8.88)

Josephus even references a "sort of brass which is said to be more valuable than gold."[19] Although brass was understood to be less valuable than gold or silver, it nonetheless had its own intrinsic value.

Plutarch. The Greek historian Plutarch (ca. 46–120 CE) discusses how patinas and colorations in brass were of interest to some and sometimes subject to criticism:

> Theon, taking up the conversation, said, "We have heard another more artful account, how a worker in bronze at Corinth, when he had come upon a hoard containing much gold, fearing detection, broke it off a little at a time and stealthily mixed it with his bronze, which thus acquired a wondrous composition. He sold it for a goodly price since it was very highly esteemed for its colour and beauty. However, both this story and that are fiction, but there was apparently some process of combination and preparation; for even now they alloy gold with silver and produce a peculiar and extraordinary, and, to my eyes, a sickly paleness and an unlovely perversion."[20] (*De Pythiae oraculis* 2)

18. Frederick J. Murphy, *Pseudo-Philo: Rewriting the Bible* (Oxford: Oxford University Press, 1993), 32.
19. Josephus, *Ant.* 7.106.
20. Plutarch, *Moralia*, ed. F. C. Babbitt (Medford: Harvard University Press, 1936), 5:264–65.

Although certain uses of electrum (described in more detail in Chapter 15) in weapons and art could have been more valuable than gold alone, this does not appear to be the case with coinage. As we examine New Testament texts below, this reference may be helpful in explaining the nature of Jesus' metallic feet in Rev 1:15 and 2:18.

New Testament Texts

First-century Jewish writers appropriated the language and hierarchy of metals to communicate the idea of increasing purity through testing. One commentator notes, "The related idea that the purity of a person's trust in God was tested by adversity as precious metal was tested by fire was a commonplace of Jewish thought, and the notion of faith tested by (fiery) adversity appears in the NT as well."[21] By analyzing New Testament texts we will demonstrate that *a hierarchy of metals was operative behind references to coinages in the first century*. This section briefly examines Matthew, Acts, 1 Corinthians, 1 Peter, and Revelation.

The Gospel of Matthew. Our first canonical reference to a hierarchy of metals comes from the Gospel of Matthew (10:9) and provides specific directions from Jesus for the Twelve apostles on their mission to the towns of Israel. Jesus forbids that they take "gold or silver or copper for your belts."[22] There is nothing in the context to suggest that the reference to money has any so-called deeper meaning. What is significant to observe is that gold comes first, then silver, and lastly copper.

The Book of Acts. Silver and gold are mentioned together three times in Acts. Of these three, Acts 3:6 and 20:33 refer to "silver and gold" as coin money. Paul's reference to "gold or silver" in his speech (Acts 17:29) is especially significant because he was speaking to a Greek audience in Areopagus. One of the dominant themes of his speech is idolatry and Paul is keen to lay out a series of negative and positive propositions about what the God of Israel is like:

> Being then God's offspring, we ought not to think that the divine being is like gold or silver or stone, an image formed by the art and imagination of man. (Acts 17:29)

21. Achtemeier, *1 Peter*, 102 n. 36.

22. The Greek of Matt 10:9 reads: Μὴ κτήσησθε χρυσὸν μηδὲ ἄργυρον μηδὲ χαλκὸν εἰς τὰς ζώνας ὑμῶν (acquire no gold or silver or copper for your belts).

Of all the materials used to make physical idols or artistic images of God, Paul selects "gold and silver" and stone. What this demonstrates is that a widely traveled Jew such as Paul was able to identify these metals as being associated with the divine in the minds of those attending the Areopagus. It confirms that the hierarchy of metals contributed and hindered how divinity was conceptualized by many Roman citizens, especially non-Jews.

1 Corinthians. The reference to gold and silver in 1 Corinthians draws explicit attention to the process of refinement and purity:

> For no one can lay a foundation other than that which is laid, which is Jesus Christ. Now if anyone builds on the foundation with gold, silver, precious stones, wood, hay, straw—each one's work will become manifest, for the Day will disclose it, because it will be revealed by fire, and the fire will test what sort of work each one has done. (1 Cor 3:11–14)

In this text, the eschatological Day of the Lord will be equivalent to the process of refinement. The Day of the Lord will reveal that nature of what people have built through fire. This text might be assuming that the audience of the first century was familiar with counterfeit coins that could not be completely tested for purity until they were melted and the elements were separated.

1 Peter. The book of 1 Peter provides another clear reference to the process of refining precious metals and the concept of purity:

> In this you rejoice, though now for a little while, if necessary, you have been grieved by various trials, so that the tested genuineness of your faith—more precious than gold that perishes though it is tested by fire—may be found to result in praise and glory and honor at the revelation of Jesus Christ. (1 Pet 1:6–7)

In this quote a comparison is at work between faith and gold. Both require testing in order to achieve greater purity and value. Of course, gold is perishable whereas faith is not. Thus, faith is more precious than the most precious metal known to the Greco-Roman world. By utilizing the metal which was the most valuable, the value of faith is held up above all perishable items of the world.

Revelation. The ESV translates Rev 1:15 as "his [Jesus'] feet were like *burnished bronze*" (also Rev 2:18). However, the word likely emphasizes the shininess of the metal and not its content. The word used for Jesus' feet is rather unique. One lexicon notes the following: "In the two references with χαλκολίβανον in the NT (Rev 1:15 and Rev 2:18) the emphasis is upon the lustrous appearance of the metal. A satisfactory equivalent may be 'bright bronze' or 'shining metal'."[23]

The fact that Jesus' feet are depicted as consisting of precious metal is significant because the early disciples of Jesus believed that he was equivalent to Yahweh, as indicated by their worship of him.[24] The one God who received worship from early Christians was worshipped as the Father and the Son. The concept that Yahweh was utterly pure was common in Jewish thought. For Jesus' feet to be anything other than the most valuable metal would have been strikingly out of place. As Josephus comments it was possible to have a bronze-like metal that had the appearance of gold. Such bronze could be even more valuable than gold itself (*Ant.* 7.106). The historical context supports the conclusion that Jesus' feet were visually stunning due to the shininess of the metal and possibly made of brass or electrum that looked like gold.

Implications for Studying the New Testament

In this chapter we have demonstrated that the social world of the New Testament was a world in which metals had an inherent hierarchy of values and that this hierarchy was used to communicate the presence of purity or the lack thereof. First, the act of refining metals is repeatedly used to describe the effect of Jesus' purifying actions and his presence among his people. Using this language, sin is purged away even as impurities are removed from gold. This is why the language of metals, as understood in the first century, appears in Christian contexts related to suffering and to eschatological judgment. Second, the hierarchy of metals that was required for proper cultic worship to Yahweh in Israel is appropriated by the apocalyptic portrait of Jesus in the book of Revelation. Here, the concept of purity is important because it is ascribed to the person of the risen Lord Jesus in an apocalyptic message. This is important evidence that points to early Christians depicting Jesus in symbols typically reserved for Yahweh—displaying a form of proto-Trinitarianism.

23. Johannes P. Louw and Eugene Albert Nida, *Greek–English Lexicon of the New Testament: Based on Semantic Domains*, 2nd ed. (New York: United Bible Societies, 1996), 1:26.

24. "In the earliest observable stages of Christian worship in the New Testament, devotion is offered to God the Father and to (and through) Jesus" (Larry Hurtado, *At the Origins of Christian Worship: The Context and Character of Earliest Christian Devotion* [Grand Rapids: Eerdmans, 1999], 63).

Summary

Jewish perspectives of precious metals were informed not only by contemporary economics but by theological principles derived from Scripture. For example, a hierarchy of metals lies very close to the center of how holiness was perceived in the Jerusalem Temple. The very holiness of Yahweh and his approachability through the Temple is communicated through a hierarchy of metals. References to combinations of coin types often follow a pattern: gold is first, silver is second, and copper is third. This pattern may be reversed but it generally holds true. The hierarchy of metals in first-century texts draws upon first-century values of metals as well as the Hebrew Scriptures (Septuagint). Overall we are developing the argument that coins are cultural texts that are best interpreted by giving careful attention to the role of author, text, and reader. This chapter focused on the world of the text—the coin itself. The first-century hierarchy of metals had an impact on perceptions of purity and impurity for first-century Jews of various sects. There are three dominant sources for the propagation of cultural memes that shaped approaches to the hierarchy of metals: (1) the Septuagint, (2) Greco-Roman literature, and (3) coinage.

Section III

The World Behind the Coin: Power

Chapter 13

Power and Identity

Roman emperors used images on statues, sculptures, temples, and especially coins to communicate how they saw themselves and how they wanted others to see them. This chapter will describe how Roman emperors used coins as political tools to control identity and the Empire.

Introduction

Coins were an important tool used by those in power to shape the public identities of themselves and their family.[1] Coins were tools for shaping their own identity as well as the identity of others. Perhaps the best way to capture how coins were an expression of the emperor's public identity is to consider how contemporary corporations invest in managing their brand-names. The emperor's public identity was constantly being managed for the sake of the benefaction system and political control. This emperor's identity also extended beyond himself to include his family. One scholar argues that coins in the imperial period commemorated the fame, achievements, and virtues "of the reigning emperor and his family."[2]

In the first century there was still a latent memory of the Republic and there were occasional voices who objected to the strong centralized powerhouse that was the Roman Emperor. The Empire could not be ruled with an iron fist. Mercenary tactics could work at the frontlines of the Empire but rarely with citizens who were protected by law. Coins provided emperors with a tool of communication that was not threatening or outwardly coercive.

1. "What coinage most obviously provides is an enormous range of self-defined and explicit representations of public/official/communal identities, principally civic in nature" (Howgego, "Coinage and Identity," 1).

2. Jonathan Williams, "The Republican Identity of Roman Imperial Coinage: 1st to mid-3rd Centuries AD," in *Money and Identity: Lectures About History, Design, and Museology of Money*, ed. R. Cunz (Hannover: [Numismatische Kommission der Länder in der Bundesrepublik Deutschland, 2007), 60.

Close to the center of the Roman emperor's identity was the concept of divinity.[3] After the turn from Republic to Empire during the years of Julius Caesar and Augustus, power was maintained through the imperial cult. One scholar explains, "Rather than rely on brute force and the markers of personal ascendency, the imperial strategy was to link the traditional ideology of Roman rule with the imperial house."[4] N. T. Wright comments on the power of the Emperor's divine identity by rhetorically asking, "Who needs armies when they have worship?"[5] One qualifier remains: the imperial cult was not monolithic and it is more accurate to speak of imperial cults (in the plural) because of its diversity. Even so, there is enough continuity across the imperials cults to use the singular for the sake of simplicity.

The task of this chapter is to consider how and why Roman emperors used coinage to communicate and shape public perceptions of their identity. This will proceed along three general lines of inquiry. Each of the areas addressed will be broad in scope and introductory in nature for the purpose of facilitating interdisciplinary work between New Testament studies and numismatics. First, we will consider how coins shaped the identity of the emperor. Second, we will consider how coins shaped the identity of the emperor's family. Third, we will examine how and why coins were used to shape the identity of previous emperors.

Fiction and Reality

As we proceed to highlight some of the ways in which coins functioned as tools to influence and create a socially constructed identity, it will be helpful to nuance our study with a critical question about identity and the concept of the "self" in the first-century Roman Empire. The one critical question to ask is whether the historian of the first century is caught in a dilemma with only two alternatives: Does a coin that purports to portray a ruler's identity give access to a real self, or is that self a fiction?[6] After all, the faces depicted on many coins were "sometimes realistic, sometimes

3. Temple imagery are "a clear demonstration of the primacy of religion in the expression of identity on coins" (Howgego, "Coinage and Identity," 4).

4. Nystrom, "We Have No King but Caesar," 35.

5. N. T. Wright as quoted by Judith Diehl, "Anti-Imperial Rhetoric in the New Testament," in McKnight and Modica, eds., *Jesus Is Lord, Caesar Is Not*, 54.

6. Here I appropriate a discussion about texts and the self in antiquity and apply it to coinage (D. Brakke, M. L. Satlow, and S. Weitzman, eds., *Religion and the Self in Antiquity* [Bloomington: Indiana University Press, 2005], 4–5).

idealised."[7] In other words, do the portraits, symbolism, authority, and honor allow those in power to shape an identity that is fictional or real? It is important that the historian should not get caught in a false dichotomy here. The problem is a both/and issue, not an either/or. One scholar notes that "Hellenistic royal portraits aimed to express royal appearance, which was made to consist of a variable combination of reality and royal image."[8] This issue is particularly acute because the portraits of emperors and their families are so detailed that the structure of noses and the particulars of hairstyles could be seen.[9]

The best way to approach this question is with the two elements of critical realism. First, the coin is a tool of propaganda that is being used to create an identity or self that is largely socially constructed. This means that the historian must have a critical eye throughout the process of interpretation. Second, viewing the coin as a cultural text should not obscure the fact that a real person acted in history to express themselves. Taking these two points into consideration means that work must be done with as many primary sources as possible. This also forces the interpreter to consider a robust hermeneutic and methodology. When approaching coins as cultural texts one should view the identity they communicate as social construction *and* a reflection of a real person's individuality.

Socially constructed identity through coinage relied upon the Greco-Roman appreciation of portraiture. Portraits typically featured a profile facing right that included the head and neck.[10] This allowed larger coins to provide details that reflected social changes and cultural memes. Thus, the larger context of social history and culture must be considered when pursuing analysis of specific coins.

Shaping Their Own Identity

Emperors used coinage to shape their own public identity. The most important source for constructing identities was the past.[11] By using iconography

7. Brennan, Turner, and Wright, *Faces of Power*, 7.

8. R. R. R. Smith, *Hellenistic Royal Portraits* (Oxford: Oxford University Press, 1988), 32.

9. "Da die Porträts im allgemeinen sehr realistisch sind, können wir auf solchen Münzen tatsächlich antiken Menschen ins Gesicht schauen" (Reiser, "Numismatik und Neues Testament," 461).

10. C. E. King, "Roman Portraiture: Images of Power," in *Roman Coins and Public Life Under the Empire: E. Togo Salmon Papers II*, ed. G. M. Paul and M. Ierardi (Ann Arbor, MI: University of Michigan Press, 1999), 124.

11. Howgego, "Coinage and Identity in the Roman Provinces," 5.

and images of themselves that drew upon people (such as Alexander the Great) and the Roman pantheon, the emperor could shape his identity into something that was accepted and even desired by the Empire. There are three key motifs that will aid those seeking to understand how emperors used coinage to shape their own identity: (1) Alexander the Great and (2) the Roman pantheon, and (3) physiognomy.

One of the dominant motifs used by emperors to shape their own identity was allusions to Alexander the Great of Macedonia (356–323 BCE). By connecting themselves with Alexander the Great, Roman emperors were associating themselves with a shared past. This shared past connected the Roman emperor with all of the virtues of Hellenism. In fact, the last series of coins (tetradrachmas and drachmas) that portrayed Alexander the Great were minted in the early first century by a Roman named Aesillas, quaestor of Macedonia.[12] The retrospective eschatology of the Roman Empire meant that emperors and citizens alike sought to look as far back as Alexander the Great to understand the public identity of the emperor.

A second dominant motif used by emperors to shape their public identity was combining their portrait with elements of the Roman pantheon. These references to deities were sometimes attached to mythological stories such as the founding of Rome. Like the references to Alexander, these connections identified the emperor as fulfilling an ancient trajectory of leadership. An important qualification must be noted here: the messages did not explicitly say that the emperors were divine. The Roman senate had to approve of apotheosis. For example, the Senate denied apotheosis to Caligula.[13] One scholar concludes: "With the exception of Caligula and Commodus, the emperors were careful to avoid official deification while alive."[14] However, the text and images on coins were strongly suggestive of concepts associated with the divine. For example, a star appeared in the sky during the Olympic games held in honor of Julius Caesar in 44 BCE.[15] This star was interpreted as a divine sign. Augustus used the image of a star or comet to connect himself to the "Divine Julius."[16] The key idea is that while emperors did not officially claim deification, they unofficially claimed it by associating themselves with imagery that could only point to one conclusion.

12. Stewart, *Faces of Power*, 328.
13. Kreitzer, *Striking New Images*, 91.
14. Nystrom, "We Have No King but Caesar," 32.
15. Kreitzer, *Striking New Images*, 84.
16. Ibid., 89.

A third motif used by emperors to shape their public identity was the details of their physical features as seen in images, also known as physiognomy. In the chapter on propaganda and Roman images, the topic of physiognomy was introduced under the heading of human portraits. Physiognomy allowed people to make a judgment about people's character and potential for leadership based on their physical qualities such as their nose or forehead. The historian Pliny the Elder, in his *Natural History*, quotes Aristotle (thinking he is quoting Trogus) on the topic of physiognomy:

> Where the forehead is broad, it is significant of a dull and sluggish understanding beneath; and where it is small, it indicates an unsteady disposition. A rounded forehead denotes an irascible temper, it seeming as though the swelling anger had left its traces there. Where the eye-brows are extended in one straight line, they denote effeminacy in the owner, and when they are bent downwards towards the nose, an austere disposition. On the other hand, when the eye-brows are bent towards the temples, they are indicative of a sarcastic disposition; but when they lie very low, they denote malice and envy. Long eyes are significant of a spiteful, malicious nature and where the corners of the eyes next the nose are fleshy, it is a sign also of a wicked disposition. If the white of the eye is large, it bears tokens of impudence, while those who are incessantly closing the eyelids are inconstant. (*NH* 11.114)

This perspective as exemplified by Pliny the Elder was an important element in Roman portraits, sculpture, and coinage in the imperial period up to the third century CE.[17] One author argues: "the physiognomic consciousness that developed permeated the Greco-Roman thought world."[18] When it comes to coinage, the male portraiture of the imperial period is characterized by realism and strongly drawn features.[19]

We conclude this section with a conceptual nuance: the Roman Emperors in the Julio-Claudian dynasty (the first five emperors) wanted to be *mythological*. This nuance may help to explain some of the reluctance to accept worship and the strong desire to be publicly identified with the divine through images on coins, statues, and temples. One scholar explains: "All mythology served to claim a position within a wider world with reference

17. Jane Fejfer, *Roman Portraits in Context* (Berlin: de Gruyter, 2008), 268; Mikeal C. Parsons, *Body and Character in Luke and Acts: The Subversion of Physiognomy in Early Christianity* (Grand Rapids: Baker, 2006), 17.

18. Parsons, *Body and Character in Luke and Acts*, 17.

19. Fejfer, *Roman Portraits in Context*, 268.

to a shared past, and sometimes articulated specific relationships with other Greek cities or with Rome."[20] Thus, to be mythological was to claim a position on the hierarchy of power that drew from the ancient past and the stories of the gods associated with it. Coins provided images that connected the present particulars of each emperor with timeless universals (myths). By being publicly identified as mythological, the emperor was publicly viewed as the fulfillment of all of the Empire's shared stories, history, and desires.

Shaping the Identity of Their Family

Emperors sought to shape the public identity of their family. The imperial cult is often thought of as consisting of worship of the Emperor alone. However, it was actually the imperial family that functioned as the head of the benefaction system. Beginning with Caesar Augustus, the imperial family was de-privatized and became a state family.[21] While many Roman coins sought to appropriate the past (retrospective), the dynastic imagery of families was future oriented (prospective).[22] One scholar notes that this was based on the concept that "the general well-being of the Roman state depended on the stability and continuation of the imperial family."[23] The broad theme of the emperor's family on coinage was an integral part of coins functioning as a cultural text that projected a world of meaning. By projecting an image of the virtuous imperial family those in power could project an image of the world as Rome desired it to look.[24]

The continuity of the Roman Empire through the future family of the emperor corresponds with the concept of the emperor as "father." The public image of the imperial family reinforced the concept that the emperor was the father of the people. Caesar was not only the head of the Roman state, he was the "Father of his country"—the *Pater Patria*, a term used first for Julius Caesar that became an official title for the emperor alone after the reign of Augustus.[25]

20. Howgego, "Coinage and Identity in the Roman Provinces," 6.

21. Eva Maria Lassen, "The Use of the Father Image in Imperial Propaganda and 1 Corinthians 4:14–21," *TynBul* 42 (1991): 132.

22. Judith Ginsburg, *Representing Agrippina: Constructions of Female Power in the Early Roman Empire* (Oxford: Oxford University Press, 2005), 61.

23. Ibid., 61 n. 22.

24. Brennan, Turner, and Wright, *Faces of Power*, 7.

25. Diane G. Chen, *God as Father in Luke–Acts*, SBL 92 (New York: Lang, 2006), 34.

There are several examples of emperors using coinage to shape the public identity of their family members. Caligula tried to have his three sisters associated with the "personifications of Securitas, Concordia, and Fortuna."[26] Claudius (41–54 CE) sought to identify his mother Livia as associated with the divine qualities of justice, piety, and health (Iustitia, Pietas, and Salus) through a series of three coins.[27]

One of the inscriptions from Neapolois, the port of Philippi, identifies Cornelia Asprilla as a priestess of Livia Augusta (wife of Augustus).[28] Eventually Livia's grandson, the emperor Claudius, and the senate decreed her a goddess.[29]

The emperor Domitian responded to the death of his 10-year-old-son by proclaiming the boy and his mother Domitia to be gods. On one denarius from the mint in Rome, the deceased son is portrayed as a young Jupiter seated on a globe and playing with seven stars.[30] This particular image also appears on a gold aureus.[31] If the infant son is to be understood as a god (Jupiter), then Domitia is the mother of god. One might also understand by inference that Domitian is the lord of the heavens.

Antonia Minor (or Antonia the Younger; 36 BCE to 37 CE) is another popular Roman woman who appeared on at least three Roman coins, eleven or more provincial issues in the East, and seven tokens.[32] She was the daughter of Mark Antony and wife of Nero Claudius Drusus, the brother of Emperor Tiberius. Antonia was granted the highest honors by Caligula because she exposed a plot by Sejanus to murder Emperor Tiberius. As a reward, Caligula granted her the status of "Vestal Virgin," which allowed her to be supported at the expense of the state, among other things.[33]

26. Kreitzer, *Striking New Images*, 90.

27. Ibid., 94. See RIC Tiberius 43.

28. Lynn Cohick, "Philippians and Empire: Paul's Engagement with Imperialism and the Imperial Cult," in McKnight and Modica, eds., *Jesus Is Lord, Caesar Is Not*, 169.

29. Ibid., 173.

30. RIC 209a.

31. RIC 213, Vagi 1160.

32. Kokkinos, *Antonia Augusta*, 87.

33. Ibid., 96.

Shaping the Identity of Previous Emperors

Emperors used coinage to shape the identity of previous emperors, including ancient rulers such as Alexander the Great. Why would one emperor mint coins with the portrait of a former emperor? Broadly speaking we can state that emperors sought to locate portraits of themselves within the spectrum of continuity that stretched far back into Hellenistic history.

One reason for wanting to be publicly identified with previous emperors is that honor for those in the past elevated the status of all emperors, thus making it easier for the current emperor to maintain power. Second, such an act reinforced the idea that the current emperor was the benefactor of the whole world—even his predecessors. Third, this act of appropriating what was ancient was part of the "retrospective eschatology" that characterized much of the Roman world in the first century.[34] This was a worldview in which "people looked back from a 'golden age' that had already arrived and saw the whole story of how they had arrived at that point."[35]

Nero issued coins that identified his adoptive father Claudius as a god. However, Nero annulled this order and it was later restored by the emperor Vespasian.[36] Vespasian sought to solidify his identity and status as emperor by creating a parallel between his defeat of Jerusalem and Octavian's defeat of Antony at Actium almost one hundred years earlier.[37]

The desire to use coinage to affect memories and shape public identity is also evident in the destruction of coinage from previous emperors who were hated. For example, Claudius sought to erase Caligula's coins, thereby erasing the public record of his achievements.[38] The Roman historian Dio Cassius (ca. 155–235 CE) states, "despising the memory of Caligula they passed a decree that all the bronze that had his image stamped on it should be melted down" (Dio 60.22.3). This destruction of coinage also supports the thesis that Roman imperial coins were "commemorative monuments to the emperor."[39] In summary, coins were used positively by emperors who wanted the public to identify them with previous emperors. Negatively, coins of despised emperors were sometimes destroyed because these coins were perceived as part of their public record.

34. Wright, *Simply Jesus*, 32.

35. Ibid.

36. Kreitzer, *Striking New Images*, 95.

37. Esler, "God's Honour and Rome's Triumph," 240.

38. A. A. Barrett, "The Invalidation of Currency in the Roman Empire: The Claudian Demonetization of Caligula's Aes'," in Paul and Ierardi, eds., *Roman Coins*, 85.

39. Williams, "The Republican Identity of Roman Imperial Coinage," 58.

Implications for Studying the New Testament

The connection between the use of coins to shape public identity and the New Testament is abundantly clear when we examine how the earliest Christians engaged their contemporary culture's language of economics. Following the death and resurrection of Jesus, Christians used economics to influence social formation and identity, albeit in significantly different ways from the peoples around them.

What was true for Caesar was also true for Christians: economic matters are ways of talking about social relationships.[40] Whereas Caesar and his family utilized the power of coinage to shape their public identity, Christians engaged in discussions of wealth that also communicated identity. One New Testament scholar states it this way: "economic attitudes and practices contributed to early Christian social formation and self-definition."[41]

We noted above that "economic attitudes and practices contributed to early Christian social formation and self-definition."[42] This author goes on to state that this self-definition took place within the context of the plurality of "ancient society."[43] One powerful example of this is Paul's view of givers and gifts of money. Typically, the act of giving away money would make a person a patron. But this was not necessarily the case in the "divine economy" of relationships amongst early Christians.[44] In this economy, spiritual goods (such as the Gospel) were more valuable than money because they carried "spiritual capital."[45] On the basis of this, Paul rhetorically asks the question (1 Cor 9:11): "If we have sown spiritual things among you, is it too much if we reap material things from you?" Paul explains the economic value of the Gospel as having implications for the church (1 Cor 9:14): "the Lord commanded that those who proclaim the gospel should get their living by the gospel." This same view is communicated by Paul in Romans (15:27): "For if the Gentiles have come to share in their spiritual blessings, they ought also to be of service

40. Stephen C. Barton, "Money Matters: Economic Relations and the Transformation of Value in Early Christianity," in Longenecker and Liebengood, eds., *Engaging Economics*, 42.

41. Ibid., 38.

42. Ibid.

43. Ibid.

44. David E. Briones, *Paul's Financial Policy: A Socio-Theological Approach*, LNTS 494 (London: T&T Clark, 2013), 17.

45. Ibid.

to them in material blessings." This language reflects practices in the micro-economy amongst the disciples. This practice in turn, reflects their identity as recipients of the spiritual gift of the gospel.

Summary

This chapter sought to identify and explain how coins were used by those in power, especially emperors, to create public personas. The presence of the emperor's family on coinage (wives, mothers, grandmothers, sisters, etc.) along with previous emperors, locks together with themes of Roman peace, harmony, and economic prosperity. All of these served to present the world as Rome would like it to be, if the world would see it through the lens of their coinage.

Like much of Roman eschatology, coins were used to connect those in power with antiquity. If we can agree that identity was "somehow correlated with 'Greekness'" then we can explain that this was mediated through associations with Alexander the Great and the Roman pantheon.[46] The relationship between contemporary Roman rulers and rulers of antiquity like Alexander the Great provided an important element of legitimacy and identity. Identity could be conveyed through portraits because they were assumed to capture the essence of a person. The artistic features and details reflected the nature of the person.

We have also identified how Roman coins and their message of patronage help illuminate important cultural values that early Christians engaged in complex ways as they sought to communicate the grace of God to Jews and Gentiles. What this chapter adds to our overall argument is an understanding of how early Christians as well as Roman emperors used aspects of economics for self-definition.

46. Howgego, "Coinage and Identity in the Roman Provinces," 7.

Chapter 14

Power and Presence

Imagery on coins was used to communicate power through a portrait that created personal presence throughout the entire Roman Empire. This personal presence was an extension of Caesar Augustus's claim to divinity.

Introduction

We begin by noting that Caesar Augustus (63 BCE–14 CE) was the first Roman ruler to claim a superhuman or divine status.[1] The presence of power in the Greco-Roman world emanated directly from Caesar. Presence was communicated not only through coins but through statues and other visual imagery. Coins were an important part of cultivating the cult of personality that placed the emperor at the top of the patron–client benefaction pyramid. The world of power communicated with the world in front of the coin with intentionality. Coins often stressed three qualities of the emperor: (1) his moral virtues, (2) his military victories, and (3) his divine election by the gods.[2] *In this chapter we will demonstrate that the image of Caesar Augustus on coins was designed to communicate the Roman-religion concept of omnipresence.*

Central to this argument is the idea that coins were cultural texts that attempted to project or communicate the propaganda of those in power. Caesar exercised his power to some extent in shaping how he was depicted on the most commonly seen cultural text in the first century—coinage. In this way coins could function as a cultural lens through which the world could be seen. Those in power sought to take advantage of this communicative power so as to impose their worldview upon the Empire. In this worldview, the emperor was linked to the world of the divine.

1. Zanker, *The Power of Images*, 24.

2. J. E. Lendon, *Empire of Honour: The Art of Government in the Roman World* (Oxford: Oxford University Press, 1997), 10–11.

Where Caesar was on one side and Venus (or some other god) was on the other, the connection was clear. One numismatic scholar concludes: "every coin links its imperial figure to the divine world."[3] Those in power wanted the populace to read the coins in a particular way. If their reading was accepted, then it was clear that Caesar had one foot in this world and one foot in the realm of the Greco-Roman pantheon. This is why it is important to begin with an analysis of the Roman gods.

Omnipresence of the Roman Gods

As we have just seen it is most helpful to begin, not with Caesar Augustus, but with the pantheon of Roman gods. The first thing we will establish is that the gods were understood to have the quality of omnipresence.[4] One way to state this position is to say that because the Roman gods formed a "part of the citizen body," they were as omnipresent as the people were.[5] Wherever the Romans were, the gods were. While the gods inhabited certain locales, there were so many gods that they collectively became omnipresent. This section explores two points that support the conclusion that the Roman gods had the collective quality of omnipresence.

First, the Romans referred to gods in terms of groups rather than individuals. While a single god may have been thought to inhabit a particular grove or temple, the collective of the gods was present in every place. Greek and Roman cities tended to have "a group of deities who were believed to have special fondness for the city."[6] Technically speaking, a single god may not have the quality of omnipresence, but the popular way of referring to groups of gods would have made that point moot. The altar dedicated "to an unknown god" in Athens (Acts 17:23) is further evidence that votive offerings and worship were given to deities that were unknown but presumed to be present in some manner.

3. Brennan, Turner, and Wright, *Faces of Power*, 7.

4. The gods could be "benevolent or malevolent toward mankind; their existence and omnipresence were no guarantee of divine goodwill" (Valerie M. Warrior, *Roman Religion*, CIRC [Cambridge: Cambridge University Press, 2006], 5).

5. "One way of expressing this relationship has been to say that in some sense the gods were regarded as forming part of the citizen body, sharing in its victories and celebrations, joining with mortal citizens in the commensality that followed blood sacrifice" (Greg Woolf, "Divinity and Power in Ancient Rome," in *Religion and Power: Divine Kingship in the Ancient World and Beyond*, ed. N. Brisch, OIS 4 [Chicago: The Oriental Institute of Chicago, 2008], 239).

6. Ibid.

Second, to some people, the gods were understood to be metaphors or "philosophical abstractions" rather than beings with an actual ontology.[7] If the gods were understood to be abstract qualities or ideas, they would naturally take on universal qualities. Philosophical abstractions such as justice, love, and power would have been thought to be universal—requiring only a short leap to be conceived as omnipresent.

Third, to other people, the gods were understood to be anthropomorphic or "real." Where and when this was true, some thought the gods could appear anywhere. This seems to be the case when Paul and Barnabas arrived at Lystra. After Paul heals a crippled man, the crowds said "the gods have come down to us in the likeness of men!" (Acts 14:11). The crowds concluded that Barnabas was Zeus and Paul was Hermes (Acts 14:12). Before this, the Latin poet Ovid wrote that Zeus and Hermes had visited the region and were denied hospitality.[8] This too supports the conclusion that the gods could appear as humans anywhere and at any time.

Fourth, by the time of the first century, most of the Empire had been influenced by "Hellenistic cosmopolitanism."[9] The world of the first century was awash with new ideas, philosophies, and gods of the vastly different people groups subsumed under the wave of Roman peace. This mix of ideas resulted in people questioning classical Greco-Roman gods of the Pantheon. The static gods of the Pantheon who were bound to a particular place were rejected as a source of personal aid. Most of the attention that the Pantheon continued to receive, such as images on coins, was a result of politics, not personal spirituality.

To summarize, while the gods of the Roman pantheon were localized and geographically limited, there was another set of ideas that competed for what constituted divinity in the hearts and minds of the average person of the Roman Empire. While any individual god would have been subject to limitations, the cosmopolitan mix of ideas in the first century resulted in the gods being understood collectively. Given this particular framework in which divinities were regularly transformed by the changing cultures, it is not hard to see how the gods could be localized as individuals

7. Plato understood the gods to be philosophical abstractions in the fourth century BCE (Antonia Tripolitis, *Religions of the Hellenistic-Roman Age* [Grand Rapids: Eerdmans, 2002], 14).

8. Ovid, *Metam.* 8.620–724. For commentary see David W. J. Gill, "Acts and Roman Religion," in *The Book of Acts in Its Graeco-Roman Setting*, ed. D. W. J. Gill and C. Gempf (Grand Rapids: Eerdmans, 1994), 82.

9. Tripolitis, *Religions of the Hellenistic-Roman Age*, 15.

and omnipresent as a collective. Given the colloquial nature of Roman religion, such paradoxes should not be surprising. Again, the biblical studies specialist should take care not to read systematic approaches to Christian theology into first-century Roman religion.

The Omnipresence of the Roman Emperor

The most salient point of the section above is that the gods of the Roman pantheon had qualities of omnipresence. They were both localized and yet everywhere. In this section we will argue that Roman Emperor's claim to divinity appropriated these same qualities.

Prior to the first century BCE, the connection between military rulers and divinity was indirect.[10] The military reforms of Gaius Marius (156–86 BCE) changed the citizen-based military into a semi-professional military that was loyal to their commander.[11] The commander acted as a patron who provided for the needs of the clients or military personnel. These factors led to the rise of military leaders who portrayed themselves as having divine qualities. This eventually led to the rise of the emperor cult in which Caesar was worshipped as a divine being. In order for ruler cults to build upon and replace traditional god cults, there had to be some elements of continuity about how divinity was conceived.

Caesar was at the top of an expansive hierarchy. However, this pyramid was very accessible to the average citizen. This is why Paul, a Roman citizen, could make an appeal directly to Caesar (Acts 25:10–12). Greco-Roman religion as a whole was chaotic and required a single and simple organizing principle—that principle was the Roman imperial cult with Caesar at its head. Davies explains the situation in this way: "In some sense, the whole pressure of Roman religion was to impose the supremacy of the imperial cult as the principle of order in the seemingly endless profusion of cults, native and foreign, new and old, which characterized the ancient Near East and the other lands of the Empire."[12]

Roman religion required a recognizable and easily understood point of singularity in order maintain social order and unify the Empire. What is important for readers of today's world to understand is that Roman religion must be understood as an institution of objectivity and social cohesion, rather than contemporary (modern-day) subjective spirituality. It is too easy to transpose Judeo-Christian frameworks of omnipresence onto the religion of Roman emperor worship.

10. Pollini, *From Republic to Empire*, 72.
11. Ibid.
12. Davies, *Death, Burial, and Rebirth*, 140.

We are also not arguing that the cult of the emperor fulfilled the spiritual needs of the average individual of the Empire. What we are arguing is that the cult of the emperor provided a singularity around which political and social activities could culminate. With respect to the spiritual needs of the people, the mystery cults and philosophies played an important role.[13]

But did Caesar himself understand that he was communicating qualities of omnipresence to the masses of the Empire? We cannot speculate as to the psychological intentions of any ancient ruler. However, we can highlight historical evidence that points to intentionality.

The interaction between power and presence is reflexive. The reflexive act of communication through coinage is based on representational art of themselves through portraits and vignettes. One numismatic scholar explains that coins are "a means of active self-definition."[14] Those who produced coins with images of themselves or aspects of their rule communicated certain things to (or among) themselves. Some coins had inscriptions so cryptic that they would only have been understandable to a small circle of people in power.[15] For example, those who ruled provinces within the Roman Empire may have wanted to ingratiate themselves with Rome or Caesar by putting Caesar on their coins. Classics scholar Paul Zanker explains: "Even those in power are affected by the image they project. Their image of themselves and of the role they play in public life are strongly influenced by their own slogans, and of course also by their opponents' slogans."[16]

The reflexive nature of images on coinage added power and honor to those who had power and honor. Coins were a way for those in power to honor themselves or those above them in the patron–client hierarchy. In the case of the Roman Emperor, the coins portraying themselves communicated to themselves (reflexively) that they were divine and ensured that everyone in the entire Empire felt their personal presence.

If the cult of the Emperor was to have any unifying effect upon the entire Empire, it had to reach everyone with the message that Caesar could be worshipped right where they were. In the next section we will see that coins provided the perfect medium to communicate this message.

13. For an accessible introduction to Greco-Roman mystery cults and the spiritual appeal of philosophy in the first century see Tripolitis, *Religions of the Hellenistic-Roman Age*, 1–6.

14. Howgego, *Ancient History from Coins*, 44.

15. Zanker, *The Power of Images*, 14.

16. Ibid., 3.

Omnipresence Through Coinage

Thus far we have established two points in this chapter. First, the gods of the Roman pantheon were, collectively, understood to have qualities similar to omnipresence. Second, we can conclude that the Roman pantheon and mythology supported the Roman imperial cult. Next we will see that the Emperor sought to express this quality of divine-like omnipresence through coinage. This personal and divine presence that extended everywhere can be observed in the following three arenas: (1) in every building, (2) in every transaction, and (3) in every family.

First, we see that coins were only part of a larger strategy to make Caesar present in every building. Later writers such as Severian of Gabala (ca. 380–408 CE) thought that the emperor's image must be present in every place so that his direct authority would be upon every transaction in the courts, markets, meeting-houses, and theatres.[17] Coins are only one example of a large attempt to literally etch Caesar's image on public buildings. One scholar notes that "In addition to temples, statues of emperors might be located on baths, gymnasia, theatres, porticoes, and homes."[18]

Second, we see that coins provided a mechanism through which Caesar could be present in every financial transaction. One scholar argues that the presence of Caesar's image was so important to the subjects of the Empire that "a coin could not reliably circulate in the market-place without the emperor's head upon it."[19] This forms the foundation for understanding the role of coinage in Rome and local cities.

Third, we note that coins communicated the power and presence of Caesar in every city (the *polis*). Coins communicated that Caesar was above all cities. Despite the independence that some cities exercised, one might also argue that cities were *administrative* units rather than *autonomous* units.[20] There was a very wide disparity in the power that was exercised by city or providential officials and Caesar (or Pompey, Antony, or Octavian). One historian explains: "They [the Senatorial families] were often staggeringly rich, but had nonetheless no access to real power."[21] While local officials might have fought minor battles over local politics, the real power always lay with Caesar in Rome.

17. Severian, *de Mund. Creat. Or*. 6.5 (= PG 56.489). For an English quotation see Lendon, *Empire of Honour*, 19.

18. Carter, *The Roman Empire and the New Testament*, 77.

19. Lendon, *Empire of Honour*, 19.

20. Howgego, *Ancient History from Coins*, 43.

21. Zanker, *The Power of Images*, 15.

Our argument has focused largely on Caesar Augustus making himself omnipresent through coinage, but evidence also points to similar efforts by Tiberius, the Roman Emperor from 14–37 CE. According to the first-century historian Suetonius, if anyone brought a coin bearing the image of the emperor into a brothel, he was liable for the death penalty.[22] We can extrapolate from this record that the law was supposing that such an act against Caesar's image was equivalent to an act against Caesar himself. This is surprising because there is "no precedent for it with regard to images of gods on coins."[23] The law is based upon a direct relationship between Caesar and his image on the coin. Even if such a law was not in effect during the reign of later emperors, it points to a very quick development, even if it was short-lived.[24]

Implications for Studying the New Testament

How did the earliest Hellenistic-Gentile converts to Christianity understand their worship and belief in the risen Lord Jesus? These early Christian Gentiles would have included people such as the proconsul in Acts 13:12, the jailer in Acts 16:26–33, as well as Dionysius and Damaris in Acts 17:34. Initially, they must have appropriated some of their own cultural resources, culture, and background. This would have been particularly true for those Gentiles who were not associated with a synagogue and fall under the category of "God-fearer." This chapter provides some historical context for suggesting that the earliest Gentile converts to Christianity might have partially appropriated ideas such as the omnipresence of Caesar as they began to worship the risen Lord Jesus.

Just as Jewish believers in Jesus appropriated sources such as the Septuagint as an "initial conceptual resource" for early (proto) Christology and worship, so also Hellenistic-Gentile believers must have appropriated their own cultural resources to express their fledgling faith.[25] This young

22. Dio Cassius, *Roman History: Books 71–80*, LCL 177 (Cambridge, MA: Harvard University Press, 1927), 321. This law or laws like it may have led to the development of tokens for use in brothels called Spintria (often with pornographic imagery).

23. Williams, "Religion and Roman Coins," 158.

24. "It seems to belong to a new, and short-lived, category of offense particular to the emperor and his image" (ibid.).

25. For references to "initial conceptual resources" see Larry Hurtado's foreword in the new edition of Wilhelm Bousset, *Kyrios Christos: A History of the Belief in Christ from the Beginnings of Christianity to Irenaeus*, trans. John E. Steely (Waco: Baylor University Press, 2013).

Christian movement would have been composed of small congregations of Gentile Christians that reflected the "character of the various locales, and also the varying ethnic groups and social classes from which converts came."[26]

Whatever may be said of the "parting of the ways" between Judaism and Christianity at the end of the first century and beginning of the second, the timeframe we are interested in here consists more of *merging* than *diverging*.[27] Those Gentiles who converted to following Jesus likely formed some rudimentary gathering in homes that would have eventually included God-fearers, Jews, and others who were more informed about texts and traditions from the Hebrew scriptures and the prophets involved in following Jesus (e.g. Agabus in Acts 11:28; 21:10). These sources would have provided Hellenistic-Gentiles with better words and concepts with which they could progress in their understanding of Jesus and Christian monotheism. As Paul's letters were distributed and the close of the New Testament canon approached, these appropriations of emperor worship became less and less influential.

Summary

The fact that Roman Emperors such as Augustus used coins to communicate their divine qualities is rather indisputable. One scholar concludes, "The emperor was a figure, or an idea, capable of provoking a strong religious response in a variety of ways."[28] This chapter has sought to develop and focus this idea by using the theological concept of omnipresence as defined by first-century Roman mythological religion. Coins functioned as a political tool that created unity out of the vast number of people groups that composed the Roman Empire. Emperor worship was one of the primary tools used to achieve this unity, or at least the illusion of it. But emperor worship required that the object to be worshipped (Caesar) be available whenever and wherever the subjects of the Empire lived. If we stay within the framework of Roman religion we can see how the spread of Caesar's image was a communicative act based on his divine qualities and his omnipresence.

26. Larry Hurtado, "Interactive Diversity: A Proposed Model of Christian Origins," *Journal of Theological Studies* 64 (2013): 453.

27. For a critique of the "parting of the ways" language see Anders K. Petersen, "At the End of the Road—Reflections on a Popular Scholarly Metaphor," in Ådna, ed., *The Formation of the Early Church*, 45–72, esp. 55.

28. Williams, "Religion and Roman Coins," 157.

Chapter 15

POWER AND PRODUCTION

This chapter demonstrates that minting or producing coins was a public display of governmental power. This establishes important ideas for understanding the role of political autonomy, economic factors, and the acquisition of raw materials for production.

Introduction

The ability of a province or city to mint its own money communicated an element of independence and power. Some have concluded that "coinage is the symbol of national sovereignty."[1] The effort to mint coins reflects a broad pattern of localized minting that accelerated after Alexander the Great.[2] Coinage itself came into being "around the late 7th century BCE in western Asia Minor."[3] The "Lex Seyrig" dictates that "no state issued coin in its own name if it was ruled by another."[4] For example, when the Jews rebelled against Rome in 66–70 CE, they began to mint their own coins.[5] Speaking more broadly, *The Handbook of Economic Sociology* states that producing coins is a "public symbol of political sovereignty."[6] While this statement requires a bit of nuancing when applied to the first

1. Romanoff, *Jewish Symbols*, xi. Similarly, Reiser, "Numismatik und Neues Testament," 458. "Das Recht zur Münzprägung ist eines der wichtigsten Hoheitsrechte eines Staates oder Gemeinwesens."

2. Meadows, "The Spread of Coins in the Hellenistic World," 169.

3. Ibid., 170.

4. The Lex Seyrig (also called lex seyrigiana) is named after Henry Seyrig. (Andrew Meadows, "Money, Freedom, and Empire in the Hellenistic World," in *Money and Its Uses in the Ancient Greek World*, ed. A. Meadows and K. Shipton [Oxford: Oxford University Press, 2004], 53).

5. Kreitzer, *Striking New Images*, 19. Also see 1 Macc 15:6.

6. B. G. Carruthers, "The Sociology of Money and Credit," in *The Handbook of Economic Sociology*, ed. N. J. Smelser and R. Swedberg, 2nd ed. (Princeton: Princeton University Press, 2005), 355–78. Similarly, Christopher Howgego, *Ancient History from Coins*, AWW (London: Routledge, 1995), 41 and 62.

century, it is a helpful idea nonetheless. Just how much independence and power was communicated by minting coins likely varied from city to city. Economically speaking, cities benefited from the profits and prestige of minting coins.[7] After describing the relationship between power and the production of coinage, we will explore some details of minting, including melting metals and mining.

The primary sources bearing on the acquisition of raw materials for coinage from the first century are scant. The most important source that refers to mining operations is Pliny the Elder's (23–79 CE) volume entitled *Naturalis Historia* (*NH*). This volume gives an account of gold and silver mining throughout the Roman Empire. Another source is Strabo (64 BCE to ca. 21 CE) who wrote about mining operations near Pontus in Γεωγραφια (*Geographia*). Seemingly mundane topics such as mining operations continue to be of interest to Classicists and historians because of the interconnectedness and relevancy of economic data from all ages.

Autonomy and Production

To produce coinage was an opportunity to communicate an element of autonomy, identity, and power. This section proceeds by viewing the minters of coins as authors of cultural texts that communicate autonomy and power, as relative as that might be. They are not authors in the sense that they made decisions about imagery and inscriptions, but they provided an important element of authorship, namely craftsmanship and skill. Minting coins was a demonstration of technological skill for any culture. In fact, minting coins is one of the "oldest forms of mass production."[8] Quality coinage reflects the ability to produce thousands of identical objects, something with great beauty and artistry. There was a certain simplicity to the process, but this should not be overstated.[9] This section will first consider autonomy and the production of imperial coins and second we will consider the production of city-coinage.

Imperial Production

One important fact that connects power and production in the Roman Empire was the control of the mints. The two most common places that imperial coins were minted in the first century were Rome and Lugdulum

7. Hollander, "The Demand for Money in the Late Roman Republic," 127.

8. Philip Grierson, *Numismatics* (Oxford: Oxford University Press), 3. Similarly Meadows, "The Spread of Coins in the Hellenistic World," 173.

9. "Minting was a relatively simple activity, and could take place almost anywhere" (Ariel, "Identifying the Mints, Minters, and Meanings," 385).

(modern day Lyon, France). The minting of silver and gold coins in the name of the emperor was done by imperial mints, which were directly under his control.[10] Its imperial mint helped to make Lugdunum the most important city of the western Roman Empire. During the economic reforms of Nero, the mint for silver and gold was transferred from Lyon to Rome.[11] It was only when cities or states came under the favor of the emperor that they were allowed to produce their own silver and gold coins. As noted in previous chapters, the use of Latin inscriptions would indicate that coins had "semi-official status."[12]

Another matter to consider is the *theory* that coin designs required approval. We do not know much about the process of minting and governmental approval. Sometimes cities sought permission from the emperor and sometimes from other Roman officials.[13] Coins were produced through casting and molds. Casting was one of the first coin production techniques used in Rome. Casting involved pouring liquid metal into molds, both open and closed, creating an unstruck piece of metal called a flan.[14] The flan was put on an anvil and a hammer was used to force a negative into the soft metal. This process was often uneven and created coins with off-center images and rough edges.[15] But before this process could begin, it is likely that a large-scale three-dimensional model was created. This model would have been sent out for the approval of the magistrates in charge of the treasury. Although, one scholar laments that "this procedure cannot be confirmed in any detail," it would fit with the fact that official likenesses of the emperor always came from Rome.[16] If this is true, it would only serve to support the conclusion that production of coinage was inseparable from power in Rome.

10. Kreitzer, *Striking New Images*, 50.

11. Butcher and Ponting also note that it is possible that the mint was shifted back to Lyon at some point or that metal flans from Lyon were shipped to Rome ("The Denarius in the First Century," 560–61).

12. Kreitzer, *Striking New Images*, 50.

13. Mark A. Chancey, "City Coins and Roman Power in Palestine," in *Religion and Society in Roman Palestine: Old Questions, New Approaches*, ed. D. R. Edwards (New York: Routledge, 2004), 103.

14. Meshorer, *Jewish Coins of the Second Temple Period*, 61.

15. Reiser, "Numismatik und Neues Testament," 458.

16. Laura Breglia, *Roman Imperial Coins: Their Art and Technique* (New York: Praeger, 1968), 8.

Polis Production

When a city (*polis*) took the initiative to coin money on their authority, they produced what is called city-coinage. This coinage was characterized by (1) bronze or copper content, (2) small denominations, and (3) localized circulation.[17] The problem with this terminology is that the degree of autonomy that any city had under the Roman Empire was relative. One scholar suggests that some so called city-coinage is really pseudo-autonomous or quasi-autonomous.[18] In the Greek city of Mylasa (now Milas in modern Turkey), the imperial coins bear the name of a certain Grammateus during the time of Augustus, but after that they are without a magistrate's name.[19] The city did not have to have a rare Roman official designation of "free" in order to view their identity as unique among other cities.[20] This definition would apply to Judaea (Palestine) as well: all coins minted in this geographical area would be considered city-coinage.

When Rome allowed cities to mint their own coinage, such an act must be understood within a context of patronage and power. When Rome allowed cities such as Ephesus and Pergamum to produce their own "brief commemorative issues," this achieved two politically expedient purposes.[21] First, it allowed the individual cities to express their own prestige and identity. Second, this gift consolidated political power by demonstrating that the emperor was the ultimate gift giver over the cities of the Empire. Furthermore, some cities created syncretistic relationships between deities and political figures. In Ephesus, Agrippina the Younger was sometimes portrayed like Diana.

The argument that minting was a public display of power can be extended by pointing to the place where it was restricted—Judaea. Although Jews in Judaea were able to mint their own copper coins, they were not allowed to mint their own silver and gold coins.[22] The possibility of populist uprising in the likeness of the Maccabean revolt was likely the reason that minting of gold and silver was restricted. The ability to mint coinage was an action of autonomy and this autonomy had to be held in check.

17. Sigismund, "Small Change?," 317.

18. Ibid.

19. Barclay V. Head, *Catalogue of Greek Coins in the British Museum: Caria, Cos, Rhodes*, vol. 14 (London: British Museum, 1897), lxiv.

20. Sigismund, "Small Change?," 317.

21. Kreitzer, *Striking New Images*, 107.

22. Craig Keener, *The IVP Bible Background Commentary: New Testament* (Downers Grove: InterVarsity, 1993), 105.

Economics and Production

With great power comes great responsibility. Surprisingly, this maxim helps to explain very little of the motivation behind some of the production of first-century coinage. The modern concept of rulers acting out of a sense of responsibility for the masses was not a powerful force in the first century. Provincial rulers and emperors were motivated by a matrix of things, to be sure. Responsibility for those under their rule might have occasionally been at work. But this should be viewed as subordinate to economic motivations. Rulers often needed to produce coinage in small denominations in order to save money or to pursue actions through the state to further their own interests. The economic motivations for production of coinage were driven by the financial needs of those in power rather than the perceived needs of the populace.[23] When the silver content in denarii was reduced and then subsequently raised, it is possible that this was due to public pressure, but not out of charity for the populace.[24]

When coins of small denominations were produced it allowed the government to make more precise payments. If silver coinage was the only thing available for the government to pay for services and equipment, it would have been easy to overpay. Smaller coins made of bronze allowed rulers to save money by producing fractional currency and having it on hand.[25]

Fractional currency would have been used for two important reasons related to economics. First, it would have been used to pay soldiers. Herod the Great minted fractional money to pay his standing army.[26] Second, it would have been used to pay for the manual labor required by building projects. Both of these reasons reflect the needs and interests of the state rather than those of the populace. In fact, one of the operating principles for understanding coinage in the first century BCE is that "there is no firm evidence that contemporary rulers were disturbed by periodic storages of small change for transactions in local markets."[27]

23. "Since the state always had the power to raise taxes, create new sources of revenue, confiscate property, and, indeed, mint (or debase) its own coins, it did not necessarily have to keep precautionary money balances commensurate with its level of uncertainty" (Hollander, "The Demand for Money in the Late Roman Republic," 127).

24. For a discussion of the debasement of silver denarii in 64 CE see Butcher and Ponting, "The Denarius in the First Century," 561–62.

25. Donald T. Ariel, "The Coins of Herod the Great in the Context of the Augustan Empire," in *IJS Studies in Judaica: Conference Proceedings of the Institute of Jewish Studies*, ed. M. J. Geller et al., vol. 6 (Leiden: Brill, 2009), 113 and 116.

26. Ibid., 113.

27. Ibid., 116.

It can be demonstrated that, as a general rule, coins with less value were given less care in the manufacturing process. On the whole, it is important to qualify that "the quality of first-century coinage is uneven."[28] Despite this broad conclusion, several facts stand out. Quality control was imposed on the manufacturing of silver coins but was never applied to bronze coins.[29] Thus bronze coins are "often of poor quality."[30] Bronze or copper coins are associated with small denominations and the region of Judaea. Copper communicated a lack of purity and thus little attention was given to it.

Likewise, silver and gold communicated the presence of purity and more attention was given to them in the areas of aesthetics and quality. However, it is important to point out that in the context of the wider Roman Empire, bronze denominations such as the sestertius were large and well suited for long inscriptions, displays of the die-cutter's skill, and imperial propaganda.[31]

When coins appear that have low copper content, as opposed to lead, one cannot immediately conclude that lead was cheaper or in greater abundance. This is because copper was an important metal for making weapons and a country at war may have prioritized copper for war making rather than for coins.[32] The term *orichalcum* or *aurichalcum* (ὀρείχαλκος) refers to a bronze alloy or mixture of copper and tin that was specifically used to manufacture Roman imperial coins, including the sestertii and dupondii under Augustus.[33] The term *orichalcum* does not appear in the New Testament or the Septuagint.

Electrum is a naturally occurring alloy or mixture of gold and silver, with trace amounts of other metals such as copper. It was originally thought to be "an element in its own right."[34] Electrum can sometimes have a pale gold or amber color. When it appears naturally, the proportions of metallic content will vary. When used on coinage, the electrum may have been present as a foil that covered or coated slugs made of lead or other metals.

28. Crawford, *Roman Republican Coinage*, 2:572.

29. Ibid., 2:573.

30. Ibid.

31. "Because of its large size, the sestertius was a perfect vehicle for the die-cutter to express his skill and expertise" (Kreitzer, *Striking New Images*, 115).

32. Meshorer, *Jewish Coins of the Second Temple Period*, 60.

33. Aune, *Revelation 1–5*, 96. For comments on the *sestertii* and *dupondii* of Augustus see Crawford, *Roman Republican Coinage*, 2:573.

34. Hudson, "Coins of the Bible," 86.

Although the earliest coins of the sixth and seventh centuries BCE used electrum, it was not used for coins in circulation in Judaea in the first century.[35] Some suspect that electrum was not used for coinage because it was relatively difficult to control the consistency of the metallic content (silver and gold elements). This inconsistency in metallic content would have changed the value of each coin. However, some evidence has indicated that some content in early electrum coins was controlled.[36]

Electrum is only referenced indirectly in the New Testament but it should not be disregarded as irrelevant. The Greek word for electrum occurs in the LXX translation of Ezek 1:27 (ὡς ὄψιν ἠλέκτρου) and is translated by the NET as "amber."[37] The tenth-century CE Byzantine lexicon commonly referred to as *Suidas* also relates electrum (ἤλεκτρον) to the word (χαλκολίβανον) *chalkolibanon*—a word for polished or burnished metal.[38] What makes this somewhat confusing is that the Greek word χαλκολίβανον is translated in the ESV as "fine bronze" or "fine brass." Electrum (containing silver and gold) could be polished to look like bronze or brass and this accounts for the occasional confusion about terminology.

Raw Materials and Production

This section will demonstrate that it required significant power to acquire raw materials such as silver and gold for a series of coins. Acquiring the raw materials needed to produce coinage was not an easy task. A small issue or short run of a given series would only have produced "a few thousand" coins whereas a large run would have produced tens of thousands of coins.[39] There are three ways to access the raw materials needed to mint coins: (1) mining for precious metals, (2) melting existing coins, and (3) over-striking. In addition, we will consider (4) counter-marks as an example of power being exercised by the state.

35. John H. Kroll, "The Monetary Use of Weighed Bullion in Archaic Greece," in Harris, ed., *Monetary Systems of the Greeks and Romans*, 17; also see R. W. Wallace, "The Origin of Electrum Coinage," *AJA* 91 (1987): 385–90.

36. Howgego, *Ancient History from Coins*, 4.

37. Also Ezek 1:4 and 8:2.

38. *EDNT*, 3:453, s.v. χαλκολίβανον. For further discussion of electrum and philological notes on χαλκολίβανον see David E. Aune, *Revelation 1–5*, WBC 52a (Nashville: Thomas Nelson, 1998), 96.

39. Kreitzer, *Striking New Images*, 102.

Mining for Raw Materials

The process of mining provided raw materials such as lead, copper, tin, iron, silver, and gold. These materials would then have to be purified in a process called smelting. Smelting refined the metal so that it could be poured into molds and casts. In general, it is difficult to reconstruct the details of the Roman system of mining for metals. This is because of the paucity of extant documents and archeological evidence.[40] Mining is often discussed in the context of quarries because the Romans did not distinguish between the two. This is evident in the fact that the term *metallum* (μέταλλον) applied to quarries and mines.[41]

What is clear is that the Roman system of mining required a vast and complex infrastructure. This included soldiers to guard valuables, slaves and possibly soldiers to provide labor, and even aqueducts to carry the vast amounts of water needed for the process of cleaning and clearing rock. In addition, the laborers had to be provided with pay, food, and tools.[42]

There were two types of mining, opencast mining and underground mining.[43] Open-cast mining is similar to surface mining and utilizes a giant open pit to excavate material. Underground mining requires tunnels dug into the side of mountains or hills to access materials deep underground.

Mining had been decentralized under the Republic but had become centralized under the Empire.[44] There are inscriptions that indicate that copper and silver mines were overseen by the Roman state in South-Western Spain.[45] Locally, the mines were controlled by a freedman or equestrian procurator.[46] Just how much power the mining procurator held seems to have depended upon their social status or political influence. As noted above, mining and quarries were viewed together. Metals were required for armor and weapons of war and marble was required for building.

40. Alfred M. Hirt, *Imperial Mines and Quarries in the Roman World: Organizational Aspects 27 BC–AD 235*, OCM (Oxford: Oxford University Press, 2010), 8.

41. Ibid., 6.

42. For organizational implications of mining see ibid., 45.

43. See Meshorer, *Jewish Coins of the Second Temple Period*, 61 for pictures of various molds.

44. Sutherland and Carson, eds., *The Roman Imperial Coinage*, 2.

45. For details on underground mining in South-Western Spain see Hirt, *Imperial Mines and Quarries*, 41.

46. Ibid., 2.

When metals were extracted from the earth, they were often smelted and cast into ingots or bars. This process of smelting may have taken place at a location removed from the immediate location of the mining operation. Cast molds for gold ingots have been found with the imperial title: C(ai) Caesaris Aug(usti) Germanici Imp(eratoris) ex Noric(is).[47] However, the geographical distance between the mining operation and the smelter creates uncertainties about original ownership of the mine and its legal context.

What is important to note is that the mining operations were ultimately owned and controlled by the Roman state through imperial administrators.[48] It is possible that some operations were owned by private individuals or municipalities but this is not a widely held view. There may also have been a system in place that allowed the Roman state to lease mines to interested parties.

Melting for Raw Materials

Melting coins was another way of acquiring previous raw materials. This was not necessarily a demonstration of prejudice toward images on certain coins or a previous ruler. Sometimes melting existing coins to create new ones was simply an expression of current economic realities. If existing coinage was of a high silver content, it could be melted and combined with alloys to provide a cheap source of raw materials. The opposite is also true. Sometimes coins survived the melting pot not because of the images or inscriptions on them, but because their silver content was known to be so low that it was not worth melting them.[49] For example, the Mark Antony legionary series survived for several hundred years, well into the era of the New Testament, due to its inferior quality.[50] In addition to melting coins, other items such as cultic objects, building ornaments, bullion, and jewelry could be melted if they were made of valuable metals.

Over-striking for Raw Materials

When raw materials for new coins could not be acquired, coins of all shapes and sizes would be over-struck. To be clear, *overstriking* is distinct from a *doublestrike* which simply means that there was an error in the

47. Ibid., 103.

48. Heather Ann Pundt, *Mining Culture in Roman Dacia: Empire, Community, and Identity at the Gold Mines of Alburnus Maior ca. 107–270 C.E.* (MA diss., Portland State University, 2012), 37.

49. "In short, the Mark Antony legionary series survived partly due to their inferior quality as silver-based coins" (Kreitzer, *Striking New Images*, 36).

50. Ibid.

original production process. Overstriking means that an old coin was used as raw material to make a new coin. These could include foreign coins.[51] This was an alternative to melting down coins and bullion to make new blanks.[52]

On silver coins especially, the former images are often visible because the minters did not want to remove any of the precious metal from the weight of the coin.[53] Copper coins were less valuable and less dependent upon weight. This meant that the copper could be filed down and the former image removed before it was re-struck.[54] As a result, it is much harder to identify the original coin used for copper overstrikes. Thicker coins were ideal for re-striking because they would not easily break. Thinner coins were more fragile in nature and more susceptible to breaking apart or cracking because of an attempted over-strike. One of the most important periods of over-striking was the Bar-Kochba War (132–135 CE).

Lead coins may have been used by moneyers for trial production.[55] Lead coins are rare and are often poorly preserved because of how easily lead is corroded by organic acids that are found naturally in soil.[56] Corrosion on ancient lead coins usually produces a white color. Lead coins may have the following traits that are indicative of trial coins rather than actual coins: (1) only struck on one side, (2) evidence of re-striking, and (3) lack of a precise design.[57]

Countermarks are different from over-striking in that additional punch marks were added to coins without destroying the whole. Countermarks were used for the purposes of legitimizing coinage in a certain locale or possibly for showing deference to a particular ruler. Countermarks appear on a wide range of Roman imperial and provincial coins. Countermarks

51. Howgego, *Ancient History from Coins*, 24.

52. Crawford, *Roman Republican Coinage*, 2:573.

53. Meshorer, *Jewish Coins of the Second Temple Period*, 97.

54. "That the bronze coins should weigh a specific amount was not as important and therefore the original designs would be filed off before the coins were re-struck with the new ones" (ibid., 97).

55. Discoveries of lead coins in new hoards since 1980 have led to an increased knowledge among collectors and scholars (Oliver D. Hoover, "A New Hellenistic Lead Issue from the Southern Levant," *INR* 4 [2009]: 51).

56. For a discussion of the lead coins used in the Second Temple period by King Janneus see: J. A. Goldstein, "The Hasmonean Revolt and the Hasmonean Dynasty," in *The Cambridge History of Judaism: The Hellenistic Age, Vol. 2*, ed. W. D. Davies and L. Finkelstein (Cambridge: Cambridge University Press, 1989), 335–38.

57. Meshorer, *Jewish Coins of the Second Temple Period*, 56.

are present on coinage from the fourth century BCE. The countermarks used by Rome may have been the origin for the famous "mark of the beast" referenced twice in Revelation.[58]

Implications for Studying the New Testament

The connection between coin production and the study of the New Testament is not especially strong. However, there is one noteworthy implication of the broad thesis that the ability to mint money communicated power and autonomy. The important point to consider is that the first people to receive coinage from imperial, provincial, and city-based minting were often soldiers receiving their government salary.[59] Coinage itself was only issued by Rome to enable it to make payments such as the ones it made to soldiers.[60] During the civil wars of 68–69 CE, Galba, Otho, and Vitellius all issued large amounts of denarii.[61]

These facts are important for New Testament studies because Roman soldiers played an important part in spreading the gospel. Roman army personnel play a role in Luke–Acts, as well as Matthew and Mark. In Matt 8:5–13 and Luke 7:1–10, the faith of a centurion is lauded by Jesus over and against the faith of Israel. In contrast, the centurion in Mark 15:37 who states, "Truly this was a son of god," may have been mocking Jesus while ironically speaking the truth. In Luke 23:47, a centurion proclaims that "certainly this man was innocent!" The narrative of Cornelius in Acts 10:1–48 is connected to Peter's understanding of the gospel itself. Overall, the army is presented rather positively in the New Testament. In his recent monograph, Kyrychenko argues that the centurion was a well-known representative of imperial power and the conversion of a centurion in Luke–Acts anticipates the mission to the Gentile world.[62]

58. May, "The Empire Strikes Back," 84.

59. For comments on the logistical problems of paying soldiers for Alexander the Great see Meadows, "The Spread of Coins in the Hellenistic World," 171.

60. For a discussion on the financial reasons for Rome's coinage see Meadows, "The Spread of Coins in the Hellenistic World," 180.

61. Butcher and Ponting, "The Denarius in the First Century," 562.

62. Alexander Kyrychenko, *The Roman Army and the Expansion of the Gospel: The Role of the Centurion in Luke–Acts*, BZNW 203 (Berlin: de Gruyter, 2014), passim.

Summary

This chapter has sought to explore the sources of raw materials and production that constitute an important element in the world behind the coin. The details of political autonomy, economics, and raw materials all point to the fact that producing coins was a display of governmental power. This power was exercised at various levels, sometimes from Rome and sometimes locally. The connection between power and production is so strong that it is almost axiomatic that money was generally never minted for the benefit of the populace or the marketplace but for the benefit of rulers.

Section IV

Conclusion

Chapter 16

CONCLUSION

In the first century, coins were the most powerful tool of communication available because any message communicated would have a wide audience that would stretch across all socio-economic and cultural groups. The academic discipline of numismatics will provide those interested in New Testament exegesis and early Christian origins a rich source of material for further research.

This volume has sought to make such data more readily available by providing an accessible gateway into the niche discipline of numismatics. The central idea supporting the volume is that coins are cultural texts. As cultural texts, coins provide worlds of meaning that must be interpreted. Coins should be understood as media through which someone was communicating something to someone else.

Chapter 1 argued that coins are cultural texts that require a robust and careful hermeneutic. This chapter established a methodology for the whole project by drawing from the domain of speech-act theory. This theory of communication seeks to identify how words are projected by a speaker to an audience who receives and interprets the communication. Speech-act theory has three loci: (1) the speaker, (2) the words being communicated, (3) and the audience. We noted that this theory for speech may also be applied to writing. We then took the step of applying speech-act theory to the communication projected by coinage, consisting of the combination of image and inscription.

The chapters in Section I argued that the world *in front* of the coin, specifically the Roman Empire, was the audience that regularly read coins as cultural texts and tools of mass communication. The chapters in Section II argued that the world *of* the coin is a cultural text primarily characterized by propaganda. The chapters in Section III argued that the world *behind* the coin or the author(s) of coins used them primarily to communicate something about their power.

The entire book is focused on the student of the New Testament who wants to draw conclusions from numismatic research in order to support a particular reading or exegetical conclusion. The central point offered here is that when making exegetical conclusions based on numismatic evidence, one must exercise great caution.

The dangers of parallels between the biblical text and historical data are well known to some but the matter is serious enough to require some repetition.[1] In the academy, the greatest temptation is to give too much weight to historical evidence. Many an exegete has fallen into the trap of using speculative historical data to arrive at conclusions about portions of the biblical text that are nonsensical when read in light of the whole text. In other words, exercise caution so that numismatic evidence is not used to force readings and twist the meaning of ancient texts. In the pulpit, the greatest temptation is to give too little weight to historical evidence that will explain or enlighten how a text in the New Testament was understood by the original audience of the first century.

While recognizing the need for caution when drawing conclusions based on shaky evidence, each chapter in the three core sections sought to bridge the gap between numismatics and New Testament studies with a section on implications. Here is a list of some of the more salient connections:

1. In the chapter on coins as cultural texts (Chapter 1), we observed how scholars refer to coins as texts. This chapter sought to sharpen this language by defining coins as cultural texts.
2. In the chapter on coins as speech-acts (Chapter 2), we continued to define coins as cultural texts within the framework of speech-act theory. Coins are cultural texts that project worlds and works of meaning that require interpretation.
3. In the chapter on coins as currency (Chapter 3), we introduced some of the basic facts about the complexities of coinage in the first century.
4. In the chapter on coins as context (Chapter 4), we demonstrated that coins are part of the literary and historical context of the New Testament. Those who pursue exegetical studies will need to consider coins as woven into the fabric of the New Testament and particularly the four gospels.

1. Neil Elliott and Mark Reasoner, eds., *Documents and Images for the Study of Paul* (Minneapolis: Fortress, 2011), 1–2.

5. In the chapter on payment and trust (Chapter 5), we observed how coinage functioned within a web of community relationships. These relationships were particularly important for the earliest Christians.
6. In the chapter on payment and fear (Chapter 6), we saw that some first-century Christians feared their present economic system and they understood it to be a tool of Satan.
7. In the chapter on payment and taxes (Chapter 7), we examined how the payment of taxes was a communicative act with layers of potential religious and social implications for the taxpayers, depending on the context.
8. In the chapter on propaganda and inscriptions (Chapter 8), we explored the question as to whether the use of "sacred names" (*nomina sacra*) by Christian scribes and manuscript copyists are imitations of the divine abbreviations found on coins.
9. In the chapter on propaganda and dating (Chapter 9), we saw that the data from coinage confirms that a majority of people in the first century were familiar with contemporaneously inhabiting various frameworks of time.
10. In the chapter on propaganda and Roman images (Chapter 10), we explored how coins were used to support participation in the pyramid of patron–client relationships that extended from Caesar all the way down to the poor.
11. In the chapter on propaganda and Jewish images (Chapter 11), the data from coins suggested that some rulers from Judaea understood their role to be messianic. This is significant for understanding Jesus' own claims as well as his self-understanding.
12. In the chapter on propaganda and metallurgy (Chapter 12), we saw that the language of purity communicated by the hierarchy of metals was used for early Christian worship of the risen Lord Jesus.
13. In the chapter on power and identity (Chapter 13), we observed that coins were an important tool used by those in power to shape public identities. Likewise, economic language was used amongst early Christians to describe the spiritual value of the gift of the gospel.
14. In the chapter on power and presence (Chapter 14), we suggested that the use of coins to spread the presence of the emperor may have been appropriated by the earliest Gentile converts to Christianity.
15. In the chapter on power and production (Chapter 15), we saw that the Roman military would have been an important force for spreading imperial coinage as well as the gospel.

As we near our conclusion, we observe that change comes in paradigms. One scholar suggests: "It is probably only a matter of time before our paradigm for understanding Second Temple Judaism shifts again."[2] This is particularly true when the evidence lies only in or on the coin itself.[3] In other words, one should seek out corroborating evidence from other historical information or sources in order to strengthen one's scholarship. Historical inquiry for New Testament studies will be based on *probability*. With respect to numismatics evidence: "One must be careful neither to overestimate nor to underestimate the evidence."[4]

We end with the warning that "coins and inscriptions are no substitute" for responsible, careful, and accurate New Testament exegesis.[5] The exegete must be aware of the danger posed by placing too much weight on numismatics and other ancillary historical disciplines. The careful exegete of coins and the New Testament must allow both to speak on their own terms before integrating the data—a difficult task indeed.

2. Kevin Vanhoozer, *Jesus, Paul, and the People of God: A Theological Dialogue with N. T. Wright*, ed. N. Perrin and R. B. Hays (Downers Grove: InterVarsity, 2011), 240.

3. Such is the case with "countermarks" or coins that were re-stamped for ideological purposes. However, no external ancient documents discuss their role or function (May, "The Empire Strikes Back," 87).

4. Baruch Kanael, "Ancient Jewish Coins and Their Historical Importance," *BA* (1963): 38.

5. D. A. Carson, *New Testament Commentary Survey*, 7th ed. (Grand Rapids: Baker Academic, 2013), 76.

Appendix

Events Related to First-Century Numismatics

(Most dates are approximate)

600 BCE	Money introduced in Greece and surrounding Mediterranean
500 BCE	Established coinage in Greece, Italy, and Hellenized areas of Persian Empire
300 BCE	Silver coins are introduced into the coinage system in Rome
211 BCE	Introduction of denarius as coinage
145 BCE	Value of a denarius is changed from ten to sixteen assarion (asses)
139 BCE	Coins are increasingly political due to pressure from the introduction of secret ballot voting in Roman assemblies
46 BCE	Standard gold coins are introduced into the Roman economy
44 BCE	First living person (Caesar) appears on Roman coinage
40 BCE	Mint at Rome is shut down due to politics and civil war
25 BCE	Mint at Rome is reopened
11 BCE	Names of private moneyers (minters) disappear from coins
54 CE	Names of non-imperial individuals disappear from coins under reign of Emperor Claudius
64 CE	Nero reconstructs the coinage system of the Empire following the great fire of Rome; coins increased in artistic excellence
70 CE	A special tax is introduced by Rome upon the Jewish people in Judaea called the *Fiscus Judaicus*

Bibliography

Achtemeier, Paul J. *1 Peter: A Commentary on First Peter*. Hermeneia. Minneapolis: Fortress, 1996.

Ameling, W. "Die Jüdische Diaspora Kleinasiens und der 'Epigraphic Habit'." Pages 253–82 in *Jewish Identity in the Greco-Roman World*. Edited by J. Frey et al. AJEC 71. Leiden: Brill, 2007.

Ariel, Donald T. "The Coins of Herod the Great in the Context of the Augustan Empire." Pages 113–26 in *IJS Studies in Judaica: Conference Proceedings of the Institute of Jewish Studies*, Vol. 6. Edited by M. J. Geller et al. Leiden: Brill, 2009.

———. "Identifying the Mints, Minters and Meanings of the First Jewish Revolt Coins." Pages 373–97 in *The Jewish Revolt Against Rome: Interdisciplinary Perspectives*. Edited by Mladen Popović. Leiden: Brill, 2012.

Ariel, Donald T., and Jean-Philippe Fontanille. *The Coins of Herod: A Modern Analysis and Die Classification*. AJC 79. Leiden: Brill, 2012.

Aune, David E. *Revelation 1–5*. WBC 52a. Nashville: Thomas Nelson, 1998.

Austin, J. L. *How to Do Things With Words*. 2nd ed. Oxford: Oxford University Press, 1962.

The Babylonian Talmud, Volumes 1–10: Original Text, Edited, Corrected, Formulated, and Translated into English. Translated by Michael L. Rodkinson. Boston: The Talmud Society, 1918.

Bailey, Daniel P. "Arch of Titus." *EDEJ* 375–76.

Barrett, A. A. "The Invalidation of Currency in the Roman Empire: The Claudian Demonetization of Caligula's Aes." Pages 83–93 in *Roman Coins and Public Life Under the Empire: E. Togo Salmon Papers II*. Edited by G. Paul and M. Ierardi. Ann Arbor: University of Michigan Press, 1999.

Bartholomew, Craig G. *Where Mortals Dwell: A Christian View of Place for Today*. Grand Rapids: Baker, 2011.

Barton, Stephen C. "Money Matters: Economic Relations and the Transformation of Value in Early Christianity." Pages 37–59 in *Engaging Economics: New Testament Scenarios and Early Christian Reception*. Edited by B. Longenecker and K. D. Liebengood. Grand Rapids: Eerdmans, 2009.

Betlyon, John Wilson. "Numismatics and Archaeology." *BA* (1985): 162–65.

Billings, J. Todd. *The Word of God for the People of God: An Entryway to the Theological Interpretation of Scripture*. Grand Rapids: Eerdmans, 2010.

Bird, Michael F. *Are You the One Who Is to Come? The Historical Jesus and the Messianic Question*. Grand Rapids: Baker, 2009.

Blackburn, W. Ross. *The God Who Makes Himself Known: The Missionary Heart of the Book of Exodus*. NSBT 28. Downers Grove: InterVarsity, 2012.

Boatwright, Mary T. *Hadrian and the Cities of the Roman Empire*. Princeton: Princeton University Press, 2003.

Bock, Darrell L. *Luke*. IVPNTC. Downers Grove: InterVarsity, 1994.

———. *Luke 9:51—24:53*. 2 vols. BECNT. Grand Rapids: Baker, 1996.

Bockmuehl, Markus. *Seeing the Word: Refocusing New Testament Study*. STI. Grand Rapids: Baker, 2006.

Botha, Pieter J. J. *Orality and Literacy in Early Christianity*. BPC 5. Eugene: Cascade, 2010.

Bousset, Wilhelm. *Kyrios Christos: A History of the Belief in Christ from the Beginnings of Christianity to Irenaeus*. Translated by John E. Steely. Baylor University Press, 2013.

Brakke, D., M. L. Satlow, and S. Weitzman, eds. *Religion and the Self in Antiquity*. Bloomington: Indiana University Press, 2005.

Breglia, Laura. *Roman Imperial Coins: Their Art and Technique*. New York: Frederick E. Praeger, 1968.

Brenk, Frederick E. "Hierosolyma: The Greek Name of Jerusalem." *Glotta* 87 (2011): 1–22.

Brennan, Peter, Michael Turner, and Nicholas L. Wright. *Faces of Power: Imperial Portraiture on Roman Coins*. Sydney: The University of Sydney/Nicholson Museum, 2007.

Brighton, Mark A. "The Sicarii in Acts: A New Perspective." *JETS* 54 (2011): 547–58.

———. *The Sicarii in Josephus's Judean War: Rhetorical Analysis and Historical Observations*. EJL 27. Atlanta: Society of Biblical Literature, 2009.

Briones, David E. *Paul's Financial Policy: A Socio-Theological Approach*. LNTS 494. London: T&T Clark, 2013.

Burnett, Andrew. *Coins*. Interpreting the Past. Berkeley: University of California Press, 1991.

Butcher, Kevin, and M. Ponting. "The Denarius in the First Century." Pages 557–68 in *Proceedings of the XIV International Numismatic Congress: Glasgow 2009*. Edited by N. Holmes. Glasgow, 2011.

Caccamo Caltabiano, Maria, L. Campagna, and A. Pinzone, eds. *Nuove prospsettive della ricerca sulla Sicilia del III sec. a.C.: archeologia, numismatica, storia*. Messina: Dipartimento di Scienze dell'Antichità dell'Università degli Studi di Messina, 2004.

Carruthers, B. G. "The Sociology of Money and Credit." Pages 355–78 in *The Handbook of Economic Sociology*. Edited by N. J. Smelser and R. Swedberg. 2nd ed. Princeton: Princeton University Press, 2005.

Carson, D. A. *The Gospel According to John*. PNTC. Grand Rapids: InterVarsity, 1991.

———. *New Testament Commentary Survey*. 7th ed. Grand Rapids: Baker Academic, 2013.

Carter, E. J. "Toll and Tribute: A Political Reading of Matthew 17:24–27." *JSNT* 25 (2003): 413–31.

Carter, Warren. *The Roman Empire and the New Testament: An Essential Guide*. Nashville: Abingdon, 2006.

Cassius, Dio. *Roman History: Books 71–80*. LCL 177. Cambridge, MA: Harvard University Press, 1927).

Chancey, Mark A. "City Coins and Roman Power in Palestine." Pages 103–12 in *Religion and Society in Roman Palestine: Old Questions, New Approaches*. Edited by D. R. Edwards. London: Routledge, 2004.

———. "The Epigraphic Habit of Hellenistic and Roman Galilee." Pages 83–94 in *Religion, Ethnicity, and Identity in Ancient Galilee: A Region in Transition*. Edited by J. Zangenberg, H. W. Attridge and D. B. Martin. WUNT 210. Tübingen: Mohr Siebeck, 2007.

———. *Greco-Roman Culture and the Galilee of Jesus*. SNTSMS 134. Cambridge: Cambridge University Press, 2005.

Charlesworth, James H. *The Old Testament Pseudepigrapha*. 2 vols. New York: Yale University Press, 1983–85.

Chen, Diane G. *God as Father in Luke–Acts*. SBL 92. New York: Lang, 2006.

Christ, Karl. *Antike Numismatik: Einführung und Bibliographie*. Darmstadt: Wissenschaftliche Buchgesellschaft, 1972.

Cohen, Edward E. "Elasticity of the Money Supply at Athens." Pages 66–83 in *Monetary Systems of the Greeks and Romans*. Edited by W. V. Harris. Oxford: Oxford University Press, 2008.

Cohick, Lynn. "Philippians and Empire: Paul's Engagement with Imperialism and the Imperial Cult." Pages 165–82 in *Jesus Is Lord, Caesar Is Not: Evaluating Empire in New Testament Studies*. Edited by S. McKnight and J. B. Modica. Downers Grove: InterVarsity, 2013.

Collins, J. J. *The Apocalyptic Imagination: An Introduction to Jewish Apocalyptic Literature*. 2nd ed. Grand Rapids: Eerdmans, 1998.

———. *Daniel: A Commentary on the Book of Daniel*. Hermeneia. Minneapolis: Augsburg, 1993.

Cooley, Alison E. *The Cambridge Manual of Latin Epigraphy*. Cambridge: Cambridge University Press, 2012.

———. *Res Gestae Divi Augusti: Texts, Translation, and Commentary*. Cambridge: Cambridge University Press, 2009.

Corbier, Mireille. "Writing in Roman Public Space." Pages 13–48 in *Written Space in the Latin West: 200 BC to AD 300*. Edited by G. Sears, P. Keegan, R. Laurence. London: Bloomsbury, 2013.

Corley, Bruce, Steve Lemke, and Grant Lovejoy. *Biblical Hermeneutics: A Comprehensive Introduction to Interpreting Scripture*. 2nd ed. Nashville: B&H, 2002.

Crawford, Michael H. *Roman Republican Coinage II*. 2 vols. Cambridge: Cambridge University Press, 1974.

Dahmen, Karsten. *The Legend of Alexander the Great on Greek and Roman Coins*. New York: Routledge, 2007.

Davies, Jon. *Death, Burial, and Rebirth in the Religions of Antiquity*. RFCC. London: Routledge, 2003.

DeBloois, Nanci. "Coins in the New Testament." Pages 239–51 in *Masada and the World of the New Testament*. Edited by John F. Hall and John W. Welch. Provo, UT: BYU Studies, 1997.

Deissmann, Adolf, and Lionel Richard Mortimer Strachan. *Light from the Ancient East the New Testament Illustrated by Recently Discovered Texts of the Graeco-Roman World*. London: Hodder & Stoughton, 1910.

deSilva, David A. *Honor, Patronage, Kinship, and Purity: Unlocking New Testament Culture*. Downers Grove: InterVarsity, 2000.

Deutsch, Robert. "Coinage of the First Jewish Revolt Against Rome: Iconography, Minting Authority, Metallurgy." Pages 361–71 in *The Jewish Revolt against Rome: Interdisciplinary Perspectives*. Edited by Mladen Popović. Leiden: Brill, 2012.

Diehl, Judith. "Anti-Imperial Rhetoric in the New Testament." Pages 38–81 in *Jesus Is Lord, Caesar Is Not: Evaluating Empire in New Testament Studies*. Edited by S. McKnight and J. B. Modica. Downers Grove: InterVarsity, 2013.

Duncan-Jones, Richard. *Money and Government in the Roman Empire*. Cambridge: Cambridge University Press, 1994.

———. *Structure and Scale in the Roman Economy*. Cambridge: Cambridge University Press, 1990.

Dunn, J. D. G. "Preface." Pages vii–x in *Jews and Christians: The Parting of the Ways: A.D. 70 to 135*. Edited by J. D. G. Dunn. WUNT 66. Grand Rapids: Eerdmans, 1999.

Dutch, Robert S. *The Educated Elite in 1 Corinthians: Education and Community Conflict in Graeco-Roman Context*. JSNTSup 271. London: T&T Clark, 2005.

Ebbott, Mary. *Imagining Illegitimacy in Classical Greek Literature*. Lanham: Lexington Books, 2003.

Edwards, James R. "A Nomen Sacrum in the Sardis Synagogue." *JBL* 128 (2009): 813–21.

Ehrensperger, Kathy. "Speaking Greek Under Rome: Paul, the Power of Language and the Language of Power." *Neot* 46 (2012): 9–28.

Elkins, Nathan T. "Coins, Context, and an Iconographic Approach for the 21st Century." Pages 25–46 in *Coins in Context I: New Perspectives for the Interpretation of Coin Finds*. Edited by H. V. Kaenel and F. Kemmers. SFMA 23. Mainz: Philipp Von Zabern, 2009.

———. "The Trade in Fresh Supplies of Ancient Coins: Scale, Organization, and Politics." Pages 91–107 in *All the King's Horses: Essays on the Impact of Looting and the Illicit Antiquities Trade on Our Knowledge of the Past*. Edited by P. K. Lazrus and A. W. Barker. Washington, DC: Society for American Archaeology Press, 2012.

Elliott, Matthew A. *Faithful Feelings: Rethinking Emotion in the New Testament*. Grand Rapids: Kregel, 2006.

Elliott, Neil, and Mark Reasoner, eds. *Documents and Images for the Study of Paul*. Minneapolis: Fortress Press, 2011.

Esler, Philip F. "God's Honour and Rome's Triumph: Responses to the Fall of Jerusalem in 70 CE in Three Jewish Apocalypses." Pages 233–47 in *Modelling Early Christianity: Social-Scientific Studies of the New Testament in Its Context*. Edited by P. E. Esler. London: Routledge, 1995.

———. "Rome in Apocalyptic and Rabbinic Literature." Pages 9–33 in *The Gospel of Matthew in Its Roman Context*. London: T&T Clark, 2005.

Evans, Craig A. *Luke*. UBCS. Grand Rapids: Baker, 1990.

Evans, Jane DeRose. *The Art of Persuasion: Political Propaganda from Aeneas to Brutus*. Ann Arbor: University of Michigan Press, 1992.

Feeney, Denis. *Caesar's Calendar: Ancient Time and the Beginnings of History*. SCL 65. Berkeley: University of California Press, 2007.

Fejfer, Jane. *Roman Portraits in Context*. Berlin: de Gruyter, 2008.

Fernández, Miguel P. *An Introductory Grammar of Rabbinic Hebrew*. Translated by J. Elwolde. Leiden: Brill, 1997.

Figueira, Thomas. "Review of Coins, Bodies, Games, and Gold." *AJP* 121 (2000): 642–46.

Foster, Paul. "Vespasian, Nerva, Jesus, and the *Fiscus Judaicus*." Pages 303–20, 454–58 in *Israel's God and Rebecca's Children: Christology and Community in Early Judaism and Christianity*. Edited by D. B. Capes, A. D. DeConick. H. K. Bond, and T. A. Miller. Waco: Baylor, 2007.

Foxhall, Lin. *Olive Cultivation in Ancient Greece: Seeking the Ancient Economy*. Oxford: Oxford University Press, 2007.

Friesen, Steven J. *Imperial Cults and the Apocalypse of John: Reading Revelation in the Ruins*. Oxford: Oxford University Press, 2001.

Garland, David. *1 Corinthians*. BECNT. Grand Rapids: Baker, 2003.

Geis, Michael L. *Speech Acts and Conversational Interaction*. Cambridge: Cambridge University Press, 1995.

Gill, David W. J. "Acts and Roman Religion." Pages 79–104 in *The Book of Acts in Its Graeco-Roman Setting*. Edited by D. W. J. Gill and C. Gempf. Grand Rapids: Eerdmans, 1994.

Ginsburg, Judith. *Representing Agrippina: Constructions of Female Power in the Early Roman Empire*. Oxford: Oxford University Press, 2005.

Gitler, Haim. "Coins." *EDEJ* 479–82.

Gleaves, G. Scott. *Did Jesus Speak Greek? The Emerging Evidence of Greek Dominance in the First-Century Palestine*. Eugene, OR: Wipf & Stock, 2015.

Goldstein, J. A. "The Hasmonean Revolt and the Hasmonean Dynasty." Pages 292–351 in *The Cambridge History of Judaism: The Hellenistic Age*. Edited by W. D. Davies and L. Finkelstein. Cambridge: Cambridge University Press, 1989.

Goodenough, Erwin R. *Jewish Symbols in the Greco-Roman Period: Abridged Edition*. Translated by J. Neusner. Princeton: Princeton University Press, 1988.

Goodman, Martin. "Coinage and Identity: The Jewish Evidence." Pages 163–66 in *Coinage and Identity in the Roman Provinces*. Edited by C. Howgego, V. Heuchert, and A. Burnett. Oxford: Oxford University Press, 2005.

Goodman, Nelson. *Languages of Art: An Approach to a Theory of Symbols*. Indianapolis: Hackett, 1976.

Green, J. B., and L. M. McDonald, eds. *The World of the New Testament: Cultural, Social, and Historical Contexts*. Grand Rapids: Baker, 2013.

Grierson, Philip. *Numismatics*. Oxford: Oxford University Press, 1975.

Grünewald, Thomas. *Bandits in the Roman Empire: Myth and Reality*. London: Routledge, 1999.

Hachlili, Rachel. *Jewish Funerary Customs, Practices and Rites in the Second Temple Period*. JSJSup 94. Leiden: Brill, 2005.

Hallo, William W., and K. Lawson Younger. *The Context of Scripture*. 3 vols. Leiden: Brill, 1997.

Hannah, Robert. *Greek and Roman Calendars: Constructions of Time in the Classical World*. London: Duckworth, 2005.

Harl, Kenneth W. *Coinage in the Roman Economy, 300 B.C. to A.D. 700*. Ancient Society and History. Baltimore: The Johns Hopkins University Press, 1996.

Harris. William V. *Ancient Literacy*. Cambridge, MA: Harvard University Press, 1989.

———, ed. *The Monetary Systems of the Greeks and Romans*. Oxford: Oxford University Press, 2008.

Hart, H. St J. "The Coin of 'Render unto Caesar.'" Pages 249–64 in *Jesus and the Politics of His Day*. Cambridge: Cambridge University Press, 1984.

Head, Barclay V. *Catalogue of Greek Coins in the British Museum: Attica, Megaris, Aegina*. London: British Museum, 1888.

———. *Catalogue of Greek Coins in the British Museum: Caria, Cos, Rhodes*. London: British Museum, 1897.

Heemstra, Marius. *Fiscus Judaicus and the Parting of the Ways*. WUNT 277. Tübingen: Mohr Siebeck, 2010.

Hekster, Olivier. "Coins and Messages: Audience Targeting on Coins of Different Denominations?" Pages 20–35 in *Representation and Perception of Roman Imperial Power*. Edited by L. de Blois et al. Leiden: Brill, 2003.

Hendin, David. *Ancient Scale Weights and Pre-Coinage Currency of the Near East*. New York: Amphora, 2007.

———. *Cultural Change: Jewish, Christian, and Islamic Coins of the Holy Land*. New York: American Numismatic Society, 2011.

———. "Current Viewpoints on Ancient Jewish Coinage: A Bibliographic Essay." *CBR* 11 (2013): 246–301.

———. "Four New Jewish Lead Coins or Tokens." *INJ* 13 (1994–1999): 63–65.

———. *Guide to Biblical Coins*. 5th ed. New York: Amphora, 2010.

———. "A New Coin Type of Herod Antipas." *INJ* 15 (2003–2006): 56–61.

Hendin, David, and Nathan Bower. "Irregular Coins of Judaea, First Century BCE—First Century CE: New Insights from Comparisons of Stylistic, Physical, and Chemical Analysis." *AJN* 2nd Series 23 (2011): 35–54.

Hezser, Catherine. *Jewish Literacy in Roman Palestine*. TSAJ 81. Tübingen: Mohr Siebeck, 2001.

Hiebert, Robert J. V., trans. *A New English Translation of the Septuagint and the Other Greek Translations Traditionally Included Under That Title: Genesis*. Oxford: Oxford University Press, 2009.

Hillyer, Norman. *1 & 2 Peter, Jude*. UBCS. Grand Rapids: Baker, 2011.

Hirt, Alfred M. *Imperial Mines and Quarries in the Roman World: Organizational Aspects 27 BC–AD 235*. OCM. Oxford: Oxford University Press, 2010.

Hollander, David B. "The Demand for Money in the Late Roman Republic." Pages 112–36 in *The Monetary Systems of the Greeks and Romans*. Edited by W. V. Harris. Oxford: Oxford University Press, 2008.

———. *Money in the Late Roman Republic*. CSCT. Leiden: Brill, 2007.

Hoover, Oliver D. "A New Hellenistic Lead Issue from the Southern Levant." *INR* 4 (2009): 51–56.

Hopkins, Keith. "Taxes and Trade in the Roman Empire: 200 BC to AD 400." *JRS* 70 (1980): 101–25.

Horsley, Richard A. *Bandits, Prophets, and Messiahs: Popular Movements at the Time of Jesus*. Harrisburg: Trinity Press International, 1999.

Horsley Richard A., and Neil A. Silberman. *The Message and the Kingdom: How Jesus and Paul Ignited a Revolution and Transformed the Ancient World*. 1997. Repri., Minneapolis: Augsburg Fortress, 2002.

Howgego, Christopher. *Ancient History from Coins*. AAW. London: Routledge, 1995.

———. "Coinage and Identity in the Roman Provinces." Pages 1–17 in *Coinage and Identity in the Roman Provinces*. Edited by C. Howgego, V. Heuchert, and A. Burnett. Oxford: Oxford University Press, 2005.

Hudson, Stan. "Coins of the Bible." *BSP* 9 (1980): 85–94.

Hurtado, Larry. *At the Origins of Christian Worship: The Context and Character of Earliest Christian Devotion*. Grand Rapids: Eerdmans, 1999.

———. *The Earliest Christian Artifacts: Manuscripts and Christian Origins*. Grand Rapids: Eerdmans, 2006.

———. "Interactive Diversity: A Proposed Model of Christian Origins." *Journal of Theological Studies* 64 (2013): 453.

Incigneri, Brian J. *The Gospel to the Romans: The Setting and Rhetoric of Mark's Gospel*. BIS 65. Leiden: Brill, 2003.

Jensen, Morten H. *Herod Antipas in Galilee*. 2nd ed. WUNT 215. Tübingen: Mohr Siebeck, 2010.

———. "Message and Minting: The Coins of Herod Antipas in Their Second Temple Context as a Source for Understanding the Religio-Political and Socio-Economic Dynamics of Early First Century Galilee." Pages 277–314 in *Religion, Ethnicity, and Identity in Ancient Galilee*. Edited by J. Zangenberg, H. W. Attridge, and D. B. Martin. WUNT 210. Tübingen: Mohr Siebeck, 2007.

Jones, A. H. M. "Numismatics and History." Pages 13–33 in *Essays in Roman Coinage Presented to Harold Mattingly*. Edited by R. A. G. Carson and C. H. V. Sutherland. Oxford: Oxford University Press, 1956.

Judge, E. A. *The First Christians in the Roman World: Augustan and New Testament Essays*. WUNT 229. Tübingen: Mohr Siebeck, 2008.

Kanael, Baruch. "Ancient Jewish Coins and Their Historical Importance." *BA* (1963): 38–62.

Keener, Craig. *The IVP Bible Background Commentary: New Testament*. Downers Grove: InterVarsity, 1993.

Keith, Chris. *Jesus' Literacy: Scribal Culture and the Teacher from Galilee*. LNTS. London: T&T Clark, 2011.

Kemmers, Fleur, and Nanouschka Myberg. "Rethinking Numismatics: The Archaeology of Coins." *Archaeological Dialogues* 18 (2011): 87–108.

Kidner, Derek. *Ezra and Nehemiah: An Introduction and Commentary*. TOTC 12. Downers Grove: InterVarsity, 1979.

King, C. E. "Roman Portraiture: Images of Power." Pages 123–36 in *Roman Coins and Public Life Under the Empire: E. Togo Salmon Papers II*. Edited by G. M. Paul and M. Ierardi. Ann Arbor, MI: University of Michigan Press, 1999.

Klawans, Zander H. *Handbook of Ancient Greek and Roman Coins*. Edited by K. E. Bresset. Atlanta: Whitman, 2012.

Kloner, Amos. *The Necropolis of Jerusalem in the Second Temple Period*. ISACR 8. Leuven: Peeters, 2007.

Kokkinos, Nikos. *Antonia Augusta: Portrait of a Great Roman Lady*. London: Routledge, 1992.

Krmnicek, Stefan. "Das Konzept der Objektbiographie in der antiken Numismatik." Pages 47–59 in *Coins in Context I: New Perspectives for the Interpretation of Coin Finds*. Edited by H. V. Kaenel and F. Kemmers. SFMA 23. Mainz: Philipp Von Zabern, 2009.

Krmnicek, Stefan, and Nathan T. Elkins. "Dinosaurs, Cocks, and Coins: An Introduction to 'Art in the Round.'" Pages 7–22 in *Art in the Round: New Approaches to Ancient Coin Iconography*. Edited by Nathan T. Elkins and Stefan Krmnicek. TAF 16. Rahden: Marie Leidorf, 2014.

Kugel, James L. *Traditions of the Bible: A Guide to the Bible As It Was at the Start of the Common Era*. Cambridge, MA: Harvard University Press, 2009.

Kurke, Leslie. *Coins, Bodies, Games, and Gold: The Politics of Meaning in Archaic Greece*. Princeton: Princeton University Press, 1999.

———. "Herodotus and the Language of Metals." *Helios* 22 (1995): 35–64.

Kreitzer, Larry J. *Striking New Images: Roman Imperial Coinage and the New Testament World*. JSNTSup 134. Sheffield: Sheffield Academic, 1996.

Kroll, John H. "The Monetary Use of Weighed Bullion in Archaic Greece." Pages 12–37 in *Monetary Systems of the Greeks and Romans*. Edited by W. V. Harris. Oxford: Oxford University Press, 2008.

Kyrychenko, Alexander. *The Roman Army and the Expansion of the Gospel: The Role of the Centurion in Luke–Acts*. BZNW 203. Berlin: de Gruyter, 2014.

Lampe, Peter. "Paul, Patrons, and Clients." Pages 457–87 in *Paul in the Greco-Roman World: A Handbook*. Edited by J. P. Sampley. Harrisburg: Trinity Press International, 2003.

Lassen, Eva Maria. "The Use of the Father Image in Imperial Propaganda and 1 Corinthians 4:14–21." *TynBul* 42 (1991): 127–36.

Law, Timothy M. *When God Spoke Greek: The Septuagint and the Making of the Christian Bible*. Oxford: Oxford University Press, 2013.

Lendon, J. E. *Empire of Honour: The Art of Government in the Roman World*. Oxford: Oxford University Press, 1997.

Liddell, H. G. *A Lexicon: Abridged from Liddell and Scott's Greek–English Lexicon*. Oak Harbor, WA: Logos Research Systems, 1996.

Lipschits, Oded, and David Vanderhooft. "Yehud Stamp Impressions in the Fourth Century BCE: A Time of Administrative Consolidation?" Pages 75–94 in *Judah and the Judeans in the Fourth Century BCE*. Edited by O. Lipschits, G. N. Knoppers, and R. Albertz. Winona Lake: Eisenbrauns, 2007.

Lotz, John Paul. "The HOMONOIA Coins of Asia Minor and Ephesians 1:21." *TynBul* 50 (1999): 173–88.

Louw, Johannes P., and Eugene Albert Nida. *Greek-English Lexicon of the New Testament: Based on Semantic Domains*. 2nd ed. New York: United Bible Societies, 1996.

Lubetski, Meir, and Edith Lubetski, eds. *New Inscriptions and Seals Relating to the Biblical World*. ABS 19. Atlanta: SBL, 2012.

Luz, Ulrich. *Matthew 21–28: A Commentary*. Hermeneia. Minneapolis: Augsburg Fortress, 2005.

MacDonald, David. "The Worth of the Assarion." *Historia: Zeitschrift für Alte Geschichte* 38 (1989): 120–23.

MacGeough, Kevin. *The Romans: New Perspectives*. Santa Barbara: ABC-CLIO, 2004.

Magness, Jodi. *The Archaeology of Qumran and the Dead Sea Scrolls*. Grand Rapids: Eerdmans, 2002.

———. *Stone and Dung, Oil and Spit: Jewish Daily Life in the Time of Jesus*. Grand Rapids: Eerdmans, 2011.

Manders, Erika. *Coining Images of Power: Patterns in the Representation of Roman Emperors on Imperial Coinage, AD 193–284*. Leiden: Brill, 2012.

Markus, Joel. "The Jewish War: The *Sitz Im Leben* of Mark." *JBL* 111 (1992): 441–62.

Marx, Werner G. "Money Matters in Matthew." *BSac* 136 (1979): 148–57.

Mason, Steve. *Flavius Josephus: Translation and Commentary*. Vol. 1b, *Judean War 2*. Edited by Steve Mason. BJP 1b. Leiden: Brill, 2008.

———. *Flavius Josephus: Translation and Commentary*. Vol. 9, *Life of Josephus*. Edited by Steve Mason. BJP 9. Leiden: Brill, 2001.

May, David M. "The Empire Strikes Back: The Mark of the Beast in Revelation." *RevExp* 106 (2009): 83–98.

McLaren, James S. "Going to War Against Rome: The Motivation of the Jewish Rebels." Pages 129–53 in *The Jewish Revolt Against Rome: Interdisciplinary Perspectives*. Edited by Mladen Popović. JSJSup 154. Leiden: Brill, 2011.

McLean, Bradley H. *An Introduction to Greek Epigraphy of the Hellenistic and Roman Periods from Alexander the Great Down to the Reign of Constantine (323 BC–AD 337)*. Ann Arbor: University of Michigan Press, 2002.

Meacham, William. "On the Archaeological Evidence for a Coin-on-Eye Jewish Burial Custom in the First Century A.D." *BA* (1986): 56–59.

Meadows, Andrew. "Money, Freedom, and Empire in the Hellenistic World." Pages 53–64 in *Money and Its Uses in the Ancient Greek World*. Edited by A. Meadows and K. Shipton. Oxford: Oxford University Press, 2004.

———. "The Spread of Coins in the Hellenistic World." Pages 169–94 in *Explaining Money and Financial Innovation*. Edited by P. Bernholz and R. Vaubel. FMPS 39. London: Springer, 2014.

Meshorer, Ya'akov. *Ancient Jewish Coinage*. Vol. 2, *Herod the Great through Bar Cochba*. New York: Amphora, 1981.

———. *Jewish Coins of the Second Temple Period*. Tel-Aviv: Am Hassefer, 1967.

———. *A Treasury of Jewish Coins: From the Persian Period to Bar Kokhba*. Jerusalem: Yad Ben-Zvi Press. Nyack: Amphora, 2001.

Metcalf, William E., ed., *The Oxford Handbook of Greek and Roman Coinage*. Oxford: Oxford University Press, 2012.

Millard, Alan. "Latin in First-Century Palestine." Pages 451–58 in *Solving Riddles and Untying Knots: Biblical, Epigraphic and Semitic Studies in Honor of Jonas C. Greenfield*. Edited by A. Berlin et al. Winona Lake: Eisenbrauns, 1995.

Mitch, Curtis, and Edward Sri. *The Gospel of Matthew*. CCSS. Grand Rapids: Baker, 2010.

Mitchell, T. *The Bible in the British Museum: Interpreting the Evidence*. London: British Museum Press, 1988.

Morris, Leon. *1 and 2 Thessalonians: An Introduction and Commentary*. Downers Grove: InterVarsity, 1984.

Mounce, Robert H. *Matthew*. UBCS. Grand Rapids: Baker, 2011.

Murphy, Catherine M. *Wealth in the Dead Sea Scrolls and in the Qumran Community*. STDJ 40. Leiden: Brill, 2001.

Murphy, Frederick J. *Pseudo-Philo: Rewriting the Bible*. Oxford: Oxford University Press, 1993.

Niang, Aliou C. *Faith and Freedom in Galatia and Senegal: The Apostle Paul, Colonists and Sending Gods*. Leiden: Brill, 2009.

Nolland, John. *The Gospel of Matthew*. NIGTC. Grand Rapids: Eerdmans, 2005.

Nystrom, David. "We Have No King but Caesar: Roman Imperial Ideology and the Imperial Cult." Pages 23–37 in *Jesus Is Lord, Caesar Is Not: Evaluating Empire in New Testament Studies*. Edited by S. McKnight and J. B. Modica. Downers Grove: InterVarsity, 2013.

Oakes, Peter. "Methodological Issues in Using Economic Evidence in Interpretation of Early Christian Texts." Pages 9–34 in *Engaging Economics: New Testament Scenarios and Earl Christian Reception*. Edited by B. W. Longenecker and K. D. Liebengood. Grand Rapids: Eerdmans, 2009.

Oakman, Douglas. "Jesus and Agrarian Palestine: The Factor of Debt." Pages 63–84 in *The Social World of the New Testament*. Edited by J. Neyrey and E. Stewart. Peabody, MA: Hendrickson, 2008.

Oster, Richard E. "Numismatics Windows into the Social World of Early Christianity: A Methodological Inquiry." *JBL* 101 (1982): 195–223.

———. "'Show Me a Denarius': Symbolism of Roman Coinage and Christian Beliefs." *ResQ* 28 (1986): 107–15.

Ostler, Nicholas. *Ad Infinitum: A Biography of Latin*. New York: Walker & Co., 2007.

Parsons, Mikeal C. *Body and Character in Luke and Acts: The Subversion of Physiognomy in Early Christianity*. Grand Rapids: Baker Academic, 2006.

Patterson, David. *Hebrew Language and Jewish Thought*. London: RoutledgeCurzon, 2005.

Patterson, John. "Military Organization and Social Change in the Later Roman Republic." Pages 92–112 in *War and Society in the Roman World*. Edited by J. Rich and G. Shipley. London: Routledge, 1993.

Pearce, Sarah K. "Philo on the Nile." Pages 137–57 in *Jewish Identity in the Greco-Roman World*. Edited by J. Frey et al. AJEC 71. Leiden: Brill, 2007.

Petersen, Anders K. "At the End of the Road—Reflections on a Popular Scholarly Metaphor." Pages in 45–72 *The Formation of the Early Church*. Edited by J. Ådna. WUNT 183. Tübingen: Mohr Siebeck, 2005,

Petersen, Allan R. "The Archaeology of Khirbet Qumran." Pages 249–60 in *Qumran Between the Old and New Testaments*. Edited by F. H Cryer and T. L. Thompson. JSOTSup 290. Sheffield: Sheffield Academic, 1998.

Petrey, Sandy. *Speech Acts and Literary Theory*. London: Routledge, 1990.

Pliny the Elder. *The Natural History*. Edited by John Bostock. Medford, MA: Taylor & Francis, 1855.

Plutarch. *Moralia*. Edited by F. C. Babbitt. Medford: Harvard University Press, 1936.

Pfann, Stephan J. "Scripts and Scribal Practice." *EDEJ* 1204–7.

Pollini, John. *From Republic to Empire: Rhetoric, Religion, and Power in the Visual Culture of Ancient Rome*. OSCC 48. Norman: University of Oklahoma Press, 2012.

Porter, Stanley. "What Do We Know and How Do We Know It? Reconstructing Early Christianity From Its Manuscripts." Pages 41–70 in *Christian Origins and Greco-Roman Culture: Social and Literary Contexts for the New Testament*. Edited by S. E. Porter and A. W. Pitts. TENT 9. Leiden: Brill, 2013.

Pundt, Heather Ann. *Mining Culture in Roman Dacia: Empire, Community, and Identity at the Gold Mines of Alburnus Maior ca. 107–270 C.E.* MA diss., Portland State University, 2012.

Reiser, Marius. "Numismatik und Neues Testament." *Biblica* 81 (2000): 457–88.

Reynolds, Bennie H., III. *Between Symbolism and Realism: The Use of Symbolic and Non-Symbolic Language in Ancient Jewish Apocalypses 333–63 B.C.E.* JAJSup 8. Göttingen: Vandenhoeck & Ruprecht, 2012.

Rhodes, P. J. "The Non-literary Written Sources." Pages 45–63 in *A Companion to the Classical Greek World*. Edited by K. H. Kinzl. BCAW. Oxford: Blackwell, 2010.

Riches, John K., and David C. Sim, eds. *The Gospel of Matthew in Its Roman Imperial Context*. LTNS 276. London: T&T Clark, 2005.

Ricoeur, Paul. *Hermeneutics and the Human Sciences: Essays on Language, Action and Interpretation*. Translated by John B. Thompson. Cambridge: Cambridge University Press, 1981.

Romanoff, Paul. *Jewish Symbols on Ancient Jewish Coins*. Philadelphia: Dropsie College, 1944.

Rogerson, John. "Ancient Israel to the Fall of the Second Temple." Pages 214–65 in *A Handbook of Ancient Religions*. Edited by John R. Hinnells. Cambridge: Cambridge University Press, 2007.

Rossi, Cesare, Flavio Russo, and Ferruccio Russo. *Ancient Engineers' Inventions: Precursors of the Present*. HMMS 8. Naples: Springer, 2009.

Sanders, Ed. "Paul Between Judaism and Hellenism." Pages 74 to 90 in *Saint Paul Among the Philosophers*. Edited by Jack Caputo. Bloomington: Indiana University Press, 2009.

Sayles, Wayne G. *Ancient Coin Collecting IV: Roman Provincial Coins* (Iola: Krause, 1998.

Scheid, John. *An Introduction to Roman Religion*. Translated by J. Lloyd. Bloomington: Indiana University Press, 2003.

Schnelle, Udo. "Das frühe Christentum und die Bildung." *NTS* 41 (2015): 113–43.

Schniedewind, William M. *A Social History of Hebrew: Its Origins Through the Rabbinic Period*. AYBRL. New Haven: Yale University Press, 2013.

Scott, James M. *2 Corinthians*. UBCS. Grand Rapids: Baker, 2011.

Seaford, Richard. *Money and the Early Greek Mind: Homer, Philosophy, Tragedy*. Cambridge: Cambridge University Press, 2004.

Seebohm, Thomas M. *Hermeneutics: Method and Methodology*. CPS. Norwell: Kluwer Academic, 2004.

Senior, Donald. *The Gospel of Matthew*. Nashville: Abingdon, 1997.

Seo, Pyung Soo. *Luke's Jesus in the Roman Empire and the Emperor in the Gospel of Luke*. Eugene, OR: Wipf & Stock, 2015.

Sigismund, Marcus. "Small Change? Coins and Weights as a Mirror of Ethnic, Religious and Political Identity in First and Second Century C.E. Tiberias?" Pages 315–36 in *Religion, Ethnicity, and Identity in Ancient Galilee: A Region in Transition*. Edited by J. Zangenberg, H. W. Attridge and D. B. Martin. WUNT 210. Tübingen: Mohr Siebeck, 2007.

Smith, R. R. R. *Hellenistic Royal Portraits*. Oxford: Oxford University Press, 1988.

Sperber, Daniel. "Mark 7:42 and Its Metrological Background: A Study in Ancient Syriac Versions." *NovT* 9 (1967): 178–90.

———. "Palestinian Currency Systems During the Second Commonwealth." *Jewish Quarterly Review* 56 (1966): 273–301.

Spinelli, Marianna. "The 'Soma' of the God: Subtypes as Qualification of the Corporal Gestures of the Main Subject on the *Kaulonia* Coins." Pages 793–800 in *Identity and Connectivity: Proceedings of the 16th Symposium on Mediterranean Archaeology*. BAR 2581. Oxford: Archaeopress, 2013.

Stewart, Andrew. *Faces of Power: Alexander's Image and Hellenistic Politics*. Berkeley: University of California Press, 1993.

Stone, Michael E. *Ancient Judaism: New Visions and Views*. Grand Rapids: Eerdmans, 2011.

Sutherland, C. H. V., and R. A. G. Carson, eds. *The Roman Imperial Coinage: From 31 BC to AD 69*. London: Spink & Son, 1984.

Syon, Danny. "The Bronze Coinage of Tyre: The First Years of Autonomy." *AJN* Second Series 20 (2008): 295–304.

Tellbe, Mikael. "The Temple Tax as a Pre-70 CE Identity Marker." Pages 19–44 in *The Formation of the Early Church*. Edited by J. Ådna. WUNT 183. Tübingen: Mohr Siebeck, 2005.

Theissen, Gerd. *Lokalkolorit und Zeitgeschichte in den Evangelien. Ein Beitrag zur Geschichte der synoptischen Tradition*. NTOA 8. Göttingen: Vandenhoeck & Ruprecht, 1989.

Travers, Scott A. *The Coin Collector's Survival Manual*. 6th ed. New York: Random House, 2008.

Tripolitis, Antonia. *Religions of the Hellenistic-Roman Age*. Grand Rapids: Eerdmans, 2002.

Ulrich, E. C. "The Qumran Biblical Scrolls—The Scriptures of Late Second Temple Judaism." Pages 67–87 in *The Dead Sea Scrolls in Their Historical Context*. Edited by T. Lim. London: T&T Clark, 2004.

Vagi, David L. *Coinage and History of the Roman Empire*. 2 vols. London: Fitzroy Dearborn, 1999.

VanderKam, James C. *Calendars in the Dead Sea Scrolls: Measuring Time*. London: Routledge, 1998.

Vanhoozer, Kevin J. *Is There a Meaning in This Text? The Bible, the Reader, and the Morality of Literary Knowledge*. Grand Rapids: Zondervan, 1998.

———. *Jesus, Paul, and the People of God: A Theological Dialogue with N. T. Wright*. Edited by N. Perrin and R. B. Hays. Downers Grove: InterVarsity, 2011.

———. "What Is Everyday Theology? How and Why Christians Should Read Culture." Pages 15–60 in *Everyday Theology: How to Read Cultural Texts and Interpret Trends*. Grand Rapids: Baker Academic, 2007.

Vermes, Geza. *The Dead Sea Scrolls in English*. Rev. and extended 4th ed. Sheffield: Sheffield Academic, 1995.

Victor, Royce M. *Colonial Education and Class Formation in Early Judaism: A Postcolonial Reading*. LSTS. London: T&T Clark, 2010.

von Reden, Sitta. *Money in Classical Antiquity*. KTAH. Cambridge: Cambridge University Press, 2010.

Wallace, R. W. "The Origin of Electrum Coinage." *AJA* 91 (1987): 385–90.

Wallace-Hadrill, A. "Image and Authority in the Coinage of Augustus." *JRS* 67 (1986): 66–87.

Warrior, Valerie M. *Roman Religion*. CIRC. Cambridge: Cambridge University Press, 2006.

Weissenrieder, Annette, and Friederike Wendt. "Images as Communication: The Methods of Iconography." Pages 3–49 in *Picturing the New Testament: Studies in Ancient Visual Images*. WUNT 2/193. Edited by A. Weissenrieder, F. Wendt, and P. von Gemünden. Tübingen: Mohr Siebeck, 2005.

Wells, David. *Above All Earthly Pow'rs: Christ in a Postmodern World*. Grand Rapids: Eerdmans, 2005.

Wenkel, David H. "When the Apostles Became Kings: Ruling and Judging the Twelve Tribes of Israel in the Book of Acts." *BTB* 42 (2012): 114–23.

Wheaton, D. H. "Money: In the New Testament." Pages 780–82 in *The New Bible Dictionary*. Edited by R. W. Wood and I. H. Marshall. 3rd ed. Downers Grove: InterVarsity, 1996.

Wiese, Heike. *Numbers, Language, and the Human Mind*. Cambridge: Cambridge University Press, 2003.

Williams, Jonathan. "Religion and Roman Coins." Pages 143–63 in *A Companion to Roman Religion*. Edited by J. Rüpke. BCAW. Oxford: Blackwell, 2007.

———. "The Republican Identity of Roman Imperial Coinage: 1st to mid–3rd Centuries AD." Pages 57–72 in *Money and Identity: Lectures About History, Design, and Museology of Money*. Edited by R. Cunz. Hannover, 2007.

Winter, Bruce W. "The Enigma of Imperial Cultic Activities and Paul in Corinth." Pages 49–72 in *Greco-Roman Culture and the New Testament*. Edited by D. E. Aune and F. E. Brenk. NovTSup 143. Leiden: Brill, 2012.

Witherington, Ben, III. *1 and 2 Thessalonians: A Socio-Rhetorical Commentary*. Grand Rapids: Eerdmans, 2006.

———. *Jesus, Paul and the End of the World*. Downers Grove: InterVarsity, 1992.

Wolff, Samuel R. "Mortuary Practices in the Persian Period of the Levant." *Near Eastern Archaeology* 65 (2002): 131–37.

Woolf, Greg. "Divinity and Power in Ancient Rome." Pages 235–52 in *Religion and Power: Divine Kingship in the Ancient World and Beyond*. Edited by N. Brisch. OIS 4. Chicago: The Oriental Institute of Chicago, 2008.

Wright, Brian J. "Ancient Literacy in New Testament Research: Incorporating a Few More Lines of Enquiry." *TrinJ* 36 (2015): 1–29.

Wright, N. T. *The Resurrection of the Son of God: Christian Origins and the Question of God*. London: SPCK, 2003.

———. *Simply Jesus: Who He Was, What He Did, Why It Matters*. London: SPCK, 2011.

Zangenberg, Jürgen K. "Archaeology, Papyri, and Inscriptions." Pages 322–66 in *Early Judaism: A Comprehensive Overview*. Edited by J. J. Collins and D. C. Harlow. Grand Rapids: Eerdmans, 2012.

Zanker, Paul. *The Power of Images in the Age of Augustus*. Translated by Paul Shapiro. Jerome Lectures 16. Ann Arbor: University of Michigan Press, 1988.

Index of References

Index of Authors